The 2023 Keto Diet

Cookbook for Beginners

1200 Easy & Tasty Keto Diet Recipes for Low-Carb Homemade Cooking(with 30-DAY MEAL PLAN)

Celestina Russell

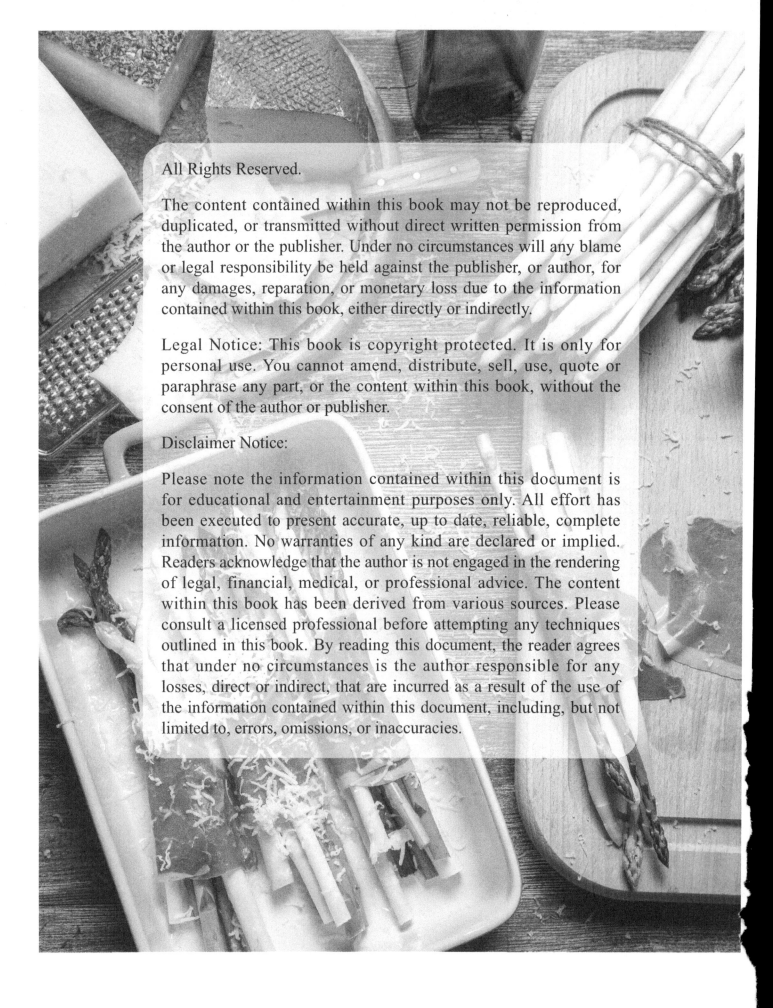

CONTENTS

Chapter 3 Vegan, Vegetable & Meatless Recipes 25

Chapter 4 Fish And Seafood Recipes 44

Chapter 5 Poultry Recipes 56

Chapter 6 Pork, Beef & Lamb Recipes 76

Chapter 7 Soups, Stew & Salads Recipes 95

Chapter 8 Sauces And Dressing Recipes 107

Chapter 9 Desserts And Drinks Recipes 114

INTRODUCTION

Hello, everyone! I'm so glad that you've bought this keto diet cookbook. Welcome to learn how to make healthy and delicious food with keto diet with me! I'm Celestina Russell. From a very early age, fitness and healthy diet have been very important to me influenced by my parents. So I majored in nutrition in college, which enabled me to learn more scientific and nutritious lifestyles. After graduation, I worked as a nutrition consultant in a food company for 9 years. During this period, I did a lot of research on how to mix food nutritionally and how to maximize their nutritional value. After having children in 2012, in order to have more time to take care of children, I quit this job and became a freelance writer. Based on my research on healthy lifestyle over the years, I wrote these in my own books, hoping to help those in need.

This keto diet cookbook starts with a brief introduction of keto diet, which can help people who don't know keto diet master it easily. If you don't know how to start this new diet pattern, you might as well try the 30-day diet plan in the cookbook first. After trying it, I believe you will love this healthy and simple diet. Let's get started now!

Chapter 1 Basic Information of Keto Diet

What Is Keto Diet?

The keto diet is a very low carb, high fat diet. It can be effective for weight loss and certain health conditions, like diabetes, cancers. It involves drastically reducing carbohydrate intake and replacing it with fat. This reduction in carbs puts your body into a metabolic state called ketosis. When this happens, your body becomes incredibly efficient at burning fat for energy. It also turns fat into ketones in the liver, which can supply energy for the brain. Keto diets can cause significant reductions in blood sugar and insulin levels. Along with the increased ketones, the benefits of keto diet will gradually emerge.

Different Types of Keto Diets

There are several versions of the keto diet, including:

• Standard keto diet (SKD): This is a very low carb, moderate protein and high fat diet. It typically contains 70% fat, 20% protein, and only 10% carbs;

• Cyclical keto diet (CKD): This diet involves periods of higher carb refeeds, such as 5 keto days followed by 2 high carb days.

• Targeted keto diet (TKD): This diet allows you to add carbs around workouts.

• High protein keto diet: This is similar to a standard keto diet, but includes more protein. The ratio is often 60% fat, 35% protein, and 5% carbs.

What to Eat or Not on A Keto Diet?

Here are typical foods to enjoy on a keto diet:

1. Meat and poultry

2. Fish and sea food

3. Cheese

4. Natural fats: olive oil, avocado oil

5. Vegetables: tomatoes, onions, eggplant, lettuce, other green veggies

Food to Avoid:

1. Bread, tortillas, muffins, bagels, pancakes

2. Pasta and rice

3. Cakes, cookies, and other baked goods

4. Some condiments or sauces: barbecue sauce, honey mustard, teriyaki sauce, ketchup, etc.

5. Sugar and anything made with sugar

6. Most fruits and fruit juice

All in all, you should eat more meat, poultry, fish, eggs and other protein-rich foods and fresh leafy vegetables. Avoid sugar and foods high in carbohydrates.

Benefits of Keto Diet

1. Keto diet can help you lose weight. A keto diet is an effective way to lose weight without counting calories or tracking your food intake.

2. The keto diet can help you lose excess fat, which is closely linked to type 2 diabetes, pre-diabetes, and metabolic syndrome.

3. Some research suggests that the diet could improve outcomes of traumatic brain injuries.

4. Recent research suggests a keto or low-carb diet may help reduce or even reverse NAFLD(non-alcoholic fatty liver disease).

5. The keto diet is currently being explored as an additional treatment for cancer, because it may help slow tumor growth.

6. The keto diet may help reduce symptoms of Alzheimer's disease and slow its progression.

Now that you understand the benefits and science behind the keto diet, you're ready to get started. This keto diet recipes cookbook will provide you with what you need to succeed with the keto diet—simple cooking, weight loss, and long-term success!

BASIC KITCHEN CONVERSIONS & EQUIVALENTS

DRY MEASUREMENTS CONVERSION CHART

3 TEASPOONS = 1 TABLESPOON = 1/16 CUP

6 TEASPOONS = 2 TABLESPOONS = 1/8 CUP

12 TEASPOONS = 4 TABLESPOONS = 1/4 CUP

24 TEASPOONS = 8 TABLESPOONS = 1/2 CUP

36 TEASPOONS = 12 TABLESPOONS = 3/4 CUP

48 TEASPOONS = 16 TABLESPOONS = 1 CUP

METRIC TO US COOKING CONVERSIONS

OVEN TEMPERATURES

120 °C = 250 °F

160 °C = 320 °F

180° C = 350 °F

205 °C = 400 °F

220 °C = 425 °F

LIQUID MEASUREMENTS CONVERSION CHART

8 FLUID OUNCES = 1 CUP = 1/2 PINT = 1/4 QUART

16 FLUID OUNCES = 2 CUPS = 1 PINT = 1/2 QUART

32 FLUID OUNCES = 4 CUPS = 2 PINTS = 1 QUART = 1/4 GALLON

128 FLUID OUNCES = 16 CUPS = 8 PINTS = 4 QUARTS = 1 GALLON

BAKING IN GRAMS

1 CUP FLOUR = 140 GRAMS

1 CUP SUGAR = 150 GRAMS

1 CUP POWDERED SUGAR = 160 GRAMS

1 CUP HEAVY CREAM = 235 GRAMS

VOLUME

1 MILLILITER = 1/5 TEASPOON

5 ML = 1 TEASPOON

15 ML = 1 TABLESPOON

240 ML = 1 CUP OR 8 FLUID OUNCES

1 LITER = 34 FL. OUNCES

WEIGHT

1 GRAM = .035 OUNCES

100 GRAMS = 3.5 OUNCES

500 GRAMS = 1.1 POUNDS

1 KILOGRAM = 35 OUNCES

US TO METRIC COOKING CONVERSIONS

1/5 TSP = 1 ML

1 TSP = 5 ML

1 TBSP = 15 ML

1 FL OUNCE = 30 ML

1 CUP = 237 ML

1 PINT (2 CUPS) = 473 ML

1 QUART (4 CUPS) = .95 LITER

1 GALLON (16 CUPS) = 3.8 LITERS

1 OZ = 28 GRAMS

1 POUND = 454 GRAMS

BUTTER

1 CUP BUTTER = 2 STICKS = 8 OUNCES = 230 GRAMS = 8 TABLESPOONS

WHAT DOES 1 CUP EQUAL

1 CUP = 8 FLUID OUNCES

1 CUP = 16 TABLESPOONS

1 CUP = 48 TEASPOONS

1 CUP = 1/2 PINT

1 CUP = 1/4 QUART

1 CUP = 1/16 GALLON

1 CUP = 240 ML

BAKING PAN CONVERSIONS

1 CUP ALL-PURPOSE FLOUR = 4.5 OZ

1 CUP ROLLED OATS = 3 OZ 1 LARGE EGG = 1.7 OZ

1 CUP BUTTER = 8 OZ 1 CUP MILK = 8 OZ

1 CUP HEAVY CREAM = 8.4 OZ

1 CUP GRANULATED SUGAR = 7.1 OZ

1 CUP PACKED BROWN SUGAR = 7.75 OZ

1 CUP VEGETABLE OIL = 7.7 OZ

1 CUP UNSIFTED POWDERED SUGAR = 4.4 OZ

BAKING PAN CONVERSIONS

9-INCH ROUND CAKE PAN = 12 CUPS

10-INCH TUBE PAN =16 CUPS

11-INCH BUNDT PAN = 12 CUPS

9-INCH SPRINGFORM PAN = 10 CUPS

9 X 5 INCH LOAF PAN = 8 CUPS

9-INCH SQUARE PAN = 8 CUPS

Chapter 2 Appetizers, Snacks & Side Dishes Recipes

Chapter 2 Appetizers, Snacks & Side Dishes Recipes

Zucchini And Cheese Gratin

Servings: 8 | Cooking Time: 15 Minutes

Ingredients:
- 5 tablespoons butter
- 1 onion, sliced
- ½ cup heavy cream
- 4 cups raw zucchini, sliced
- 1 ½ cups shredded pepper Jack cheese
- Salt and pepper to taste

Directions:
1. Place all ingredients in a mixing bowl and give a good stir to incorporate everything.
2. Pour the mixture in a heat-proof baking dish.
3. Place in a 350F preheated oven and bake for 15 minutes.
4. Serve and enjoy.

Nutrition Info:
- Per Servings 5.0g Carbs, 8.0g Protein, 20.0g Fat, 280 Calories

Zucchini Gratin With Feta Cheese

Servings: 6 | Cooking Time: 65 Minutes

Ingredients:
- Cooking spray
- 2 lb zucchinis, sliced
- 2 red bell peppers, seeded and sliced
- Salt and black pepper to taste
- 1 ½ cups crumbled feta cheese
- ⅓ cup crumbled feta cheese for topping
- 2 tbsp butter
- ¼ tsp xanthan gum
- ½ cup heavy whipping cream

Directions:
1. Preheat oven to 370ºF. Place the sliced zucchinis in a colander over the sink, sprinkle with salt and let sit for 20 minutes. Transfer to paper towels to drain the excess liquid.
2. Grease a baking dish with cooking spray and make a layer of zucchini and bell peppers in the dish overlapping one on another. Season with black pepper, and sprinkle with some feta cheese. Repeat the layering process a second time.
3. Combine the butter, xanthan gum, and whipping cream in a microwave dish for 2 minutes, stir to mix completely, and pour over the vegetables. Top with remaining feta cheese.
4. Bake the gratin for 45 minutes to be golden brown on top. Cut out slices and serve with kale salad.

Nutrition Info:
- Per Servings 4g Carbs, 14g Protein, 21g Fat, 264 Calories

Chicken Enchilada Dip

Servings: 16 | Cooking Time:240 Minutes

Ingredients:
- 2 pounds cooked rotisserie chicken, shredded
- 1 cup enchilada sauce
- ½ cup cheddar cheese
- 2 stalk green onions, sliced
- 3 tbsp olive oil
- Salt and pepper to taste

Directions:
1. Place all ingredients in the crockpot except for the green onions.
2. Give a good stir to combine everything.
3. Close the lid and cook on low for 4 hours. Mix well and adjust seasoning to taste.
4. Garnish with green onions.

Nutrition Info:
- Per Servings 1.5g Carbs, 16.2g Protein, 13.6g Fat, 178 Calories

Parmesan Crackers With Guacamole

Servings: 4 | Cooking Time: 10 Minutes

Ingredients:
- 1 cup finely grated Parmesan cheese
- ¼ tsp sweet paprika
- ¼ tsp garlic powder
- 2 soft avocados, pitted and scooped
- 1 tomato, chopped
- Salt to taste

Directions:
1. To make the chips, preheat oven to 350ºF and line a baking sheet with parchment paper.
2. Mix parmesan cheese, paprika, and garlic powder. Spoon 8 teaspoons on the baking sheet creating spaces between each mound. Flatten mounds. Bake for 5 minutes, cool, and remove to a plate.
3. To make the guacamole, mash avocado, with a fork in a bowl, add in tomato and continue to mash until mostly smooth. Season with salt. Serve crackers with guacamole.

Nutrition Info:
- Per Servings 2g Carbs, 10g Protein, 20g Fat, 229 Calories

Coconut Ginger Macaroons

Servings: 6 | Cooking Time: 20 Minutes

Ingredients:
- 2 fingers ginger root, peeled and pureed
- 6 egg whites
- 1 cup finely shredded coconut
- ¼ cup swerve
- A pinch of chili powder

- 1 cup water
- Angel hair chili to garnish

Directions:

1. Preheat the oven to 350ºF and line a baking sheet with parchment paper. Set aside.

2. Then, in a heatproof bowl, whisk the ginger, egg whites, shredded coconut, swerve, and chili powder.

3. Bring the water to boil in a pot over medium heat and place the heatproof bowl on the pot. Then, continue whisking the mixture until it is glossy, about 4 minutes. Do not let the bowl touch the water or be too hot so that the eggs don't cook.

4. Spoon the mixture into the piping bag after and pipe out 40 to 50 little mounds on the lined baking sheet. Bake the macaroons in the middle part of the oven for 15 minutes.

5. Once they are ready, transfer them to a wire rack, garnish them with the angel hair chili, and serve.

Nutrition Info:
- Per Servings 0.3g Carbs, 6.8g Protein, 3.5g Fat, 97 Calories

Spicy Chicken Cucumber Bites

Servings: 6 | Cooking Time: 5 Minutes

Ingredients:
- 2 cucumbers, sliced with a 3-inch thickness
- 2 cups small dices leftover chicken
- ¼ jalapeño pepper, seeded and minced
- 1 tbsp Dijon mustard
- ⅓ cup mayonnaise
- Salt and black pepper to taste

Directions:

1. Cut mid-level holes in cucumber slices with a knife and set aside. Combine chicken, jalapeno pepper, mustard, mayonnaise, salt, and black pepper to be evenly mixed. Fill cucumber holes with chicken mixture and serve.

Nutrition Info:
- Per Servings 0g Carbs, 10g Protein, 14g Fat, 170 Calories

Squid Salad With Mint, Cucumber & Chili Dressing

Servings: 4 | Cooking Time: 30 Minutes

Ingredients:
- 4 medium squid tubes, cut into strips
- ½ cup mint leaves
- 2 medium cucumbers, halved and cut in strips
- ½ cup coriander leaves, reserve the stems
- ½ red onion, finely sliced
- Salt and black pepper to taste
- 1 tsp fish sauce
- 1 red chili, roughly chopped
- 1 tsp swerve
- 1 clove garlic
- 2 limes, juiced
- 1 tbsp chopped coriander
- 1tsp olive oil

Directions:

1. In a salad bowl, mix mint leaves, cucumber strips, coriander leaves, and red onion. Season with salt, pepper and a little drizzle of olive oil; set aside. In the mortar, pound the coriander stems, red chili, and swerve into a paste using the pestle. Add the fish sauce and lime juice, and mix with the pestle.

2. Heat a skillet over high heat on a stovetop and sear the squid on both sides to lightly brown, about 5 minutes. Pour the squid on the salad and drizzle with the chili dressing. Toss the ingredients with two spoons, garnish with coriander, and serve the salad as a single dish or with some more seafood.

Nutrition Info:
- Per Servings 2.1g Carbs, 24.6g Protein, 22.5g Fat, 318 Calories

Bacon Mashed Cauliflower

Servings: 6 | Cooking Time: 40 Minutes

Ingredients:
- 6 slices bacon
- 3 heads cauliflower, leaves removed
- 2 cups water
- 2 tbsp melted butter
- ½ cup buttermilk
- Salt and black pepper to taste
- ¼ cup grated yellow cheddar cheese
- 2 tbsp chopped chives

Directions:

1. Preheat oven to 350ºF. Fry bacon in a heated skillet over medium heat for 5 minutes until crispy. Remove to a paper towel-lined plate, allow to cool, and crumble. Set aside and keep bacon fat.

2. Boil cauli heads in water in a pot over high heat for 7 minutes, until tender. Drain and put in a bowl.

3. Include butter, buttermilk, salt, black pepper, and puree using a hand blender until smooth and creamy. Lightly grease a casserole dish with the bacon fat and spread the mash in it.

4. Sprinkle with cheddar cheese and place under the broiler for 4 minutes on high until the cheese melts. Remove and top with bacon and chopped chives. Serve with pan-seared scallops.

Nutrition Info:
- Per Servings 6g Carbs, 14g Protein, 25g Fat, 312 Calories

Crispy Chorizo With Cheesy Topping

Servings: 6 | Cooking Time: 30 Minutes

Ingredients:
- 7 ounces Spanish chorizo
- 4 ounces cream cheese
- ¼ cup chopped parsley

Directions:

1. Preheat your oven to 325 ºF. Slice the chorizo into 30 slices

2. Line a baking dish with waxed paper. Bake the chorizo for 15 minutes until crispy. Remove from the oven and let cool. Arrange on a serving platter. Top each slice with some cream cheese.

3. Serve sprinkled with chopped parsley.

Nutrition Info:
- Per Servings 0g Carbs, 5g Protein, 13g Fat, 172 Calories

Roasted String Beans, Mushrooms & Tomato Plate

Servings: 4 | Cooking Time: 32 Minutes

Ingredients:
- 2 cups strings beans, cut in halves
- 1 lb cremini mushrooms, quartered
- 3 tomatoes, quartered
- 2 cloves garlic, minced
- 3 tbsp olive oil
- 3 shallots, julienned
- ½ tsp dried thyme
- Salt and black pepper to season

Directions:
1. Preheat oven to 450ºF. In a bowl, mix the strings beans, mushrooms, tomatoes, garlic, olive oil, shallots, thyme, salt, and pepper. Pour the vegetables in a baking sheet and spread them all around.
2. Place the baking sheet in the oven and bake the veggies for 20 to 25 minutes.

Nutrition Info:
- Per Servings 6g Carbs, 6g Protein, 2g Fat, 121 Calories

Teriyaki Chicken Wings

Servings: 9 | Cooking Time: 50 Minutes

Ingredients:
- 3 pounds chicken wings
- 1 onion, chopped
- 2 cups commercial teriyaki sauce
- 1 tablespoon chili garlic paste
- 2 teaspoons ginger paste
- Salt and pepper to taste

Directions:
1. In a heavy-bottomed pot, place on medium-high fire and lightly grease with cooking spray.
2. Pan fry chicken for 4 minutes per side. Cook in two batches.
3. Stir in remaining ingredients in a pot, along with the chicken.
4. Cover and cook on low fire for 30 minutes, stirring every now and then. Continue cooking until desired sauce thickness is achieved.
5. Serve and enjoy.

Nutrition Info:
- Per Servings 5.4g Carbs, 34.3g Protein, 5.4g Fat, 214 Calories

Crab Stuffed Mushrooms

Servings: 3 | Cooking Time: 25 Minutes

Ingredients:
- 2 tbsp minced green onion
- 1 cup cooked crabmeat, chopped finely
- ¼ cup Monterey Jack cheese, shredded
- 1 tsp lemon juice
- ¼ lb, fresh button mushrooms
- Pepper and salt to taste

- 3 tablespoons olive oil

Directions:
1. Destem mushrooms, wash, and drain well.
2. Chop mushroom stems.
3. Preheat oven to 400oF and lightly grease a baking pan with cooking spray.
4. In a small bowl, whisk well green onion, crabmeat, lemon juice, dill, and chopped mushroom stems.
5. Evenly spread mushrooms on prepared pan with cap sides up. Evenly spoon crabmeat mixture on top of mushroom caps.
6. Pop in the oven and bake for 20 minutes.
7. Remove from oven and sprinkle cheese on top.
8. Return to oven and broil for 3 minutes.
9. Serve and enjoy.

Nutrition Info:
- Per Servings 10g Carbs, 7.9g Protein, 17.3g Fat, 286 Calories

Parmesan Crackers

Servings: 6 | Cooking Time: 25 Minutes

Ingredients:
- 1 ⅓ cups coconut flour
- 1 ¼ cup grated Parmesan cheese
- Salt and black pepper to taste
- 1 tsp garlic powder
- ⅓ cup butter, softened
- ⅓ tsp sweet paprika
- ⅓ cup heavy cream
- Water as needed

Directions:
1. Preheat the oven to 350ºF.
2. Mix the coconut flour, parmesan cheese, salt, pepper, garlic powder, and paprika in a bowl. Add in the butter and mix well. Top with the heavy cream and mix again until a smooth, thick mixture has formed. Add 1 to 2 tablespoon of water at this point, if it is too thick.
3. Place the dough on a cutting board and cover with plastic wrap. Use a rolling pin to spread out the dough into a light rectangle. Cut cracker squares out of the dough and arrange them on a baking sheet without overlapping. Bake for 20 minutes and transfer to a serving bowl after.

Nutrition Info:
- Per Servings 0.7g Carbs, 5g Protein, 3g Fat, 115 Calories

Italian-style Chicken Wraps

Servings: 8 | Cooking Time: 20 Minutes

Ingredients:
- ¼ tsp garlic powder
- 8 ounces provolone cheese
- 8 raw chicken tenders
- Salt and black pepper to taste
- 8 prosciutto slices

Directions:
1. Pound the chicken until half an inch thick. Season with salt, black pepper, and garlic powder. Cut the provolone cheese into 8 strips. Place a slice of prosciutto on a flat surface. Place one

chicken tender on top. Top with a provolone strip.

2. Roll the chicken and secure with previously soaked skewers. Grill the wraps for 3 minutes per side.

Nutrition Info:
• Per Servings 0.7g Carbs, 17g Protein, 10g Fat, 174 Calories

Cajun Spiced Pecans

Servings: 10 | Cooking Time: 10 Minutes

Ingredients:
• 1-pound pecan halves
• ¼ cup butter
• 1 packet Cajun seasoning mix
• ¼ teaspoon ground cayenne pepper
• Salt and pepper to taste

Directions:
1. Place a nonstick saucepan on medium fire and melt butter.
2. Add pecans and remaining ingredients.
3. Sauté for 5 minutes.
4. Remove from fire and let it cool completely.
5. Serve and enjoy.

Nutrition Info:
• Per Servings 6.8g Carbs, 4.2g Protein, 37.3g Fat, 356.5 Calories

Dill Pickles With Tuna-mayo Topping

Servings: 12 | Cooking Time: 40 Minutes

Ingredients:
• 18 ounces canned and drained tuna
• 6 large dill pickles
• ¼ tsp garlic powder
• ⅓ cup sugar-free mayonnaise
• 1 tbsp onion flakes

Directions:
1. Combine the mayonnaise, tuna, onion flakes, and garlic powder in a bowl. Cut the pickles in half lengthwise. Top each half with tuna mixture. Place in the fridge for 30 minutes before serving.

Nutrition Info:
• Per Servings 1.5g Carbs, 11g Protein, 10g Fat, 118 Calories

Mixed Roast Vegetables

Servings: 4 | Cooking Time: 40 Minutes

Ingredients:
• 1 large butternut squash, cut into chunks
• ¼ lb shallots, peeled
• 4 rutabagas, cut into chunks
• ¼ lb Brussels sprouts
• 1 sprig rosemary, chopped
• 1 sprig thyme, chopped
• 4 cloves garlic, peeled only
• 3 tbsp olive oil
• Salt and black pepper to taste

Directions:
1. Preheat the oven to 450ºF.
2. Pour the butternut squash, shallots, rutabagas, garlic cloves,

and brussels sprouts in a bowl. Season with salt, pepper, olive oil, and toss them. Pour the mixture on a baking sheet and sprinkle with the chopped thyme and rosemary. Roast the vegetables for 15–20 minutes.

3. Once ready, remove and spoon into a serving bowl. Serve with oven roasted chicken thighs.

Nutrition Info:
• Per Servings 8g Carbs, 3g Protein, 3g Fat, 65 Calories

French Fried Butternut Squash

Servings: 6 | Cooking Time: 20 Minutes

Ingredients:
• 1 medium butternut squash
• 1 tablespoon chopped fresh thyme
• 1 tablespoon chopped fresh rosemary
• 4 tablespoons olive oil
• 1/2 teaspoon salt
• Cooking spray

Directions:
1. Heat oven to 425oF. Lightly coat a baking sheet with cooking spray.
2. Peel skin from butternut squash and cut into even sticks, about 1/2-inch-wide and 3 inches long.
3. In a medium bowl, combine the squash, oil, thyme, rosemary, and salt; mix until the squash is evenly coated.
4. Spread onto the baking sheet and roast for 10 minutes.
5. Remove the baking sheet from the oven and shake to loosen the squash.
6. Return to oven and continue to roast for 10 minutes or until golden brown.
7. Serve and enjoy.

Nutrition Info:
• Per Servings 1g Carbs, 1g Protein, 9g Fat, 86 Calories

Roasted Cauliflower With Serrano Ham & Pine Nuts

Servings: 6 | Cooking Time: 30 Minutes

Ingredients:
• 2 heads cauliflower, cut into 1-inch slices
• 2 tbsp olive oil
• Salt and chili pepper to taste
• 1 tsp garlic powder
• 10 slices Serrano ham, chopped
• ¼ cup pine nuts, chopped
• 1 tsp capers
• 1 tsp parsley

Directions:
1. Preheat oven to 450ºF and line a baking sheet with foil.
2. Brush the cauli steaks with olive oil and season with chili pepper, garlic, and salt.
3. Spread the cauli florets on the baking sheet. Roast in the oven for 10 minutes until tender and lightly browned. Remove the sheet and sprinkle the ham and pine nuts all over the cauli. Bake for another 10 minutes until the ham is crispy and a nutty aroma is perceived.
4. Take out, sprinkle with capers and parsley. Serve with

ground beef stew and braised asparagus.

Nutrition Info:
- Per Servings 2.5g Carbs, 10g Protein, 10g Fat, 141 Calories

Tofu Stuffed Peppers

Servings: 8 | Cooking Time: 10 Minutes

Ingredients:
- 1 package firm tofu, crumbled
- 1 onion, finely chopped
- ½ teaspoon turmeric powder
- 1 teaspoon coriander powder
- 8 banana peppers, top-end sliced and seeded
- Salt and pepper to taste
- 3 tablespoons oil

Directions:
1. Preheat oven to 400oF.
2. In a mixing bowl, combine the tofu, onion, coconut oil, turmeric powder, red chili powder, coriander powder, and salt. Mix until well-combined.
3. Scoop the tofu mixture into the hollows of the banana peppers.
4. Place the stuffed peppers in one layer in a lightly greased baking sheet.
5. Cook for 10 minutes.
6. Serve and enjoy.

Nutrition Info:
- Per Servings 4.1g Carbs, 1.2g Protein, 15.6g Fat, 187 Calories

Cheesy Cauliflower Bake With Mayo Sauce

Servings: 6 | Cooking Time: 27 Minutes

Ingredients:
- Cooking spray
- 2 heads cauliflower, cut into florets
- ¼ cup melted butter
- Salt and black pepper to taste
- 1 pinch red pepper flakes
- ½ cup mayonnaise
- ¼ tsp Dijon mustard
- 3 tbsp grated pecorino cheese

Directions:
1. Preheat oven to 400ºF and grease a baking dish with cooking spray.
2. Combine the cauli florets, butter, salt, black pepper, and red pepper flakes in a bowl until well mixed. Mix the mayonnaise and Dijon mustard in a bowl, and set aside until ready to serve. Arrange cauliflower florets on the prepared baking dish.
3. Sprinkle with grated pecorino cheese and bake for 25 minutes until the cheese has melted and golden brown on the top. Remove, let sit for 3 minutes to cool, and serve with the mayo sauce.

Nutrition Info:
- Per Servings 2g Carbs, 6g Protein, 35g Fat, 363 Calories

Cobb Salad With Blue Cheese Dressing

Servings: 6 | Cooking Time: 2 Hours 40 Minutes

Ingredients:
- ½ cup buttermilk
- 1 cup mayonnaise
- 2 tbsp sugar-free Worcestershire sauce
- ½ cup sour cream
- 1 ½ cup crumbled blue cheese
- Salt and black pepper to taste
- 2 tbsp chopped chives
- 6 eggs
- 1 cup water
- Ice bath
- 2 chicken breasts, boneless and skinless
- Salt and black pepper to taste
- 5 strips bacon
- 1 iceberg lettuce, cut into chunks
- 1 romaine lettuce, chopped
- 1 bibb lettuce, cored and leaves removed
- 2 avocado, pitted and diced
- 2 large tomatoes, chopped
- ½ cup crumbled blue cheese
- 2 scallions, chopped

Directions:
1. In a bowl, whisk the buttermilk, mayonnaise, Worcestershire sauce, and sour cream. Stir in the blue cheese, salt, pepper, and chives. Place in the refrigerator to chill for 2 hours.
2. Bring the eggs to boil in salted water over medium heat for 10 minutes. Once ready, drain the eggs and transfer to the ice bath. Peel and chop the eggs. Set aside.
3. Preheat the grill pan over high heat. Season the chicken with salt and pepper. Grill for 3 minutes on each side. Remove to a plate to cool for 3 minutes, and cut into bite-size chunks.
4. Fry the bacon in another pan set over medium heat until crispy, about 6 minutes. Remove, let cool for 2 minutes, and chop.
5. Arrange the lettuce leaves in a salad bowl and in single piles, add the avocado, tomatoes, eggs, bacon, and chicken. Sprinkle the blue cheese over the salad as well as the scallions and black pepper.
6. Drizzle the blue cheese dressing on the salad and serve with low carb bread.

Nutrition Info:
- Per Servings 2g Carbs, 23g Protein, 14g Fat, 122 Calories

Spiced Gruyere Crisps

Servings: 4 | Cooking Time: 10 Minutes

Ingredients:
- 2 cups gruyere cheese, shredded
- ½ tsp garlic powder
- ¼ tsp onion powder
- 1 rosemary sprig, minced
- ½ tsp chili powder

Directions:
1. Set oven to 400ºF. Coat two baking sheets with parchment paper.
2. Mix Gruyere cheese with the seasonings. Take 1 table-

spoon of cheese mixture and form small mounds on the baking sheets. Bake for 6 minutes. Leave to cool. Serve.

Nutrition Info:
• Per Servings 2.9g Carbs, 14.5g Protein, 15g Fat, 205 Calories

Garlic And Basil Mashed Celeriac

Servings: 4 | Cooking Time: 30 Minutes

Ingredients:
• 2 lb celeriac, chopped
• 4 cups water
• 2 oz cream cheese
• 2 tbsp butter
• ⅓ cup sour cream
• ½ tsp garlic powder
• 2 tsp dried basil
• Salt and black pepper to taste

Directions:
1. Bring the celeriac and water to boil over high heat on a stovetop for 5 minutes and then reduce the heat to low to simmer for 15 minutes. Drain the celeriac through a colander after.
2. Then, pour the celeriac in a large bowl, add the cream cheese, butter, sour cream, garlic powder, dried basil, salt, and pepper. Mix them with a hand mixer on medium speed until well combined.Serve with pan-grilled salmon.

Nutrition Info:
• Per Servings 6g Carbs, 2.4g Protein, 0.5g Fat, 94 Calories

Spicy Devilled Eggs With Herbs

Servings: 4 | Cooking Time: 30 Minutes

Ingredients:
• 12 large eggs
• 1 ½ cups water
• 6 tbsp mayonnaise
• Salt and chili pepper to taste
• 1 tsp mixed dried herbs
• ½ tsp sugar-free Worcestershire sauce
• ¼ tsp Dijon mustard
• A pinch of sweet paprika
• Chopped parsley to garnish
• Ice water Bath

Directions:
1. Pour the water into a saucepan, add the eggs, and bring to boil on high heat for 10 minutes. Cut the eggs in half lengthways and remove the yolks into a medium bowl. Use a fork to crush the yolks.
2. Add the mayonnaise, salt, chili pepper, dried herbs, Worcestershire sauce, mustard, and paprika. Mix together until a smooth paste has formed. Then, spoon the mixture into the piping bag and fill the egg white holes with it. Garnish with the chopped parsley and serve immediately.

Nutrition Info:
• Per Servings 0.4g Carbs, 6.7g Protein, 9.3g Fat, 112 Calories

Sweet And Hot Nuts

Servings: 12 | Cooking Time: 4 Hours

Ingredients:
• ½ pound assorted nuts, raw
• 1/3 cup butter, melted
• 1 teaspoon cayenne pepper or to taste
• 1 tablespoon MCT oil or coconut oil
• 1 packet stevia powder
• ¼ tsp salt

Directions:
1. Place all ingredients in the crockpot.
2. Give it a good stir to combine everything.
3. Close the lid and cook on low for 4 hours.

Nutrition Info:
• Per Servings 2.9g Carbs, 7.0g Protein, 21.6g Fat, 271 Calories

Parsnip And Carrot Fries With Aioli

Servings: 4 | Cooking Time: 40 Minutes

Ingredients:
• 4 tbsp mayonnaise
• 2 garlic cloves, minced
• Salt and black pepper to taste
• 3 tbsp lemon juice
• Parsnip and Carrots Fries:
• 6 medium parsnips, julienned
• 3 large carrots, julienned
• 2 tbsp olive oil
• 5 tbsp chopped parsley
• Salt and black pepper to taste

Directions:
1. Preheat the oven to 400ºF. Make the aioli by mixing the mayonnaise with garlic, salt, pepper, and lemon juice; then refrigerate for 30 minutes.
2. Spread the parsnip and carrots on a baking sheet. Drizzle with olive oil, sprinkle with salt, and pepper, and rub the seasoning into the veggies. Bake for 35 minutes. Remove and transfer to a plate. Garnish the vegetables with parsley and serve with the chilled aioli.

Nutrition Info:
• Per Servings 4.4g Carbs, 2.1g Protein, 4.1g Fat, 205 Calories

Cheddar Cheese Chips

Servings: 4 | Cooking Time: 8 Minutes

Ingredients:
• 8 oz cheddar cheese or provolone cheese or Edam cheese, in slices
• ½ tsp paprika powder

Directions:
1. Line baking sheet with foil and preheat oven to 400F.
2. Place cheese slices on a baking sheet and sprinkle the paprika powder on top.
3. Pop in the oven and bake for 8 to 10 minutes.
4. Pay an attention when the timer reaches 6 to 7 minutes as a

burnt cheese tastes bitter.

5. Serve and enjoy.

Nutrition Info:

• Per Servings 2.0g Carbs, 13.0g Protein, 19.0g Fat, 228 Calories

Crunchy Pork Rind And Zucchini Sticks

Servings: 4 | Cooking Time: 20 Minutes

Ingredients:

• Cooking spray
• ¼ cup pork rind crumbs
• 1 tsp sweet paprika
• ¼ cup shredded Parmesan cheese
• Salt and chili pepper to taste
• 3 fresh eggs
• 2 zucchinis, cut into strips
• Aioli:
• ½ cup mayonnaise
• 1 garlic clove, minced
• Juice and zest from ½ lemon

Directions:

1. Preheat oven to 425ºF and line a baking sheet with foil. Grease with cooking spray and set aside. Mix the pork rinds, paprika, parmesan cheese, salt, and chili pepper in a bowl. Beat the eggs in another bowl. Coat zucchini strips in egg, then in parmesan mixture, and arrange on the baking sheet. Grease lightly with cooking spray and bake for 15 minutes to be crispy.

2. To make the aioli, combine in a bowl mayonnaise, lemon juice, and garlic, and gently stir until everything is well incorporated. Add the lemon zest, adjust the seasoning and stir again. Cover and place in the refrigerator until ready to serve. Serve the zucchini strips with garlic aioli for dipping.

Nutrition Info:

• Per Servings 2g Carbs, 6g Protein, 14g Fat, 180 Calories

Choco And Coconut Bars

Servings: 9 | Cooking Time: 30 Minutes

Ingredients:

• 1 tbsp Stevia
• ¾ cup shredded coconut, unsweetened
• ½ cup ground nuts (almonds, pecans, or walnuts)
• ¼ cup unsweetened cocoa powder
• 4 tbsp coconut oil

Directions:

1. In a medium bowl, mix shredded coconut, nuts, and cocoa powder.

2. Add Stevia and coconut oil.

3. Mix batter thoroughly.

4. In a 9x9 square inch pan or dish, press the batter and for a 30-minutes place in the freezer.

5. Evenly divide into suggested servings and enjoy.

Nutrition Info:

• Per Servings 2.7g Carbs, 1.3g Protein, 9.3g Fat, 99.7 Calories

Mascarpone Snapped Amaretti Biscuits

Servings: 6 | Cooking Time: 25 Minutes

Ingredients:

• 6 egg whites
• 1 egg yolk, beaten
• 1 tsp vanilla bean paste
• 8 oz swerve confectioner's sugar
• A pinch of salt
• ¼ cup ground fragrant almonds
• 1 lemon juice
• 7 tbsp sugar-free amaretto liquor
• ¼ cup mascarpone cheese
• ¼ cup butter, room temperature
• ¾ cup swerve confectioner's sugar, for topping

Directions:

1. Preheat an oven to 300ºF and line a baking sheet with parchment paper. Set aside.

2. In a bowl, beat eggs whites, salt, and vanilla paste with the hand mixer while you gradually spoon in 8 oz of swerve confectioner's sugar until a stiff mixture. Add ground almonds and fold in the egg yolk, lemon juice, and amaretto liquor. Spoon the mixture into the piping bag and press out 40 to 50 mounds on the baking sheet.

3. Bake the biscuits for 15 minutes by which time they should be golden brown. Whisk the mascarpone cheese, butter, and swerve confectioner's sugar with the cleaned electric mixer; set aside.

4. When the biscuits are ready, transfer them into a serving bowl and let cool. Spread a scoop of mascarpone cream onto one biscuit and snap with another biscuit. Sift some swerve confectioner's sugar on top of them and serve.

Nutrition Info:

• Per Servings 3g Carbs, 9g Protein, 13g Fat, 165 Calories

Zesty Balsamic Chard

Servings: 6 | Cooking Time: 20 Minutes

Ingredients:

• 2 medium onions, chopped
• 6 garlic cloves, sliced
• 1/2 cup white balsamic vinegar
• 2 bunches Swiss chard, coarsely chopped
• 1/2 cup walnut halves, toasted
• 1/4 teaspoon salt
• 1/4 teaspoon pepper
• 3 tablespoons olive oil

Directions:

1. In a 6-qt. Stockpot, heat oil over medium-high heat. Add onions; cook and stir until tender. Add garlic; cook 1 minute longer.

2. Add vinegar, stirring to loosen any browned bits from pot. Add remaining ingredients; cook 4-6 minutes or until chard is tender, stirring occasionally.

Nutrition Info:

• Per Servings 4g Carbs, 4g Protein, 13g Fat, 144 Calories

Easy Garlic Keto Bread

Servings: 1 | Cooking Time: 1 Minute 30 Seconds

Ingredients:
- 1 large egg
- 1 tbsp milk
- 1 tbsp coconut flour
- 1 tbsp almond flour
- ¼ tsp baking powder
- Salt to taste

Directions:
1. Mix all ingredients in a bowl until well combined.
2. Pour into a mug and place in the microwave oven.
3. Cook for 1 minute and 30 seconds.
4. Once cooked, invert the mug.
5. Allow to cool before slicing.

Nutrition Info:
- Per Servings 3g Carbs, 4g Protein, 7g Fat, 75 Calories

Herb Cheese Sticks

Servings: 4 | Cooking Time: 15 Minutes

Ingredients:
- 1 cup pork rinds, crushed
- 1 tbsp Italian herb mix
- 1 egg
- 1 lb swiss cheese, cut into sticks
- Cooking spray

Directions:
1. Preheat oven to 350ºF and line a baking sheet with parchment paper. Combine pork rinds and herb mix in a bowl to be evenly mixed and beat the egg in another bowl. Coat the cheese sticks in egg and then generously dredge in pork rind mixture. Arrange on baking sheet. Bake for 4 to 5 minutes, take out after, let cool for 2 minutes, and serve with marinara sauce.

Nutrition Info:
- Per Servings 0g Carbs, 8g Protein, 17.3g Fat, 188 Calories

Jalapeno Popper Spread

Servings: 8 | Cooking Time: 3 Mins

Ingredients:
- 2 packages cream cheese, softened; low-carb
- 1 cup. mayonnaise
- 1 can chopped green chilies, drained
- 2 ounces canned diced jalapeno peppers, drained
- 1 cup. grated Parmesan cheese

Directions:
1. Combine cream cheese and mayonnaise in a bowl until incorporated. Add in jalapeno peppers and green chilies. In a microwave safe bowl, spread jalapeno peppers mixture and sprinkle with Parmesan cheese.
2. Microwave jalapeno peppers mixture on High about 3 minutes or until warm.

Nutrition Info:
- Per Servings 1g Carbs, 2.1g Protein, 11.1g Fat, 110 Calories

Easy Baked Parmesan Chips

Servings: 10 | Cooking Time: 10 Minutes

Ingredients:
- 1 cup grated Parmesan cheese, low fat
- 1 tablespoon olive oil

Directions:
1. Lightly grease a cookie sheet and preheat oven to 400°F.
2. Evenly sprinkle parmesan cheese on a cookie sheet into 10 circles. Place them about ½-inch apart.
3. Drizzle with oil
4. Bake until lightly browned and crisped.
5. Let it cool, evenly divide into suggested servings and enjoy.

Nutrition Info:
- Per Servings 1.4g Carbs, 2.8g Protein, 12.8g Fat, 142 Calories

Baked Vegetable Side

Servings: 4 | Cooking Time: 15 Minutes

Ingredients:
- 1 large zucchini, sliced
- 1 bell pepper, sliced
- ½ cup peeled garlic cloves, sliced
- A dash of oregano
- 4 tablespoons olive oil
- Salt and pepper to taste

Directions:
1. Place all ingredients in a mixing bowl. Stir to coat everything.
2. Place in a baking sheet.
3. Bake in a 350F preheated oven for 15 minutes.
4. Serve and enjoy.

Nutrition Info:
- Per Servings 10.0g Carbs, 3.0g Protein, 23.0g Fat, 191 Calories

Fat Burger Bombs

Servings: 6 | Cooking Time: 20 Minutes

Ingredients:
- 12 slices uncured bacon, chopped
- 1 cup almond flour
- 2 eggs, beaten
- ½ pound ground beef
- 3 tablespoons olive oil
- Salt and pepper to taste

Directions:
1. In a mixing bowl, combine all ingredients except for the olive oil.
2. Use your hands to form small balls with the mixture. Place in a baking sheet and allow it to set in the fridge for at least 2 hours.
3. Once 2 hours is nearly up, preheat oven to 400oF.
4. Place meatballs in a single layer in a baking sheet and brush the meatballs with olive oil on all sides.
5. Cook for 20 minutes.

Nutrition Info:
- Per Servings 1.9g Carbs, 19.1g Protein, 40.6g Fat, 448 Calories

Party Bacon And Pistachio Balls

Servings: 8 | Cooking Time: 45 Minutes

Ingredients:
- 8 bacon slices, cooked and chopped
- 8 ounces Liverwurst
- ¼ cup chopped pistachios
- 1 tsp Dijon mustard
- 6 ounces cream cheese

Directions:
1. Combine the liverwurst and pistachios in the bowl of your food processor. Pulse until smooth. Whisk the cream cheese and mustard in another bowl. Make 12 balls out of the liverwurst mixture.
2. Make a thin cream cheese layer over. Coat with bacon, arrange on a plate and chill for 30 minutes.

Nutrition Info:
- Per Servings 1.5g Carbs, 7g Protein, 12g Fat, 145 Calories

Onion Cheese Muffins

Servings: 6 | Cooking Time: 20 Minutes

Ingredients:
- ¼ cup Colby jack cheese, shredded
- ¼ cup shallots, minced
- 1 cup almond flour
- 1 egg
- 3 tbsp sour cream
- ½ tsp salt
- 3 tbsp melted butter or oil

Directions:
1. Line 6 muffin tins with 6 muffin liners. Set aside and preheat oven to 350oF.
2. In a bowl, stir the dry and wet ingredients alternately. Mix well using a spatula until the consistency of the mixture becomes even.
3. Scoop a spoonful of the batter to the prepared muffin tins.
4. Bake for 20 minutes in the oven until golden brown.
5. Serve and enjoy.

Nutrition Info:
- Per Servings 4.6g Carbs, 6.3g Protein, 17.4g Fat, 193 Calories

Ricotta And Pomegranate

Servings: 3 | Cooking Time: 12 Minutes

Ingredients:
- 1 cup Ricotta cheese
- 3 tablespoons olive oil
- 1/2 cup pomegranate Arils
- 2 tsp thyme, fresh
- 2 cups arugula leaves
- Pepper and salt to taste
- 1/2 tsp grated lemon zest

Directions:
1. Mix all ingredients in a bowl.
2. Toss until well combined.
3. Season with pepper and salt.

4. Serve and enjoy.

Nutrition Info:
- Per Servings 9g Carbs, 11g Protein, 25g Fat, 312 Calories

Bacon Jalapeno Poppers

Servings: 8 | Cooking Time: 10 Minutes

Ingredients:
- 4-ounce cream cheese
- ¼ cup cheddar cheese, shredded
- 1 teaspoon paprika
- 16 fresh jalapenos, sliced lengthwise and seeded
- 16 strips of uncured bacon, cut into half
- Salt and pepper to taste

Directions:
1. Preheat oven to 400oF.
2. In a mixing bowl, mix the cream cheese, cheddar cheese, salt, and paprika until well-combined.
3. Scoop half a teaspoon onto each half of jalapeno peppers.
4. Use a thin strip of bacon and wrap it around the cheese-filled jalapeno half.
5. Place in a single layer in a lightly greased baking sheet and roast for 10 minutes.
6. Serve and enjoy.

Nutrition Info:
- Per Servings 3.2g Carbs, 10.6g Protein, 18.9g Fat, 225 Calories

Sautéed Brussels Sprouts

Servings: 4 | Cooking Time: 8 Minutes

Ingredients:
- 2 cups Brussels sprouts, halved
- 1 tablespoon balsamic vinegar
- 4 tablespoons olive oil
- Salt and pepper to taste

Directions:
1. Place a saucepan on medium-high fire and heat oil for a minute.
2. Add all ingredients and sauté for 7 minutes.
3. Season with pepper and salt.
4. Serve and enjoy.

Nutrition Info:
- Per Servings 4.6g Carbs, 1.5g Protein, 16.8g Fat, 162 Calories

Tart Raspberry Crumble Bar

Servings: 9 | Cooking Time: 55 Minutes

Ingredients:
- 1/2 cup whole toasted almonds
- 1 cup almond flour
- 1 cup cold, unsalted butter, cut into cubes
- 2 eggs, beaten
- 3-ounce dried raspberries
- 1/4 teaspoon salt
- 3 tbsp MCT or coconut oil.

Directions:

1. In a food processor, pulse almonds until chopped coarsely. Transfer to a bowl.
2. Add almond flour and salt into the food processor and pulse until a bit combined. Add butter, eggs, and MCT oil. Pulse until you have a coarse batter. Evenly divide batter into two bowls.
3. In the first bowl of batter, knead well until it forms a ball. Wrap in cling wrap, flatten a bit and chill for an hour for easy handling.
4. In the second bowl of batter, add the raspberries. In a pinching motion, pinch batter to form clusters of streusel. Set aside.
5. When ready to bake, preheat oven to 375oF and lightly grease an 8x8-inch baking pan with cooking spray.
6. Discard cling wrap and evenly press dough on the bottom of the pan, up to 1-inch up the sides of the pan, making sure that everything is covered in dough.
7. Top with streusel.
8. Pop in the oven and bake until golden brown and berries are bubbly around 45 minutes.
9. Remove from oven and cool for 20 minutes before slicing into 9 equal bars.
10. Serve and enjoy or store in a lidded container for 10-days in the fridge.

Nutrition Info:
• Per Servings 3.9g Carbs, 2.8g Protein, 22.9g Fat, 229 Calories

Tasty Cream Cheese Stuffed Mushrooms

Servings: 2 | Cooking Time: 0 Mins

Ingredients:
• 12 mushrooms, keto-friendly
• 1 package cream cheese, softened; low-carb
• 1/4 cup grated Parmesan cheese
• 1/4 teaspoon ground black pepper
• 1/4 teaspoon ground cayenne pepper
• What you'll need from the store cupboard:
• 1 tablespoon olive oil
• 1 tablespoon minced garlic
• 1/4 teaspoon onion powder

Directions:
1. Preheat oven to 350 degrees F.
2. Clean mushrooms; chop stems and discard the cut ends.
3. Heat oil in a large skillet over medium heat, sauté garlic and chopped stems until crispy. Set aside.
4. In a bowl, combine mushroom mixture with cream cheese, Parmensan cheese, black pepper, onion powder and cayenne pepper, stir well.
5. Scoop the filling into each mushroom cap and transfer to a greased baking sheet.
6. Bake for 20 minutes or until liquid has formed under caps.

Nutrition Info:
• Per Servings 1.5g Carbs, 2.7g Protein, 8.2g Fat, 88 Calories

Cocktail Kielbasa With Mustard Sauce

Servings: 8 | Cooking Time: 6 Hours

Ingredients:
• 2 pounds kielbasa (Polish sausage)
• 1 jar prepared mustard
• 1 bay leaf
• Pepper to taste

Directions:
1. Slice kielbasa into bite-sized pieces.
2. Place all ingredients in the slow cooker.
3. Give a good stir to combine everything.
4. Close the lid and cook on low for 6 hours.
5. Remove the bay leaf.
6. Serve on toothpicks.

Nutrition Info:
• Per Servings 4g Carbs, 14g Protein, 20g Fat, 256 Calories

Cheese-jalapeno Mushrooms

Servings: 8 | Cooking Time: 20 Mins

Ingredients:
• 2 slices bacon
• 1 package cream cheese, softened; low-carb
• 3 tablespoons shredded Cheddar cheese
• 1 jalapeno pepper, ribs and seeds removed, finely chopped
• 8 mushrooms, stems removed and chopped and caps reserved; keto-friendly
• Salt and pepper to taste
• Cooking spray

Directions:
1. Preheat the oven to 400 degrees F.
2. In a large bowl, combine bacon, cream cheese, cheese, jalapenos, salt and pepper. Mix well.
3. Spoon the bacon filling into each mushroom cap. Then transfer the stuffed mushroom caps to a baking dish or sheet sprayed with cooking spray.
4. Bake until the mushroom caps are cooked, about 15-20 minutes.
5. Serve and enjoy.

Nutrition Info:
• Per Servings 2.5g Carbs, 6.1g Protein, 13.4g Fat, 151 Calories

Cranberry Sauce Meatballs

Servings: 2 | Cooking Time: 25 Mins

Ingredients:
• 1 pound lean ground beef
• 1 egg
• 2 tablespoons water
• 1/2 cup cauliflower rice
• 3 tablespoons minced onion
• 1 can jellied cranberry sauce, keto-friendly
• 3/4 cup chili sauce

Directions:
1. Preheat oven to 350 degrees F.
2. Mix the ground beef, egg, water, cauliflower rice and

minced onions together until well combined. Form into small meatballs and place on a rack over a foil-lined baking sheet.

3. Bake the meatballs for 20 to 25 minutes, turning halfway through.

4. Combine sauce ingredients in a large saucepan over low heat, toss with meatballs and allow to simmer on low for 1 hour.

5. Serve and garnish with parsley if desired.

Nutrition Info:
• Per Servings 8.6g Carbs, 9.8g Protein, 10.2g Fat, 193 Calories

Pecorino-mushroom Balls

Servings: 4 | Cooking Time: 20 Minutes

Ingredients:
• 2 tbsp butter, softened
• 2 garlic cloves, minced
• 2 cups portobello mushrooms, chopped
• 4 tbsp blanched almond flour
• 4 tbsp ground flax seeds
• 4 tbsp hemp seeds
• 4 tbsp sunflower seeds
• 1 tbsp cajun seasonings
• 1 tsp mustard
• 2 eggs, whisked
• ½ cup pecorino cheese

Directions:
1. Set a pan over medium-high heat and warm 1 tablespoon of butter. Add in mushrooms and garlic and sauté until there is no more water in mushrooms.

2. Place in pecorino cheese, almond flour, hemp seeds, mustard, eggs, sunflower seeds, flax seeds, and Cajun seasonings. Create 4 burgers from the mixture.

3. In a pan, warm the remaining butter; fry the burgers for 7 minutes. Flip them over with a wide spatula and cook for 6 more minutes. Serve while warm.

Nutrition Info:
• Per Servings 7.7g Carbs, 16.8g Protein, 30g Fat, 370 Calories

Asian Glazed Meatballs

Servings: 4 | Cooking Time: 35 Minutes

Ingredients:
• 1-pound frozen meatballs, thawed to room temperature
• ½ cup hoisin sauce
• 1 tablespoon apricot jam
• 2 tablespoons soy sauce
• ½ teaspoon sesame oil
• 5 tbsp MCT oil or coconut oil
• 2 tbsp water

Directions:
1. Place a heavy-bottomed pot on medium-high fire and heat coconut oil.

2. Sauté meatballs until lightly browned, around 10 minutes.

3. Stir in remaining ingredients and mix well.

4. Cover and cook for 25 minutes on low fire, mixing now and then.

5. Serve and enjoy.

Nutrition Info:
• Per Servings 6.5g Carbs, 16.3g Protein, 51.6g Fat, 536 Calories

Chapter 3 Vegan, Vegetable & Meatless Recipes

Chapter 3 Vegan, Vegetable & Meatless Recipes

Keto Cauliflower Hash Browns

Servings: 4 | Cooking Time: 30 Mins

Ingredients:
- 1 lb cauliflower
- 3 eggs
- ½ yellow onion, grated
- 2 pinches pepper
- 4 oz. butter, for frying
- What you'll need from the store cupboard:
- 1 tsp salt

Directions:

1. Rinse, trim and grate the cauliflower using a food processor or grater.
2. In a large bowl, add the cauliflower onion and pepper, tossing evenly. Set aside for 5 to 10 minutes.
3. In a large skillet over medium heat, heat a generous amount of butter on medium heat. The cooking process will go quicker if you plan to have room for 3–4 pancakes at a time. Use the oven on low heat to keep the first batches of pancakes warm while you make the others.
4. Place scoops of the grated cauliflower mixture in the frying pan and flatten them carefully until they measure about 3 to 4 inches in diameter.
5. Fry for 4 to 5 minutes on each side. Adjust the heat to make sure they don't burn. Serve.

Nutrition Info:
- Per Servings 5g Carbs, 7g Protein, 26g Fat, 282 Calories

Wild Mushroom And Asparagus Stew

Servings: 4 | Cooking Time: 25 Minutes

Ingredients:
- 2 tbsp olive oil
- 1 cup onions, chopped
- 2 garlic cloves, pressed
- ½ cup celery, chopped
- 2 carrots, chopped
- 1 cup wild mushrooms, sliced
- 2 tbsp dry white wine
- 2 rosemary sprigs, chopped
- 1 thyme sprig, chopped
- 4 cups vegetable stock
- ½ tsp chili pepper
- 1 tsp smoked paprika
- 2 tomatoes, chopped
- 1 tbsp flax seed meal

Directions:

1. Set a stockpot over medium heat and warm oil. Add in onions and cook until tender.
2. Place in carrots, celery, and garlic and cook until soft for 4 more minutes. Add in mushrooms; cook the mixture the liquid is lost; set the vegetables aside. Stir in wine to deglaze the stockpot's bottom. Place in thyme and rosemary. Pour in

tomatoes, vegetable stock, paprika, and chili pepper; add in reserved vegetables and allow to boil.
3. On low heat, allow the mixture to simmer for 15 minutes while covered. Stir in flax seed meal to thicken the stew. Plate into individual bowls and serve.

Nutrition Info:
- Per Servings 9.5g Carbs, 2.1g Protein, 7.3g Fat, 114 Calories

Guacamole

Servings: 2 | Cooking Time: 0 Minutes

Ingredients:
- 2 medium ripe avocados
- 1 tablespoon lemon juice
- 1/4 cup chopped tomatoes
- 4 tablespoons olive oil
- 1/4 teaspoon salt
- Pepper to taste

Directions:

1. Peel and chop avocados; place them in a small bowl. Sprinkle with lemon juice.
2. Add tomatoes and salt.
3. Season with pepper to taste and mash coarsely with a fork. Refrigerate until serving.

Nutrition Info:
- Per Servings 10g Carbs, 6g Protein, 56g Fat, 565 Calories

Garlic Lemon Mushrooms

Servings: 4 | Cooking Time: 20 Minutes

Ingredients:
- 1/4 cup lemon juice
- 3 tablespoons minced fresh parsley
- 3 garlic cloves, minced
- 1-pound large fresh mushrooms
- 4 tablespoons olive oil
- Pepper to taste

Directions:

1. For the dressing, whisk together the first 5 ingredients. Toss mushrooms with 2 tablespoons dressing.
2. Grill mushrooms, covered, over medium-high heat until tender, 5-7 minutes per side. Toss with remaining dressing before serving.

Nutrition Info:
- Per Servings 6.8g Carbs, 4g Protein, 14g Fat, 160 Calories

Cheesy Cauliflower Falafel

Servings: 4 | Cooking Time: 15 Minutes

Ingredients:
- 1 head cauliflower, cut into florets
- ⅓ cup silvered ground almonds
- ½ tsp mixed spice
- Salt and chili pepper to taste
- 3 tbsp coconut flour
- 3 fresh eggs
- 4 tbsp ghee

Directions:
1. Blend the cauli florets in a food processor until a grain meal consistency is formed. Pour the puree in a bowl, add the ground almonds, mixed spice, salt, chili pepper, and coconut flour, and mix until evenly combined.
2. Beat the eggs in a bowl until creamy in color and mix with the cauli mixture. Shape ¼ cup each into patties and set aside.
3. Melt ghee in a frying pan over medium heat and fry the patties for 5 minutes on each side to be firm and browned. Remove onto a wire rack to cool, share into serving plates, and top with tahini sauce.

Nutrition Info:
- Per Servings 2g Carbs, 8g Protein, 26g Fat, 315 Calories

Grilled Spicy Eggplant

Servings: 2 | Cooking Time: 20 Minutes

Ingredients:
- 2 small eggplants, cut into 1/2-inch slices
- 1/4 cup olive oil
- 2 tablespoons lime juice
- 3 teaspoons Cajun seasoning
- Salt and pepper to taste

Directions:
1. Brush eggplant slices with oil. Drizzle with lime juice; sprinkle with Cajun seasoning. Let stand for 5 minutes.
2. Grill eggplant, covered, over medium heat or broil 4 minutes. from heat until tender, 4-5 minutes per side.
3. Season with pepper and salt to taste.
4. Serve and enjoy.

Nutrition Info:
- Per Servings 7g Carbs, 5g Protein, 28g Fat, 350 Calories

Vegan Cheesy Chips With Tomatoes

Servings: 6 | Cooking Time: 15 Minutes

Ingredients:
- 5 tomatoes, sliced
- ¼ cup olive oil
- 1 tbsp seasoning mix
- For Vegan cheese
- ½ cup pepitas seeds
- 1 tbsp nutritional yeast
- Salt and black pepper, to taste
- 1 tsp garlic puree

Directions:
1. Over the sliced tomatoes, drizzle olive oil. Set oven to 200ºF.
2. In a food processor, add all vegan cheese ingredients and pulse until the desired consistency is attained. Combine vegan cheese and seasoning mixture. Toss in seasoned tomato slices to coat.
3. Set the tomato slices on the prepared baking pan and bake for 10 minutes.

Nutrition Info:
- Per Servings 7.2g Carbs, 4.6g Protein, 14g Fat, 161 Calories

Cauliflower Mac And Cheese

Servings: 7 | Cooking Time: 45 Minutes

Ingredients:
- 1 cauliflower head, riced
- 1 ½ cups shredded cheese
- 2 tsp paprika
- ¾ tsp rosemary
- 2 tsp turmeric
- 3 eggs
- Olive oil, for frying

Directions:
1. Microwave the cauliflower for 5 minutes. Place it in cheesecloth and squeeze the extra juices out. Place the cauliflower in a bowl. Stir in the rest of the ingredients.
2. Heat the oil in a deep pan until it reaches 360ºF. Add the 'mac and cheese' and fry until golden and crispy. Drain on paper towels before serving.

Nutrition Info:
- Per Servings 2g Carbs, 8.6g Protein, 12g Fat, 160 Calories

Kale Cheese Waffles

Servings: 4 | Cooking Time: 45 Minutes

Ingredients:
- 2 green onions
- 1 tbsp olive oil
- 2 eggs
- ⅓ cup Parmesan cheese
- 1 cup kale, chopped
- 1 cup mozzarella cheese
- ½ cauliflower head
- 1 tsp garlic powder
- 1 tbsp sesame seeds
- 2 tsp chopped thyme

Directions:
1. Place the chopped cauliflower in the food processor and process until rice is formed. Add kale, spring onions, and thyme to the food processor. Pulse until smooth. Transfer to a bowl. Stir in the rest of the ingredients and mix to combine.
2. Heat waffle iron and spread in the mixture, evenly. Cook following the manufacturer's instructions.

Nutrition Info:
- Per Servings 3.6g Carbs, 16g Protein, 20.2g Fat, 283 Calories

Coconut Cauliflower & Parsnip Soup

Servings: 4 | Cooking Time: 20 Minutes

Ingredients:
- 4 cups vegetable broth
- 2 heads cauliflower, cut into florets
- 1 cup parsnip, chopped
- 1 tbsp coconut oil
- 1 cup coconut milk
- ½ tsp red pepper flakes

Directions:
1. Add water in a pot set over medium-high heat and bring to a boil. Add in cauliflower florets and parsnip, cook for about 10 minutes. Add in broth and coconut oil. While on low heat, cook for an additional 5 minutes. Transfer the mixture to an immersion blender and puree.
2. Plate into four separate soup bowls; decorate each with red pepper flakes. Serve while warm.

Nutrition Info:
- Per Servings 7g Carbs, 2.7g Protein, 7.2g Fat, 94 Calories

Herb Butter With Parsley

Servings: 1 | Cooking Time: 0 Minutes

Ingredients:
- 5 oz. butter, at room temperature
- 1 garlic clove, pressed
- ½ tbsp garlic powder
- 4 tbsp fresh parsley, finely chopped
- 1 tsp lemon juice
- ½ tsp salt

Directions:
1. In a bowl, stir all ingredients until completely combined. Set aside for 15 minutes or refrigerate it before serving.

Nutrition Info:
- Per Servings 1g Carbs, 1g Protein, 28g Fat, 258 Calories

Roasted Leeks And Asparagus

Servings: 12 | Cooking Time: 25 Minutes

Ingredients:
- 3 pounds fresh asparagus, trimmed
- 2 medium leeks (white portion only), halved lengthwise
- 1-1/2 teaspoons dill weed
- 1/2 teaspoon crushed red pepper flakes
- 3 tablespoons melted butter
- 1/4 teaspoon pepper
- 1/2 teaspoon salt
- 4 ½ tablespoons olive oil

Directions:
1. Place asparagus and leeks on an ungreased 15x10x1-inch baking pan. Combine the remaining ingredients; pour over vegetables.
2. Bake at 400F for 20-25 minutes or until tender, stirring occasionally.

Nutrition Info:
- Per Servings 6g Carbs, 3g Protein, 8g Fat, 98 Calories

Sausage Roll

Servings: 6 | Cooking Time: 1 Hour And 15 Minutes

Ingredients:
- 6 vegan sausages (defrosted)
- 1 cup mushrooms
- 1 onion
- 2 fresh sage leaves
- 1 package tofu skin sheet
- Salt and pepper to taste
- 5 tablespoons olive oil

Directions:
1. Preheat the oven to 180°F/356°F assisted.
2. Defrost the vegan sausages.
3. Roughly chop the mushrooms and add them to a food processor. Process until mostly broken down. Peel and roughly chop the onions, then add them to the processor along with the defrosted vegan sausages, sage leaves, and a pinch of salt and pepper. Pour in the oil. Process until all the ingredients have mostly broken down, and only a few larger pieces remain.
4. Heat a frying pan on a medium heat. Once hot, transfer the mushroom mixture to the pan and fry for 20 minutes or until almost all of the moisture has evaporated, frequently stirring to prevent the mixture sticking to the pan.
5. Remove the mushroom mixture from the heat and transfer to a plate. Leave to cool completely. Tip: if it's cold outside, we leave the mushroom mixture outdoors, so it cools quicker.
6. Meanwhile, either line a large baking tray with baking paper or (if the pastry already comes wrapped in a sheet of baking paper) roll out the tofu skin onto the tray and cut it in half both lengthways and widthways to create 4 equal-sized pieces of tofu skin.
7. Spoon a quarter of the mushroom mixture along the length of each rectangle of tofu skin and shape the mixture into a log. Add one vegan sausage and roll into a log.
8. Seal the roll by securing the edged with a toothpick.
9. Brush the sausage rolls with olive oil and bake for 40-45 minutes until golden brown. Enjoy!

Nutrition Info:
- Per Servings 3g Carbs, 0.9g Protein, 11g Fat, 113 Calories

Vegetable Tempura

Servings: 4 | Cooking Time: 17 Minutes

Ingredients:
- ½ cup coconut flour + extra for dredging
- Salt and black pepper to taste
- 3 egg yolks
- 2 red bell peppers, cut into strips
- 1 squash, peeled and cut into strips
- 1 broccoli, cut into florets
- 1 cup Chilled water
- Olive oil for frying
- Lemon wedges to serve
- Sugar-free soy sauce to serve

Directions:
1. In a deep frying pan or wok, heat the olive oil over medium heat. Beat the eggs lightly with ½ cup of coconut flour and water. The mixture should be lumpy. Dredge the vegetables light-

ly in some flour, shake off the excess flour, dip it in the batter, and then into the hot oil.

2. Fry in batches for 1 minute each, not more, and remove with a perforated spoon onto a wire rack. Sprinkle with salt and pepper and serve with the lemon wedges and soy sauce.

Nutrition Info:
- Per Servings 0.9g Carbs, 3g Protein, 17g Fat, 218 Calories

Chard Swiss Dip

Servings: 6 | Cooking Time: 25 Minutes

Ingredients:
- 2 cups Swiss chard
- 1 cup tofu, pressed, drained, crumbled
- ½ cup almond milk
- 2 tsp nutritional yeast
- 2 garlic cloves, minced
- 2 tbsp olive oil
- Salt and pepper to taste
- ½ tsp paprika
- ½ tsp chopped fresh mint leaves

Directions:
1. Set oven to 400ºF. Spray a nonstick cooking spray on a casserole pan. Boil Swiss chard until wilted. Using a blender, puree the remaining ingredients. Season with salt and pepper. Stir in the Swiss chard to get a homogeneous mixture. Bake for 13 minutes. Serve alongside baked vegetables.

Nutrition Info:
- Per Servings 7.9g Carbs, 2.9g Protein, 7.3g Fat, 105 Calories

Garlicky Bok Choy

Servings: 4 | Cooking Time: 25 Minutes

Ingredients:
- 2 pounds bok choy, chopped
- 2 tbsp almond oil
- 1 tsp garlic, minced
- ½ tsp thyme
- ½ tsp red pepper flakes, crushed
- Salt and black pepper, to the taste

Directions:
1. Add Bok choy in a pot containing salted water and cook for 10 minutes over medium heat. Drain and set aside. Place a sauté pan over medium-high heat and warm the oil.
2. Add in garlic and cook until soft. Stir in the Bok choy, red pepper, black pepper, salt, and thyme and ensure they are heated through. Add more seasonings if needed and serve warm with cauli rice.

Nutrition Info:
- Per Servings 13.4g Carbs, 2.9g Protein, 7g Fat, 118 Calories

Creamy Artichoke And Spinach

Servings: 4 | Cooking Time: 15 Minutes

Ingredients:
- 5 tablespoons olive oil
- 1 can water-packed artichoke hearts quartered
- 1 package frozen spinach
- 1 cup shredded part-skim mozzarella cheese, divided
- 1/4 cup grated Parmesan cheese
- 1/2 teaspoon salt
- 1/4 teaspoon pepper

Directions:
1. Heat oil in a pan over medium flame. Add artichoke hearts and season with salt and pepper to taste. Cook for 5 minutes. Stir in the spinach until wilted.
2. Place in a bowl and stir in mozzarella cheese, Parmesan cheese, salt, and pepper. Toss to combine.
3. Transfer to a greased 2-qt. Broiler-safe baking dish; sprinkle with remaining mozzarella cheese. Broil 4-6 in. from heat 2-3 minutes or until cheese is melted.

Nutrition Info:
- Per Servings 7.3g Carbs, 11.5g Protein, 23.9g Fat, 283 Calories

Stuffed Portobello Mushrooms

Servings: 2 | Cooking Time: 30 Minutes

Ingredients:
- 4 portobello mushrooms, stems removed
- 2 tbsp olive oil
- 2 cups lettuce
- 1 cup crumbled blue cheese

Directions:
1. Preheat the oven to 350ºF. Fill the mushrooms with blue cheese and place on a lined baking sheet; bake for 20 minutes. Serve with lettuce drizzled with olive oil.

Nutrition Info:
- Per Servings 5.5g Carbs, 14g Protein, 29g Fat, 334 Calories

Easy Vanilla Granola

Servings: 6 | Cooking Time: 1 Hour

Ingredients:
- ½ cup hazelnuts, chopped
- 1 cup walnuts, chopped
- ⅓ cup flax meal
- ⅓ cup coconut milk
- ⅓ cup poppy seeds
- ⅓ cup pumpkin seeds
- 8 drops stevia
- ⅓ cup coconut oil, melted
- 1 ½ tsp vanilla paste
- 1 tsp ground cloves
- 1 tsp grated nutmeg
- 1 tsp lemon zest
- ⅓ cup water

Directions:
1. Set oven to 300ºF. Line a parchment paper to a baking

sheet. Combine all ingredients. Spread the mixture onto the baking sheet in an even layer. Bake for 55 minutes, as you stir at intervals of 15 minutes. Let cool at room temperature.

Nutrition Info:
• Per Servings 5.1g Carbs, 9.3g Protein, 44.9g Fat, 449 Calories

Endives Mix With Lemon Dressing

Servings: 8 | Cooking Time: 0 Minutes

Ingredients:
• 1 bunch watercress
• 2 heads endive, halved lengthwise and thinly sliced
• 1 cup pomegranate seeds
• 1 shallot, thinly sliced
• 2 lemons, juiced and zested
• 1/4 teaspoon salt
• 1/8 teaspoon pepper
• 1/4 cup olive oil

Directions:
1. In a large bowl, combine watercress, endive, pomegranate seeds, and shallot.
2. In a small bowl, whisk the lemon juice, zest, salt, pepper, and olive oil. Drizzle over salad; toss to coat.

Nutrition Info:
• Per Servings 6g Carbs, 2g Protein, 13g Fat, 151 Calories

Parsnip Chips With Avocado Dip

Servings: 6 | Cooking Time: 20 Minutes

Ingredients:
• 2 avocados, pitted
• 2 tsp lime juice
• Salt and black pepper, to taste
• 2 garlic cloves, minced
• 2 tbsp olive oil
• For Parsnip Chips
• 3 cups parsnips, sliced
• 1 tbsp olive oil
• Sea salt and garlic powder, to taste

Directions:
1. Use a fork to mash avocado pulp. Stir in fresh lime juice, pepper, 2 tbsp of olive oil, garlic, and salt until well combined. Remove to a bowl and set the oven to 300 ºF. Grease a baking sheet with spray.
2. Set parsnip slices on the baking sheet; toss with garlic powder, 1 tbsp of olive oil, and salt. Bake for 15 minutes until slices become dry. Serve alongside well-chilled avocado dip.

Nutrition Info:
• Per Servings 9.4g Carbs, 2.3g Protein, 26.7g Fat, 269 Calories

Herbed Portobello Mushrooms

Servings: 2 | Cooking Time: 10 Minutes

Ingredients:
• 2 Portobello mushrooms, stemmed and wiped clean
• 1 tsp minced garlic
• ¼ tsp dried rosemary
• 1 tablespoon balsamic vinegar
• ¼ cup grated provolone cheese
• 4 tablespoons olive oil
• Salt and pepper to taste

Directions:
1. In an oven, position rack 4-inches away from the top and preheat broiler.
2. Prepare a baking dish by spraying with cooking spray lightly.
3. Stemless, place mushroom gill side up.
4. Mix well garlic, rosemary, balsamic vinegar, and olive oil in a small bowl. Season with salt and pepper to taste.
5. Drizzle over mushrooms equally.
6. Marinate for at least 5 minutes before popping into the oven and broiling for 4 minutes per side or until tender.
7. Once cooked, remove from oven, sprinkle cheese, return to broiler and broil for a minute or two or until cheese melts.
8. Remove from oven and serve right away.

Nutrition Info:
• Per Servings 21.5g Carbs, 8.6g Protein, 5.1g Fat, 168 Calories

Tofu Sesame Skewers With Warm Kale Salad

Servings: 4 | Cooking Time: 2 Hours 40 Minutes

Ingredients:
• 14 oz Firm tofu
• 4 tsp sesame oil
• 1 lemon, juiced
• 5 tbsp sugar-free soy sauce
• 3 tsp garlic powder
• 4 tbsp coconut flour
• ½ cup sesame seeds
• Warm Kale Salad:
• 4 cups chopped kale
• 2 tsp + 2 tsp olive oil
• 1 white onion, thinly sliced
• 3 cloves garlic, minced
• 1 cup sliced white mushrooms
• 1 tsp chopped rosemary
• Salt and black pepper to season
• 1 tbsp balsamic vinegar

Directions:
1. In a bowl, mix sesame oil, lemon juice, soy sauce, garlic powder, and coconut flour. Wrap the tofu in a paper towel, squeeze out as much liquid from it, and cut it into strips. Stick on the skewers, height wise. Place onto a plate, pour the soy sauce mixture over, and turn in the sauce to be adequately coated. Cover the dish with cling film and marinate in the fridge for 2 hours.
2. Heat the griddle pan over high heat. Pour the sesame seeds

in a plate and roll the tofu skewers in the seeds for a generous coat. Grill the tofu in the griddle pan to be golden brown on both sides, about 12 minutes in total.

3. Heat 2 tablespoons of olive oil in a skillet over medium heat and sauté onion to begin browning for 10 minutes with continuous stirring. Add the remaining olive oil and mushrooms. Continue cooking for 10 minutes. Add garlic, rosemary, salt, pepper, and balsamic vinegar. Cook for 1 minute.

4. Put the kale in a salad bowl; when the onion mixture is ready, pour it on the kale and toss well. Serve the tofu skewers with the warm kale salad and a peanut butter dipping sauce.

Nutrition Info:
- Per Servings 6.1g Carbs, 5.6g Protein, 12.9g Fat, 263 Calories

Coconut Cauliflower Rice
Servings: 3 | Cooking Time: 15 Minutes

Ingredients:
- 1 head cauliflower, grated
- ½ cup heavy cream
- ¼ cup butter, melted
- 3 cloves of garlic, minced
- 1 onion, chopped
- Salt and pepper to taste

Directions:
1. Place a nonstick saucepan on high fire and heat cream and butter.
2. Saute onion and garlic for 3 minutes.
3. Stir in grated cauliflower. Season with pepper and salt.
4. Cook until cauliflower is tender, around 5 minutes.
5. Turn off fire and let it set for 5 minutes.
6. Serve and enjoy.

Nutrition Info:
- Per Servings 9g Carbs, 3g Protein, 23g Fat, 246 Calories

Cauliflower Gouda Casserole
Servings: 4 | Cooking Time: 21 Minutes

Ingredients:
- 2 heads cauliflower, cut into florets
- ⅓ cup butter, cubed
- 2 tbsp melted butter
- 1 white onion, chopped
- Pink salt and black pepper to taste
- ¼ almond milk
- ½ cup almond flour
- 1 ½ cup grated gouda cheese
- Water for sprinkling

Directions:
1. Preheat oven to 350ºF and put the cauli florets in a large microwave-safe bowl. Sprinkle with water, and steam in the microwave for 4 to 5 minutes.
2. Melt the ⅓ cup of butter in a saucepan over medium heat and sauté the onion for 3 minutes. Add the cauliflower, season with salt and black pepper and mix in almond milk. Simmer for 3 minutes.
3. Mix the remaining melted butter with almond flour. Stir into the cauliflower as well as half of the cheese. Sprinkle the

top with the remaining cheese and bake for 10 minutes until the cheese has melted and golden brown on the top. Plate the bake and serve with arugula salad.

Nutrition Info:
- Per Servings 4g Carbs, 12g Protein, 15g Fat, 215 Calories

Zucchini Noodles
Servings: 6 | Cooking Time: 15 Mins

Ingredients:
- 2 cloves garlic, minced
- 2 medium zucchini, cut into noodles with a spiralizer
- 12 zucchini blossoms, pistils removed; cut into strips
- 6 fresh basil leaves, cut into strips, or to taste
- 4 tablespoons olive oil
- Salt to taste

Directions:
1. In a large skillet over low heat, cook garlic in olive oil for 10 minutes until slightly browned. Add in zucchini and zucchini blossoms, stir well.
2. Toss in green beans and season with salt to taste; sprinkle with basil and serve.

Nutrition Info:
- Per Servings 13.5g Carbs, 5.7g Protein, 28.1g Fat, 348 Calories

Keto Enchilada Bake
Servings: 6 | Cooking Time: 20 Minutes

Ingredients:
- 1 package House Foods Organic Extra Firm Tofu
- 1 cup roma tomatoes, chopped
- 1 cup shredded cheddar cheese
- 1 small avocado, pitted and sliced
- ½ cup sour cream
- 5 tablespoons olive oil
- Salt and pepper to taste

Directions:
1. Preheat oven to 350F.
2. Cut tofu into small cubes and sauté with oil and seasoning. Set aside and reserve the oil.
3. Place the tofu in the bottom of a casserole dish.
4. Mix the reserved oil and tomatoes and pour over the tofu.
5. Sprinkle with cheese on top.
6. Bake for 20 minutes.
7. Top with avocado and sour cream toppings.
8. Serve and enjoy.

Nutrition Info:
- Per Servings 6g Carbs, 38g Protein, 40g Fat, 568 Calories

Spiced Cauliflower & Peppers
Servings: 4 | Cooking Time: 35 Minutes

Ingredients:
- 1 pound cauliflower, cut into florets
- 2 bell peppers, halved
- ¼ cup olive oil
- Sea salt and black pepper, to taste

- ½ tsp cayenne pepper
- 1 tsp curry powder

Directions:

1. Set oven to 425 ºF. Line a parchment paper to a large baking sheet. Sprinkle olive oil to the peppers and cauliflower alongside curry powder, black pepper, salt, and cayenne pepper.

2. Set the vegetables on the baking sheet. Roast for 30 minutes as you toss in intervals until they start to brown. Serve alongside mushroom pate or homemade tomato dip!

Nutrition Info:
- Per Servings 7.4g Carbs, 3g Protein, 13.9g Fat, 166 Calories

Grilled Cauliflower

Servings: 8 | Cooking Time: 20 Minutes

Ingredients:
- 1 large head cauliflower
- 1 teaspoon ground turmeric
- 1/2 teaspoon crushed red pepper flakes
- Lemon juice, additional olive oil, and pomegranate seeds, optional
- 2 tablespoons olive oil
- 2 tablespoons melted butter

Directions:

1. Remove leaves and trim stem from cauliflower. Cut cauliflower into eight wedges. Mix turmeric and pepper flakes. Brush wedges with oil; sprinkle with turmeric mixture.

2. Grill, covered, over medium-high heat or broil 4 minutes from heat until cauliflower is tender, 8-10 minutes on each side. If desired, drizzle with lemon juice and additional oil. Brush with melted butter and serve with pomegranate seeds.

Nutrition Info:
- Per Servings 2.3g Carbs, 0.7g Protein, 6.3g Fat, 66 Calories

Mushroom & Jalapeño Stew

Servings: 4 | Cooking Time: 50 Minutes

Ingredients:
- 2 tsp olive oil
- 1 cup leeks, chopped
- 1 garlic clove, minced
- ½ cup celery, chopped
- ½ cup carrot, chopped
- 1 green bell pepper, chopped
- 1 jalapeño pepper, chopped
- 2 ½ cups mushrooms, sliced
- 1 ½ cups vegetable stock
- 2 tomatoes, chopped
- 2 thyme sprigs, chopped
- 1 rosemary sprig, chopped
- 2 bay leaves
- ½ tsp salt
- ¼ tsp ground black pepper
- 2 tbsp vinegar

Directions:

1. Set a pot over medium-high heat and warm oil. Add in garlic and leeks and sauté until soft and translucent. Add in the pepper, celery, mushrooms, and carrots.

2. Cook as you stir for 12 minutes; stir in a splash of vegetable stock to ensure there is no sticking. Stir in the rest of the ingredients. Set heat to medium; allow to simmer for 25 to 35 minutes or until cooked through. Divide into individual bowls and serve while warm.

Nutrition Info:
- Per Servings 9g Carbs, 2.7g Protein, 2.7g Fat, 65 Calories

Briam With Tomato Sauce

Servings: 4 | Cooking Time: 70 Minutes

Ingredients:
- 3 tbsp olive oil
- 1 large eggplant, halved and sliced
- 1 large onion, thinly sliced
- 3 cloves garlic, sliced
- 5 tomatoes, diced
- 3 rutabagas, peeled and diced
- 1 cup sugar-free tomato sauce
- 4 zucchinis, sliced
- ¼ cup water
- Salt and black pepper to taste
- 1 tbsp dried oregano
- 2 tbsp chopped parsley

Directions:

1. Preheat the oven to 400ºF. Heat the olive oil in a skillet over medium heat and cook the eggplants in it for 6 minutes to brown on the edges. After, remove to a medium bowl.

2. Sauté the onion and garlic in the oil for 3 minutes and add them to the eggplants. Turn the heat off.

3. In the eggplants bowl, mix in the tomatoes, rutabagas, tomato sauce, and zucchinis. Add the water and stir in the salt, pepper, oregano, and parsley. Pour the mixture in the casserole dish. Place the dish in the oven and bake for 45 to 60 minutes. Serve the briam warm on a bed of cauli rice.

Nutrition Info:
- Per Servings 12.5g Carbs, 11.3g Protein, 12g Fat, 365 Calories

Tasty Cauliflower Dip

Servings: 4 | Cooking Time: 10 Minutes

Ingredients:
- ¾ pound cauliflower, cut into florets
- ¼ cup olive oil
- Salt and black pepper, to taste
- 1 garlic clove, smashed
- 1 tbsp sesame paste
- 1 tbsp fresh lime juice
- ½ tsp garam masala

Directions:

1. Steam cauliflower until tender for 7 minutes in. Transfer to a blender and pulse until you attain a rice-like consistency.

2. Place in Garam Masala, oil, black paper, fresh lime juice, garlic, salt, and sesame paste. Blend the mixture until well combined. Decorate with some additional olive oil and serve. Otherwise, refrigerate until ready to use.

Nutrition Info:
- Per Servings 4.7g Carbs, 3.7g Protein, 8.2g Fat, 100 Calories

Egg And Tomato Salad

Servings: 2 | Cooking Time: 1 Minute

Ingredients:
• 4 hard-boiled eggs, peeled and sliced
• 2 red tomatoes, chopped
• 1 small red onion, chopped
• 2 tablespoons lemon juice, freshly squeezed
• Salt and pepper to taste
• 4 tablespoons olive oil

Directions:
1. Place all ingredients in a mixing bowl.
2. Toss to coat all ingredients.
3. Garnish with parsley if desired.
4. Serve over toasted whole wheat bread.

Nutrition Info:
• Per Servings 9.1g Carbs, 14.7g Protein, 15.9g Fat, 189 Calories

Grilled Parmesan Eggplant

Servings: 4 | Cooking Time: 15 Minutes

Ingredients:
• 1 medium-sized eggplant
• 1 log fresh mozzarella cheese, cut into sixteen slices
• 1 small tomato, cut into eight slices
• 1/2 cup shredded Parmesan cheese
• Chopped fresh basil or parsley
• 1/2 teaspoon salt
• 1 tablespoon olive oil
• 1/2 teaspoon pepper

Directions:
1. Trim ends of the eggplant; cut eggplant crosswise into eight slices. Sprinkle with salt; let stand 5 minutes.
2. Blot eggplant dry with paper towels; brush both sides with oil and sprinkle with pepper. Grill, covered, over medium heat 4-6 minutes on each side or until tender. Remove from grill.
3. Top eggplant with mozzarella cheese, tomato, and Parmesan cheese. Grill, covered, 1-2 minutes longer or until cheese begins to melt. Top with basil.

Nutrition Info:
• Per Servings 10g Carbs, 26g Protein, 31g Fat, 449 Calories

Cream Of Zucchini And Avocado

Servings: 4 | Cooking Time: 35 Minutes

Ingredients:
• 3 tsp vegetable oil
• 1 onion, chopped
• 1 carrot, sliced
• 1 turnip, sliced
• 3 cups zucchinis, chopped
• 1 avocado, peeled and diced
• ¼ tsp ground black pepper
• 4 vegetable broth
• 1 tomato, pureed

Directions:
1. In a pot, warm the oil and sauté onion until translucent, about 3 minutes. Add in turnip, zucchini, and carrot and cook for 7 minutes; add black pepper for seasoning.
2. Mix in pureed tomato, and broth; and boil. Change heat to low and allow the mixture to simmer for 20 minutes. Lift from the heat. In batches, add the soup and avocado to a blender. Blend until creamy and smooth.

Nutrition Info:
• Per Servings 11g Carbs, 2.2g Protein, 13.4g Fat, 165 Calories

Tofu Sandwich With Cabbage Slaw

Servings: 4 | Cooking Time: 4 Hours 10 Minutes

Ingredients:
• ½ lb Firm tofu, sliced
• 4 low carb buns
• 1 tbsp olive oil
• Marinade
• Salt and black pepper to taste
• 2 tsp allspice
• 1 tbsp erythritol
• 2 tsp chopped thyme
• 1 Habanero, seeded and minced
• 3 green onions, thinly sliced
• 2 cloves garlic
• ¼ cup olive oil
• Slaw
• ½ small cabbage, shredded
• 1 carrot, grated
• ½ red onion, grated
• 2 tsp swerve
• 2 tbsp white vinegar
• 1 pinch Italian seasoning
• ¼ cup olive oil
• 1 tsp Dijon mustard
• Salt and black pepper to taste

Directions:
1. In a food processor, make the marinade by blending the allspice, salt, black pepper, erythritol, thyme, habanero, green onions, garlic, and olive oil, for a minute. Pour the mixture in a bowl and put the tofu in it, coating it to be covered with marinade. Place in the fridge to marinate for 4 hours.
2. Make the slaw next: In a large bowl, evenly combine the white vinegar, swerve, olive oil, Dijon mustard, Italian seasoning, salt, and pepper. Stir in the cabbage, carrot, and onion, and place it in the refrigerator to chill while the tofu marinates.
3. Frying the tofu: heat 1 teaspoon of oil in a skillet over medium heat, remove the tofu from the marinade, and cook it in the oil to brown on both sides for 6 minutes in total. Remove onto a plate after and toast the buns in the skillet. In the buns, add the tofu and top with the slaw. Close the bread and serve with a sweet chili sauce.

Nutrition Info:
• Per Servings 7.8g Carbs, 14g Protein, 33g Fat, 386 Calories

Vegan Mushroom Pizza

Servings: 4 | Cooking Time: 35 Minutes

Ingredients:
- 2 tsp ghee
- 1 cup chopped button mushrooms
- ½ cup sliced mixed colored bell peppers
- Pink salt and black pepper to taste
- 1 almond flour pizza bread
- 1 cup tomato sauce
- 1 tsp vegan Parmesan cheese
- Vegan Parmesan cheese for garnish

Directions:
1. Melt ghee in a skillet over medium heat, sauté the mushrooms and bell peppers for 10 minutes to soften. Season with salt and black pepper. Turn the heat off.
2. Put the pizza bread on a pizza pan, spread the tomato sauce all over the top and scatter vegetables evenly on top. Season with a little more salt and sprinkle with parmesan cheese.
3. Bake for 20 minutes until the vegetables are soft and the cheese has melted and is bubbly. Garnish with extra parmesan cheese. Slice pizza and serve with chilled berry juice.

Nutrition Info:
- Per Servings 8g Carbs, 15g Protein, 20g Fat, 295 Calories

Spicy Cauliflower Steaks With Steamed Green Beans

Servings: 4 | Cooking Time: 20 Minutes

Ingredients:
- 2 heads cauliflower, sliced lengthwise into 'steaks'
- ¼ cup olive oil
- ¼ cup chili sauce
- 2 tsp erythritol
- Salt and black pepper to taste
- 2 shallots, diced
- 1 bunch green beans, trimmed
- 2 tbsp fresh lemon juice
- 1 cup water
- Dried parsley to garnish

Directions:
1. In a bowl, mix the olive oil, chili sauce, and erythritol. Brush the cauliflower with the mixture. Place them on the grill, close the lid, and grill for 6 minutes. Flip the cauliflower, cook further for 6 minutes.
2. Bring the water to boil over high heat, place the green beans in a sieve and set over the steam from the boiling water. Cover with a clean napkin to keep the steam trapped in the sieve. Cook for 6 minutes. After, remove to a bowl and toss with lemon juice.
3. Remove the grilled caulis to a plate; sprinkle with salt, pepper, shallots, and parsley. Serve with the steamed green beans.

Nutrition Info:
- Per Servings 4g Carbs, 2g Protein, 9g Fat, 118 Calories

Grilled Cheese The Keto Way

Servings: 1 | Cooking Time: 15 Minutes

Ingredients:
- 2 eggs
- ½ tsp baking powder
- 2 tbsp butter
- 2 tbsp almond flour
- 1 ½ tbsp psyllium husk powder
- 2 ounces cheddar cheese

Directions:
1. Whisk together all ingredients except 1 tbsp. butter and cheddar cheese. Place in a square oven-proof bowl, and microwave for 90 seconds. Flip the bun over and cut in half.
2. Place the cheddar cheese on one half of the bun and top with the other. Melt the remaining butter in a skillet. Add the sandwich and grill until the cheese is melted and the bun is crispy.

Nutrition Info:
- Per Servings 6.1g Carbs, 25g Protein, 51g Fat, 623 Calories

Stir Fried Bok Choy

Servings: 4 | Cooking Time: 15 Minutes

Ingredients:
- 4 cloves of garlic, minced
- 1 onion, chopped
- 2 heads bok choy, rinsed and chopped
- 2 tablespoons sesame oil
- 2 tablespoons sesame seeds, toasted
- 3 tablespoons oil
- Salt and pepper to taste

Directions:
1. Heat the oil in a pot for 2 minutes.
2. Sauté the garlic and onions until fragrant, around 3 minutes.
3. Stir in the bok choy, salt, and pepper.
4. Cover pan and cook for 5 minutes.
5. Stir and continue cooking for another 3 minutes.
6. Drizzle with sesame oil and sesame seeds on top before serving.

Nutrition Info:
- Per Servings 5.2g Carbs, 21.5g Protein, 28.4g Fat, 358 Calories

Spaghetti Squash With Eggplant & Parmesan

Servings: 4 | Cooking Time: 15 Minutes

Ingredients:
- 1 tbsp butter
- 1 cup cherry tomatoes
- 2 tbsp parsley
- 1 eggplant, cubed
- ¼ cup Parmesan cheese
- 3 tbsp scallions, chopped
- 1 cup snap peas
- 1 tsp lemon zest

- 2 cups cooked spaghetti squash

Directions:

1. Melt the butter in a saucepan and cook eggplant for 5 minutes until tender. Add the tomatoes and peas, and cook for 5 more minutes. Stir in parsley, zest, and scallions, and remove the pan from heat. Stir in spaghetti squash and parmesan.

Nutrition Info:

- Per Servings 6.8g Carbs, 6.9g Protein, 8.2g Fat, 139 Calories

Greek Salad With Poppy Seed Dressing

Servings: 4 | Cooking Time: 3 Hours 15 Minutes

Ingredients:

- For the Dressing
- 1 cup poppy seeds
- 2 cups water
- 2 tbsp green onions, chopped
- 1 garlic clove, minced
- 1 lime, freshly squeezed
- Salt and black pepper, to taste
- ¼ tsp dill, minced
- 2 tbsp almond milk
- For the salad
- 1 head lettuce, separated into leaves
- 3 tomatoes, diced
- 3 cucumbers, sliced
- 2 tbsp kalamata olives, pitted

Directions:

1. Put all dressing ingredients in a food processor and pulse until well incorporated. Add in poppy seeds and mix well. Divide salad ingredients into 4 plates. Add the dressing to each and shake.

Nutrition Info:

- Per Servings 6.7g Carbs, 7.6g Protein, 15.6g Fat, 208 Calories

Spicy Tofu With Worcestershire Sauce

Servings: 4 | Cooking Time: 25 Minutes

Ingredients:

- 2 tbsp olive oil
- 14 ounces block tofu, pressed and cubed
- 1 celery stalk, chopped
- 1 bunch scallions, chopped
- 1 tsp cayenne pepper
- 1 tsp garlic powder
- 2 tbsp Worcestershire sauce
- Salt and black pepper, to taste
- 1 pound green cabbage, shredded
- ½ tsp turmeric powder
- ¼ tsp dried basil

Directions:

1. Set a large skillet over medium-high heat and warm 1 tablespoon of olive oil. Stir in tofu cubes and cook for 8 minutes. Place in scallions and celery; cook for 5 minutes until soft
2. Stir in cayenne, Worcestershire sauce, pepper, salt, and garlic; cook for 3 more minutes; set aside.

3. In the same pan, warm the remaining 1 tablespoon of oil. Add in shredded cabbage and the remaining seasonings and cook for 4 minutes. Mix in tofu mixture and serve while warm.

Nutrition Info:

- Per Servings 8.3g Carbs, 8.1g Protein, 10.3g Fat, 182 Calories

Curried Tofu

Servings: 6 | Cooking Time: 15 Minutes

Ingredients:

- 2 cloves of garlic, minced
- 1 onion, cubed
- 12-ounce firm tofu, drained and cubed
- 1 teaspoon curry powder
- 1 tablespoon soy sauce
- ¼ teaspoon pepper
- 5 tablespoons olive oil

Directions:

1. Heat the oil in a skillet over medium flame.
2. Sauté the garlic and onion until fragrant.
3. Stir in the tofu and stir for 3 minutes.
4. Add the rest of the ingredients and adjust the water.
5. Close the lid and allow simmering for 10 minutes.
6. Serve and enjoy.

Nutrition Info:

- Per Servings 4.4g Carbs, 6.2g Protein, 14.1g Fat, 148 Calories

Scrambled Eggs With Mushrooms And Spinach

Servings: 2 | Cooking Time: 15 Minutes

Ingredients:

- 2 large eggs
- 1 teaspoon butter
- 1/2 cup thinly sliced fresh mushrooms
- 1/2 cup fresh baby spinach, chopped
- 2 tablespoons shredded provolone cheese
- 1/8 teaspoon salt
- 1/8 teaspoon pepper

Directions:

1. In a small bowl, whisk eggs, salt, and pepper until blended. In a small nonstick skillet, heat butter over medium-high heat. Add mushrooms; cook and stir 3-4 minutes or until tender. Add spinach; cook and stir until wilted. Reduce heat to medium.
2. Add egg mixture; cook and stir just until eggs are thickened and no liquid egg remains. Stir in cheese.

Nutrition Info:

- Per Servings 2g Carbs, 14g Protein, 11g Fat, 162 Calories

Paprika 'n Cajun Seasoned Onion Rings

Servings: 6 | Cooking Time: 25 Minutes

Ingredients:
- 1 large white onion
- 2 large eggs, beaten
- ½ teaspoon Cajun seasoning
- ¾ cup almond flour
- 1 ½ teaspoon paprika
- ½ cups coconut oil for frying
- ¼ cup water
- Salt and pepper to taste

Directions:
1. Preheat a pot with oil for 8 minutes.
2. Peel the onion, cut off the top and slice into circles.
3. In a mixing bowl, combine the water and the eggs. Season with pepper and salt.
4. Soak the onion in the egg mixture.
5. In another bowl, combine the almond flour, paprika powder, Cajun seasoning, salt and pepper.
6. Dredge the onion in the almond flour mixture.
7. Place in the pot and cook in batches until golden brown, around 8 minutes per batch.

Nutrition Info:
- Per Servings 3.9g Carbs, 2.8g Protein, 24.1g Fat, 262 Calories

Greek-style Zucchini Pasta

Servings: 4 | Cooking Time: 15 Minutes

Ingredients:
- ¼ cup sun-dried tomatoes
- 5 garlic cloves, minced
- 2 tbsp butter
- 1 cup spinach
- 2 large zucchinis, spiralized
- ¼ cup crumbled feta
- ¼ cup Parmesan cheese, shredded
- 10 kalamata olives, halved
- 2 tbsp olive oil
- 2 tbsp chopped parsley

Directions:
1. Heat the olive oil in a pan over medium heat. Add zoodles, butter, garlic, and spinach. Cook for about 5 minutes. Stir in the olives, tomatoes, and parsley. Cook for 2 more minutes. Add in the cheeses and serve.

Nutrition Info:
- Per Servings 6.5g Carbs, 6.5g Protein, 19.5g Fat, 231 Calories

Cauliflower & Hazelnut Salad

Servings: 4 | Cooking Time: 15 Minutes + Chilling Time

Ingredients:
- 1 head cauliflower, cut into florets
- 1 cup green onions, chopped
- 4 ounces bottled roasted peppers, chopped
- ¼ cup extra-virgin olive oil
- 1 tbsp wine vinegar
- 1 tsp yellow mustard
- Salt and black pepper, to taste
- ½ cup black olives, pitted and chopped
- ½ cup hazelnuts, chopped

Directions:
1. Place the cauliflower florets over low heat and steam for 5 minutes; let cool and set aside. Add roasted peppers and green onions in a salad bowl.
2. Using a mixing dish, combine salt, olive oil, mustard, pepper, and vinegar. Sprinkle the mixture over the veggies. Place in the reserved cauliflower and shake to mix well. Top with hazelnut and black olives and serve.

Nutrition Info:
- Per Servings 6.6g Carbs, 4.2g Protein, 18g Fat, 221 Calories

Strawberry Mug Cake

Servings: 8 | Cooking Time: 3 Mins

Ingredients:
- 2 slices fresh strawberry
- 1 teaspoon chia seeds
- 1 teaspoon poppy seeds
- What you'll need from the store cupboard:
- 1/4 teaspoon baking powder
- 3 leaves fresh mint
- 2 tablespoons cream of coconut

Directions:
1. Add all the ingredients together in a mug, stir until finely combined.
2. Cook in microwave at full power for 3 minutes then allow to cool before you serve.

Nutrition Info:
- Per Servings 4.7g Carbs, 2.4g Protein, 12g Fat, 196 Calories

Zesty Frittata With Roasted Chilies

Servings: 4 | Cooking Time: 17 Minutes

Ingredients:
- 2 large green bell peppers, seeded, chopped
- 4 red and yellow chilies, roasted
- 2 tbsp red wine vinegar
- 1 knob butter, melted
- 8 sprigs parsley, chopped
- 8 eggs, cracked into a bowl
- 4 tbsp olive oil
- ½ cup grated Parmesan
- ¼ cup crumbled goat cheese
- 4 cloves garlic, minced
- 1 cup loosely filled salad leaves

Directions:
1. Preheat the oven to 400ºF. With a knife, seed the chilies, cut into long strips, and pour into a bowl.
2. Mix in the vinegar, butter, half of the parsley, half of the olive oil, and garlic; set aside. In another bowl, whisk the eggs with salt, pepper, bell peppers, parmesan, and the remaining parsley.
3. Now, heat the remaining oil in the cast iron over medium heat and pour the egg mixture along with half of the goat

cheese. Let cook for 3 minutes and when it is near done, sprinkle the remaining goat cheese on it, and transfer the cast iron to the oven.

4. Bake the frittata for 4 more minutes, remove and drizzle with the chili oil. Garnish the frittata with salad greens and serve for lunch.

Nutrition Info:
- Per Servings 2.3g Carbs, 6.4g Protein, 10.3g Fat, 153 Calories

Butternut Squash And Cauliflower Stew

Servings: 4 | Cooking Time:10 Minutes

Ingredients:
- 3 cloves of garlic, minced
- 1 cup cauliflower florets
- 1 ½ cups butternut squash, cubed
- 2 ½ cups heavy cream
- Pepper and salt to taste
- 3 tbsp coconut oil

Directions:
1. Heat the oil in a pan and saute the garlic until fragrant.
2. Stir in the rest of the ingredients and season with salt and pepper to taste.
3. Close the lid and bring to a boil for 10 minutes.
4. Serve and enjoy.

Nutrition Info:
- Per Servings 10g Carbs, 2g Protein, 38.1g Fat, 385 Calories

Bell Pepper Stuffed Avocado

Servings: 8 | Cooking Time: 10 Minutes

Ingredients:
- 4 avocados, pitted and halved
- 2 tbsp olive oil
- 3 cups green bell peppers, chopped
- 1 onion, chopped
- 1 tsp garlic puree
- Salt and black pepper, to taste
- 1 tsp deli mustard
- 1 tomato, chopped

Directions:
1. From each half of the avocados, scoop out 2 teaspoons of flesh; set aside.
2. Use a sauté pan to warm oil over medium-high heat. Cook the garlic, onion, and bell peppers until tender. Mix in the reserved avocado. Add in tomato, salt, mustard, and black pepper. Separate the mushroom mixture and mix equally among the avocado halves and serve.

Nutrition Info:
- Per Servings 7.4g Carbs, 2.4g Protein, 23.2g Fat, 255 Calories

Onion & Nuts Stuffed Mushrooms

Servings: 4 | Cooking Time: 30 Minutes

Ingredients:
- 1 tbsp sesame oil
- 1 onion, chopped
- 1 garlic clove, minced
- 1 pound mushrooms, stems removed
- Salt and black pepper, to taste
- ¼ cup raw pine nuts
- 2 tbsp parsley, chopped

Directions:
1. Set oven to 360ºF. Use a nonstick cooking spray to grease a large baking sheet. Into a frying pan, add sesame oil and warm. Place in garlic and onion and cook until soft.
2. Chop the mushroom stems and cook until tender. Turn off the heat, sprinkle with pepper and salt; add in pine nuts. Take the nut/mushroom mixture and stuff them to the mushroom caps and set on the baking sheet.
3. Bake the stuffed mushrooms for 30 minutes and remove to a wire rack to cool slightly. Add fresh parsley for garnish and serve.

Nutrition Info:
- Per Servings 7.4g Carbs, 4.8g Protein, 11.2g Fat, 139 Calories

Creamy Almond And Turnip Soup

Servings: 4 | Cooking Time: 25 Minutes

Ingredients:
- 1 tbsp olive oil
- 1 cup onion, chopped
- 1 celery, chopped
- 2 cloves garlic, minced
- 2 turnips, peeled and chopped
- 4 cups vegetable broth
- Salt and white pepper, to taste
- ¼ cup ground almonds
- 1 cup almond milk
- 1 tbsp fresh cilantro, chopped

Directions:
1. Set a stockpot over medium-high heat and warm the oil. Add in celery, garlic, and onion and sauté for 6 minutes. Stir in white pepper, broth, salt, and ground almonds. Boil the mixture. Set heat to low and simmer for 17 minutes. Transfer the soup to an immersion blender and puree. Decorate with fresh cilantro before serving.

Nutrition Info:
- Per Servings 9.2g Carbs, 3.8g Protein, 6.5g Fat, 114 Calories

Cauliflower Risotto With Mushrooms

Servings: 4 | Cooking Time: 15 Minutes

Ingredients:
- 2 shallots, diced
- 3 tbsp olive oil
- ¼ cup veggie broth
- ⅓ cup Parmesan cheese
- 4 tbsp butter

- 3 tbsp chopped chives
- 2 pounds mushrooms, sliced
- 4 ½ cups riced cauliflower

Directions:
1. Heat 2 tbsp. oil in a saucepan. Add the mushrooms and cook over medium heat for about 3 minutes. Remove from the pan and set aside.
2. Heat the remaining oil and cook the shallots for 2 minutes. Stir in the cauliflower and broth, and cook until the liquid is absorbed. Stir in the rest of the ingredients.

Nutrition Info:
- Per Servings 8.4g Carbs, 11g Protein, 18g Fat, 264 Calories

Garlic And Greens

Servings: 4 | Cooking Time: 20 Minutes

Ingredients:
- 1-pound kale, trimmed and torn
- 1/4 cup chopped oil-packed sun-dried tomatoes
- 5 garlic cloves, minced
- 2 tablespoons minced fresh parsley
- 1/4 teaspoon salt
- 3 tablespoons olive oil

Directions:
1. In a 6-qt. stockpot, bring 1 inch. of water to a boil. Add kale; cook, covered, 10-15 minutes or until tender. Remove with a slotted spoon; discard cooking liquid.
2. In the same pot, heat oil over medium heat. Add tomatoes and garlic; cook and stir 1 minute. Add kale, parsley and salt; heat through, stirring occasionally.

Nutrition Info:
- Per Servings 9g Carbs, 6g Protein, 13g Fat, 160 Calories

Sriracha Tofu With Yogurt Sauce

Servings: 4 | Cooking Time: 40 Minutes

Ingredients:
- 12 ounces tofu, pressed and sliced
- 1 cup green onions, chopped
- 1 garlic clove, minced
- 2 tbsp vinegar
- 1 tbsp sriracha sauce
- 2 tbsp olive oil
- For Yogurt Sauce
- 2 cloves garlic, pressed
- 2 tbsp fresh lemon juice
- Sea salt and black pepper, to taste
- 1 tsp fresh dill weed
- 1 cup Greek yogurt
- 1 cucumber, shredded

Directions:
1. Put tofu slices, garlic, Sriracha sauce, vinegar, and scallions in a bowl; allow to settle for approximately 30 minutes. Set oven to medium-high heat and add oil in a nonstick skillet to warm. Cook tofu for 5 minutes until golden brown.
2. For the preparation of sauce, use a bowl to mix garlic, salt, yogurt, black pepper, lemon juice, and dill. Add in shredded cucumber as you stir to combine well. Put the yogurt sauce in your fridge until ready to serve. Serve the tofu in serving plates with a dollop of yogurt sauce.

Nutrition Info:
- Per Servings 8.1g Carbs, 17.5g Protein, 25.9g Fat, 351 Calories

Tofu Stir Fry With Asparagus

Servings: 4 | Cooking Time: 30 Minutes

Ingredients:
- 1 pound asparagus, cut off stems
- 2 tbsp olive oil
- 2 blocks tofu, pressed and cubed
- 2 garlic cloves, minced
- 1 tsp cajun spice mix
- 1 tsp mustard
- 1 bell pepper, chopped
- ¼ cup vegetable broth
- Salt and black pepper, to taste

Directions:
1. Using a large saucepan with lightly salted water, place in asparagus and cook until tender for 10 minutes; drain. Set a wok over high heat and warm olive oil; stir in tofu cubes and cook for 6 minutes.
2. Place in garlic and cook for 30 seconds until soft. Stir in the rest of the ingredients, including reserved asparagus, and cook for an additional 4 minutes. Divide among plates and serve.

Nutrition Info:
- Per Servings 5.9g Carbs, 6.4g Protein, 8.9g Fat, 138 Calories

Classic Tangy Ratatouille

Servings: 6 | Cooking Time: 47 Minutes

Ingredients:
- 2 eggplants, chopped
- 3 zucchinis, chopped
- 2 red onions, diced
- 1 can tomatoes
- 2 red bell peppers, cut in chunks
- 1 yellow bell pepper, cut in chunks
- 3 cloves garlic, sliced
- ½ cup basil leaves, chop half
- 4 sprigs thyme
- 1 tbsp balsamic vinegar
- 2 tbsp olive oil
- ½ lemon, zested

Directions:
1. In a casserole pot, heat the olive oil and sauté the eggplants, zucchinis, and bell peppers over medium heat for 5 minutes. Spoon the veggies into a large bowl.
2. In the same pan, sauté garlic, onions, and thyme leaves for 5 minutes and return the cooked veggies to the pan along with the canned tomatoes, balsamic vinegar, chopped basil, salt, and pepper to taste. Stir and cover the pot, and cook the ingredients on low heat for 30 minutes.
3. Open the lid and stir in the remaining basil leaves, lemon zest, and adjust the seasoning. Turn the heat off. Plate the ratatouille and serve with some low carb crusted bread.

Nutrition Info:
- Per Servings 5.6g Carbs, 1.7g Protein, 12.1g Fat, 154 Calories

Parmesan Roasted Cabbage

Servings: 4 | Cooking Time: 25 Minutes

Ingredients:
- Cooking spray
- 1 large head green cabbage
- 4 tbsp melted butter
- 1 tsp garlic powder
- Salt and black pepper to taste
- 1 cup grated Parmesan cheese
- Grated Parmesan cheese for topping
- 1 tbsp chopped parsley to garnish

Directions:
1. Preheat oven to 400°F, line a baking sheet with foil, and grease with cooking spray.
2. Stand the cabbage and run a knife from the top to bottom to cut the cabbage into wedges. Remove stems and wilted leaves. Mix the butter, garlic, salt, and black pepper until evenly combined.
3. Brush the mixture on all sides of the cabbage wedges and sprinkle with parmesan cheese.
4. Place on the baking sheet, and bake for 20 minutes to soften the cabbage and melt the cheese. Remove the cabbages when golden brown, plate and sprinkle with extra cheese and parsley. Serve warm with pan-glazed tofu.

Nutrition Info:
- Per Servings 4g Carbs, 17.5g Protein, 19.3g Fat, 268 Calories

Portobello Mushroom Burgers

Servings: 4 | Cooking Time: 15 Minutes

Ingredients:
- 4 low carb buns
- 4 portobello mushroom caps
- 1 clove garlic, minced
- ½ tsp salt
- 2 tbsp olive oil
- ½ cup sliced roasted red peppers
- 2 medium tomatoes, chopped
- ¼ cup crumbled feta cheese
- 1 tbsp red wine vinegar
- 2 tbsp pitted kalamata olives, chopped
- ½ tsp dried oregano
- 2 cups baby salad greens

Directions:
1. Heat the grill pan over medium-high heat and while it heats, crush the garlic with salt in a bowl using the back of a spoon. Stir in 1 tablespoon of oil and brush the mushrooms and each inner side of the buns with the mixture.
2. Place the mushrooms in the heated pan and grill them on both sides for 8 minutes until tender.
3. Also, toast the buns in the pan until they are crisp, about 2 minutes. Set aside.
4. In a bowl, mix the red peppers, tomatoes, olives, feta cheese, vinegar, oregano, baby salad greens, and remaining oil; toss them. Assemble the burger: in a slice of bun, add a mushroom cap, a scoop of vegetables, and another slice of bread. Serve with cheese dip.

Nutrition Info:
- Per Servings 3g Carbs, 16g Protein, 8g Fat, 190 Calories

Roasted Brussels Sprouts With Sunflower Seeds

Servings: 6 | Cooking Time: 45 Minutes

Ingredients:
- Nonstick cooking spray
- 3 pounds brussels sprouts, halved
- ¼ cup olive oil
- Salt and ground black pepper, to taste
- 1 tsp sunflower seeds
- 2 tbsp fresh chives, chopped

Directions:
1. Set oven to 390°F. Apply a nonstick cooking spray to a rimmed baking sheet. Arrange sprout halves on the baking sheet. Shake in black pepper, salt, sunflower seeds, and olive oil.
2. Roast for 40 minutes, until the cabbage becomes soft. Apply a garnish of fresh chopped chives.

Nutrition Info:
- Per Servings 8g Carbs, 2.1g Protein, 17g Fat, 186 Calories

Bell Pepper & Pumpkin With Avocado Sauce

Servings: 4 | Cooking Time: 15 Minutes

Ingredients:
- ½ pound pumpkin, peeled
- ½ pound bell peppers
- 1 tbsp olive oil
- 1 avocado, peeled and pitted
- 1 lemon, juiced and zested
- 2 tbsp sesame oil
- 2 tbsp cilantro, chopped
- 1 onion, chopped
- 1 jalapeño pepper, deveined and minced
- Salt and black pepper, to taste

Directions:
1. Use a spiralizer to spiralize bell peppers and pumpkin. Using a large nonstick skillet, warm olive oil. Add in bell peppers and pumpkin and sauté for 8 minutes.
2. Combine the remaining ingredients to obtain a creamy mixture. Top the vegetable noodles with the avocado sauce and serve.

Nutrition Info:
- Per Servings 11g Carbs, 1.9g Protein, 20.2g Fat, 233 Calories

Roasted Asparagus With Spicy Eggplant Dip

Servings: 6 | Cooking Time: 35 Minutes

Ingredients:
- 1 ½ pounds asparagus spears, trimmed
- ¼ cup olive oil
- 1 tsp sea salt
- ½ tsp black pepper, to taste
- ½ tsp paprika
- For Eggplant Dip
- ¾ pound eggplants
- 2 tsp olive oil
- ½ cup scallions, chopped
- 2 cloves garlic, minced
- 1 tbsp fresh lemon juice
- ½ tsp chili pepper
- Salt and black pepper, to taste
- ¼ cup fresh cilantro, chopped

Directions:
1. Set the oven to 390ºF. Line a parchment paper to a baking sheet. Add asparagus spears to the baking sheet. Toss with oil, paprika, pepper, and salt. Bake until cooked through for 9 minutes.
2. Set the oven to 425 ºF. Add eggplants on a lined cookie sheet. Place under the broiler for about 20 minutes; let the eggplants to cool. Peel them and discard the stems. Place a frying pan over medium-high heat and warm olive oil. Add in garlic and onion and sauté until tender.
3. Using a food processor, pulse together black pepper, roasted eggplants, salt, lemon juice, scallion mixture, and chili pepper to mix evenly. Add cilantro for garnishing. Serve alongside roasted asparagus spears.

Nutrition Info:
- Per Servings 9g Carbs, 3.6g Protein, 12.1g Fat, 149 Calories

Creamy Vegetable Stew

Servings: 4 | Cooking Time: 32 Minutes

Ingredients:
- 2 tbsp ghee
- 1 tbsp onion garlic puree
- 4 medium carrots, peeled and chopped
- 1 large head cauliflower, cut into florets
- 2 cups green beans, halved
- Salt and black pepper to taste
- 1 cup water
- 1 ½ cups heavy cream

Directions:
1. Melt ghee in a saucepan over medium heat and sauté onion-garlic puree to be fragrant, 2 minutes.
2. Stir in carrots, cauliflower, and green beans, salt, and pepper, add the water, stir again, and cook the vegetables on low heat for 25 minutes to soften. Mix in the heavy cream to be incorporated, turn the heat off, and adjust the taste with salt and pepper. Serve the stew with almond flour bread.

Nutrition Info:
- Per Servings 6g Carbs, 8g Protein, 26.4g Fat, 310 Calories

Lemon Grilled Veggie

Servings: 4 | Cooking Time: 20 Minutes

Ingredients:
- 2/3 eggplant
- 1 zucchini
- 10 oz. cheddar cheese
- 20 black olives
- 2 oz. leafy greens
- ½ cup olive oil
- 1 lemon, the juice
- 1 cup mayonnaise
- 4 tbsp almonds
- Salt and pepper

Directions:
1. Cut eggplant and zucchini lengthwise into half inch-thick slices. Season with salt to coat evenly. Set aside for 5-10 minutes.
2. Preheat the oven to 450 degrees F.
3. Pat zucchini and eggplant slices' surface dry with a kitchen towel.
4. Line a baking sheet with parchment paper and place slices on it. Spray with olive oil on top and season with pepper.
5. Bake for 15-20 minutes or until cooked through, flipping halfway.
6. Once done, transfer to a serving platter. Drizzle olive oil and lemon juice on top.
7. Serve with cheese cubes, almonds, olives, mayonnaise and leafy greens.

Nutrition Info:
- Per Servings 9g Carbs, 21g Protein, 99g Fat, 1013 Calories

Cauliflower & Mushrooms Stuffed Peppers

Servings: 4 | Cooking Time: 40 Minutes

Ingredients:
- 1 head cauliflower
- 4 bell peppers
- 1 cup mushrooms, sliced
- 1 ½ tbsp oil
- 1 onion, chopped
- 1 cup celery, chopped
- 1 garlic cloves, minced
- 1 tsp chili powder
- 2 tomatoes, pureed
- Sea salt and pepper, to taste

Directions:
1. To prepare cauliflower rice, grate the cauliflower into rice-size. Set in a kitchen towel to attract and remove any excess moisture. Set oven to 360ºF.
2. Lightly oil a casserole dish. Chop off bell pepper tops, do away with the seeds and core. Line a baking pan with a parchment paper and roast the peppers for 18 minutes until the skin starts to brown.
3. Warm the oil over medium heat. Add in garlic, celery, and onion and sauté until soft and translucent.Stir in chili powder, mushrooms, and cauliflower rice. Cook for 6 minutes until the cauliflower rice becomes tender. Split the cauliflower mixture

among the bell peppers. Set in the casserole dish. Combine pepper, salt, and tomatoes. Top the peppers with the tomato mixture. Bake for 10 minutes.

Nutrition Info:
• Per Servings 8.4g Carbs, 1.6g Protein, 4.8g Fat, 77 Calories

Easy Cauliflower Soup

Servings: 4 | Cooking Time: 15 Minutes

Ingredients:
• 2 tbsp olive oil
• 2 onions, finely chopped
• 1 tsp garlic, minced
• 1 pound cauliflower, cut into florets
• 1 cup kale, chopped
• 4 cups vegetable broth
• ½ cup almond milk
• ½ tsp salt
• ½ tsp red pepper flakes
• 1 tbsp fresh chopped parsley

Directions:
1. Set a pot over medium-high heat and warm the oil. Add garlic and onion and sauté until browned and softened. Place in vegetable broth, kale, and cauliflower; cook for 10 minutes until the mixture boils. Stir in the pepper, salt, and almond milk; simmer the soup while covered for 5 minutes.
2. Transfer the soup to an immersion blender and blend to achieve the required consistency; top with parsley and serve immediately.

Nutrition Info:
• Per Servings 11.8g Carbs, 8.1g Protein, 10.3g Fat, 172 Calories

Fall Roasted Vegetables

Servings: 4 | Cooking Time: 45 Minutes

Ingredients:
• 1 red bell pepper, sliced
• 1 green bell pepper, sliced
• 1 orange bell pepper, sliced
• ½ head broccoli, cut into florets
• 2 zucchinis, sliced
• 2 leeks, chopped
• 4 garlic cloves, halved
• 2 thyme sprigs, chopped
• 1 tsp dried sage, crushed
• 4 tbsp olive oil
• 2 tbsp vinegar
• 4 tbsp tomato puree
• Sea salt and cayenne pepper, to taste

Directions:
1. Set oven to 425 °F. Apply nonstick cooking spray to a rimmed baking sheet. Mix all vegetables with oil, seasonings, and vinegar; shake well. Roast for 40 minutes, flipping once halfway through.

Nutrition Info:
• Per Servings 8.2g Carbs, 2.1g Protein, 14.3g Fat, 165 Calories

Garlic 'n Sour Cream Zucchini Bake

Servings: 3 | Cooking Time: 35 Minutes

Ingredients:
• 1 ½ cups zucchini slices
• 5 tablespoons olive oil
• 1 tablespoon minced garlic
• 1/4 cup grated Parmesan cheese
• 1 package cream cheese, softened
• Salt and pepper to taste

Directions:
1. Lightly grease a baking sheet with cooking spray.
2. Place zucchini in a bowl and put in olive oil and garlic.
3. Place zucchini slices in a single layer in dish.
4. Bake for 35 minutes at 390oF until crispy.
5. In a bowl, whisk well, remaining ingredients.
6. Serve with zucchini

Nutrition Info:
• Per Servings 9.5g Carbs, 11.9g Protein, 32.4g Fat, 385 Calories

Cremini Mushroom Stroganoff

Servings: 4 | Cooking Time: 15 Minutes

Ingredients:
• 3 tbsp butter
• 1 white onion, chopped
• 4 cups cremini mushrooms, cubed
• 2 cups water
• ½ cup heavy cream
• ½ cup grated Parmesan cheese
• 1 ½ tbsp dried mixed herbs
• Salt and black pepper to taste

Directions:
1. Melt the butter in a saucepan over medium heat, sauté the onion for 3 minutes until soft.
2. Stir in the mushrooms and cook until tender, about 3 minutes. Add the water, mix, and bring to boil for 4 minutes until the water reduces slightly.
3. Pour in the heavy cream and parmesan cheese. Stir to melt the cheese. Also, mix in the dried herbs. Season with salt and pepper, simmer for 40 seconds and turn the heat off.
4. Ladle stroganoff over a bed of spaghetti squash and serve.

Nutrition Info:
• Per Servings 1g Carbs, 5g Protein, 28g Fat, 284 Calories

Walnut Tofu Sauté

Servings: 4 | Cooking Time: 15 Minutes

Ingredients:
• 1 tbsp olive oil
• 1 block firm tofu, cubed
• 1 tbsp tomato paste with garlic and onion
• 1 tbsp balsamic vinegar
• Pink salt and black pepper to taste
• ½ tsp mixed dried herbs
• 1 cup chopped raw walnuts

Directions:

1. Heat the oil in a skillet over medium heat and cook the tofu for 3 minutes while stirring to brown.
2. Mix the tomato paste with the vinegar and add to the tofu. Stir, season with salt and black pepper, and cook for another 4 minutes.
3. Add the herbs and walnuts. Stir and cook on low heat for 3 minutes to be fragrant. Spoon to a side of squash mash and a sweet berry sauce to serve.

Nutrition Info:
• Per Servings 4g Carbs, 18g Protein, 24g Fat, 320 Calories

Vegetable Burritos

Servings: 4 | Cooking Time: 10 Minutes

Ingredients:
• 2 large low carb tortillas
• 2 tsp olive oil
• 1 small onion, sliced
• 1 bell pepper, seeded and sliced
• 1 large ripe avocado, pitted and sliced
• 1 cup lemon cauli couscous
• Salt and black pepper to taste
• ⅓ cup sour cream
• 3 tbsp Mexican salsa

Directions:
1. Heat the olive oil in a skillet and sauté the onion and bell pepper until they start to brown on the edges, about 4 minutes. Turn the heat off and set the skillet aside.
2. Lay the tortillas on a flat surface and top each with halves of the onion and bell pepper mixture, avocado, cauli couscous, season with salt and pepper, sour cream, and Mexican salsa. Fold in the sides of each tortilla, and roll them in and over the filling to be completely enclosed.
3. Wrap with foil, cut in halves, and serve warm.

Nutrition Info:
• Per Servings 5.4g Carbs, 17.9g Protein, 23.2g Fat, 373 Calories

Cauliflower Fritters

Servings: 6 | Cooking Time: 15 Minutes

Ingredients:
• 1 large cauliflower head, cut into florets
• 2 eggs, beaten
• ½ teaspoon turmeric
• 1 large onion, peeled and chopped
• ½ teaspoon salt
• ¼ teaspoon black pepper
• 6 tablespoons oil

Directions:
1. Place the cauliflower florets in a pot with water.
2. Bring to a boil and drain once cooked.
3. Place the cauliflower, eggs, onion, turmeric, salt, and pepper into the food processor.
4. Pulse until the mixture becomes coarse.
5. Transfer into a bowl. Using your hands, form six small flattened balls and place in the fridge for at least 1 hour until the mixture hardens.

6. Heat the oil in a skillet and fry the cauliflower patties for 3 minutes on each side.
7. Serve and enjoy.

Nutrition Info:
• Per Servings 2.28g Carbs, 3.9g Protein, 15.3g Fat, 157 Calories

Morning Granola

Servings: 8 | Cooking Time: 1 Hour

Ingredients:
• 1 tbsp coconut oil
• ⅓ cup almond flakes
• ½ cups almond milk
• 2 tbsp sugar
• 1/8 tsp salt
• 1 tsp lime zest
• 1/8 tsp nutmeg, grated
• ½ tsp ground cinnamon
• ½ cup pecans, chopped
• ½ cup almonds, slivered
• 2 tbsp pepitas
• 3 tbsp sunflower seeds
• ¼ cup flax seed

Directions:
1. Set a deep pan over medium-high heat and warm the coconut oil. Add almond flakes and toast for 1 to 2 minutes. Stir in the remaining ingredients. Set oven to 300°F. Lay the mixture in an even layer onto a baking sheet lined with a parchment paper. Bake for 1 hour, making sure that you shake gently in intervals of 15 minutes. Serve alongside additional almond milk.

Nutrition Info:
• Per Servings 9.2g Carbs, 5.1g Protein, 24.3g Fat, 262 Calories

Zucchini Lasagna With Ricotta And Spinach

Servings: 4 | Cooking Time: 50 Minutes

Ingredients:
• Cooking spray
• 2 zucchinis, sliced
• Salt and black pepper to taste
• 2 cups ricotta cheese
• 2 cups shredded mozzarella cheese
• 3 cups tomato sauce
• 1 cup packed baby spinach

Directions:
1. Preheat oven to 370°F and grease a baking dish with cooking spray.
2. Put the zucchini slices in a colander and sprinkle with salt. Let sit and drain liquid for 5 minutes and pat dry with paper towels. Mix the ricotta, mozzarella, salt, and pepper to evenly combine and spread ¼ cup of the mixture in the bottom of the baking dish.
3. Layer ⅓ of the zucchini slices on top spread 1 cup of tomato sauce over, and scatter a ⅓ cup of spinach on top. Repeat

the layering process two more times to exhaust the ingredients while making sure to layer with the last ¼ cup of cheese mixture finally.

4. Grease one end of foil with cooking spray and cover the baking dish with the foil. Bake for 35 minutes, remove foil, and bake further for 5 to 10 minutes or until the cheese has a nice golden brown color. Remove the dish, sit for 5 minutes, make slices of the lasagna, and serve warm.

Nutrition Info:
• Per Servings 2g Carbs, 7g Protein, 39g Fat, 390 Calories

Walnuts With Tofu

Servings: 4 | Cooking Time: 13 Minutes

Ingredients:
• 3 tsp olive oil
• 1 cup extra firm tofu, cubed
• ¼ cup walnuts, chopped
• 1 ½ tbsp coconut aminos
• 3 tbsp vegetable broth
• ½ tsp smashed garlic
• 1 tsp cayenne pepper
• ½ tsp turmeric powder
• Sea salt and black pepper, to taste
• 2 tsp sunflower seeds

Directions:
1. Set a frying pan over medium heat. Warm the oil. Add in tofu and fry as you stir until they brown. Pour in the walnuts; turn temperature to higher and cook for 2 minutes. Stir in the remaining ingredients, set heat to medium-low and cook for 5 more minutes. Drizzle with hot sauce and serve!

Nutrition Info:
• Per Servings 5.3g Carbs, 8.3g Protein, 21.6g Fat, 232 Calories

Zoodles With Avocado & Olives

Servings: 4 | Cooking Time: 15 Minutes

Ingredients:
• 4 zucchinis, julienned or spiralized
• ½ cup pesto
• 2 avocados, sliced
• 1 cup kalamata olives, chopped
• ¼ cup chopped basil
• 2 tbsp olive oil
• ¼ cup chopped sun-dried tomatoes

Directions:
1. Heat half of the olive oil in a pan over medium heat. Add zoodles and cook for 4 minutes. Transfer to a plate. Stir in pesto, basil, salt, tomatoes, and olives. Top with avocado slices.

Nutrition Info:
• Per Servings 8.4g Carbs, 6.3g Protein, 42g Fat, 449 Calories

Creamy Cucumber Avocado Soup

Servings: 4 | Cooking Time: 15 Minutes

Ingredients:
• 4 large cucumbers, seeded, chopped
• 1 large avocado, peeled and pitted
• Salt and black pepper to taste
• 2 cups water
• 1 tbsp cilantro, chopped
• 3 tbsp olive oil
• 2 limes, juiced
• 2 tsp minced garlic
• 2 tomatoes, evenly chopped
• 1 chopped avocado for garnish

Directions:
1. Pour the cucumbers, avocado halves, salt, pepper, olive oil, lime juice, cilantro, water, and garlic in the food processor. Puree the ingredients for 2 minutes or until smooth.

2. Pour the mixture in a bowl and top with avocado and tomatoes. Serve chilled with zero-carb bread.

Nutrition Info:
• Per Servings 4.1g Carbs, 3.7g Protein, 7.4g Fat, 170 Calories

Sautéed Celeriac With Tomato Sauce

Servings: 4 | Cooking Time: 20 Minutes

Ingredients:
• 2 tbsp olive oil
• 1 garlic clove, crushed
• 1 celeriac, sliced
• ¼ cup vegetable stock
• Sea salt and black pepper, to taste
• For the Sauce
• 2 tomatoes, halved
• 2 tbsp olive oil
• ½ cup onions, chopped
• 2 cloves garlic, minced
• 1 chili, minced
• 1 bunch fresh basil, chopped
• 1 tbsp fresh cilantro, chopped
• Salt and black pepper, to taste

Directions:
1. Set a pan over medium-high heat and warm olive oil. Add in garlic and sauté for 1 minute. Stir in celeriac slices, stock and cook until softened. Sprinkle with black pepper and salt; kill the heat. Brush olive oil to the tomato halves. Microwave for 15 minutes; get rid of any excess liquid.

2. Remove the cooked tomatoes to a food processor; add the rest of the ingredients for the sauce and puree to obtain the desired consistency. Serve the celeriac topped with tomato sauce.

Nutrition Info:
• Per Servings 3g Carbs, 0.9g Protein, 13.6g Fat, 135 Calories

Chapter 4 Fish And Seafood Recipes

Chapter 4 Fish And Seafood Recipes

Steamed Cod With Ginger

Servings: 4 | Cooking Time: 15 Minutes

Ingredients:
- 4 cod fillets, skin removed
- 3 tbsp. lemon juice, freshly squeezed
- 2 tbsp. coconut aminos
- 2 tbsp. grated ginger
- 6 scallions, chopped
- 5 tbsp coconut oil
- Pepper and salt to taste

Directions:
1. Place a trivet in a large saucepan and pour a cup or two of water into the pan. Bring to a boil.
2. In a small bowl, whisk well lemon juice, coconut aminos, coconut oil, and grated ginger.
3. Place scallions in a heatproof dish that fits inside a saucepan. Season scallions mon with pepper and salt. Drizzle with ginger mixture. Sprinkle scallions on top.
4. Seal dish with foil. Place the dish on the trivet inside the saucepan. Cover and steam for 15 minutes.
5. Serve and enjoy.

Nutrition Info:
- Per Servings 10g Carbs, 28.3g Protein, 40g Fat, 514 Calories

Cilantro Shrimp

Servings: 4 | Cooking Time: 10 Minutes

Ingredients:
- 1/2 cup reduced-fat Asian sesame salad dressing
- 1-pound uncooked shrimp, peeled and deveined
- Lime wedges
- 1/4 cup chopped fresh cilantro
- 5 tablespoon olive oil
- Salt and pepper

Directions:
1. In a large nonstick skillet, heat 1 tablespoon dressing over medium heat. Add shrimp; cook and stir 1 minute.
2. Stir in remaining dressing; cook, uncovered, until shrimp turn pink, 1-2 minutes longer.
3. To serve, squeeze lime juice over the top; sprinkle with cilantro, pepper, and salt. If desired, serve with rice.

Nutrition Info:
- Per Servings 4.7g Carbs, 32g Protein, 39g Fat, 509 Calories

Chipotle Salmon Asparagus

Servings: 2 | Cooking Time: 15 Minutes

Ingredients:
- 1-lb salmon fillet, skin on
- 2 teaspoon chipotle paste
- A handful of asparagus spears, trimmed
- 1 lemon, sliced thinly
- A pinch of rosemary
- Salt to taste
- 5 tbsp olive oil

Directions:
1. In a heat-proof dish that fits inside the saucepan, add asparagus spears on the bottom of the dish. Place fish, top with rosemary, and lemon slices. Season with chipotle paste and salt. Drizzle with olive oil. Cover dish with foil.
2. Place a large saucepan on the medium-high fire. Place a trivet inside the saucepan and fill the pan halfway with water. Cover and bring to a boil.
3. Place dish on the trivet.
4. Cover pan and steam for 10 minutes. Let it rest in pan for another 5 minutes.
5. Serve and enjoy topped with pepper.

Nutrition Info:
- Per Servings 2.8g Carbs, 35.0g Protein, 50.7g Fat, 651 Calories

Shrimp And Cauliflower Jambalaya

Servings: 4 | Cooking Time: 15 Minutes

Ingredients:
- 2 cloves garlic, peeled and minced
- 1 head cauliflower, grated
- 1 cup chopped tomatoes
- 8 oz. raw shrimp, peeled and deveined
- 1 tbsp Cajun seasoning
- Salt and pepper
- 4 tbsp coconut oil
- 1 tbsp water

Directions:
1. On medium-high fire, heat a nonstick saucepan for 2 minutes. Add oil to a pan and swirl to coat bottom and sides. Heat oil for a minute.
2. Add garlic and sauté for a minute. Stir in tomatoes and stir fry for 5 minutes. Add water and deglaze the pan.
3. Add remaining ingredients. Season generously with pepper.
4. Increase fire to high and stir fry for 3 minutes.
5. Lower fire to low, cover, and cook for 5 minutes.
6. Serve and enjoy.

Nutrition Info:
- Per Servings 7.8g Carbs, 21.4g Protein, 22.25g Fat, 314 Calories

Baked Codfish With Lemon

Serves: 4 | Cooking Time:25 Minutes

Ingredients:
- 4 fillets codfish
- 1 teaspoon salt
- 1 teaspoon pepper
- 2 tablespoons olive oil
- 2 teaspoons dried basil
- 2 tablespoons melted butter
- 1 teaspoon dried thyme
- 1/3 teaspoon onion powder
- 2 lemons, juiced
- lemon wedges, for garnish

Directions:
1. Preheat the oven to 400°F.
2. In a medium bowl combine the lemon juice, onion powder, olive oil, dried basil and thyme. Stir well. Season the fillets with salt and pepper.
3. Top each fillet into the mixture. Then place the fillets into a medium baking dish, greased with melted butter.
4. Bake the codfish fillets for 15-20 minutes. Serve with fresh lemon wedges. Enjoy!

Nutrition Info:
- Per serving: 3.9g Carbs; 21.2g Protein; 23.6g Fat; 308 Calories

Spicy Sea Bass With Hazelnuts

Servings: 2 | Cooking Time: 30 Minutes

Ingredients:
- 2 sea bass fillets
- 2 tbsp butter
- 1/3 cup roasted hazelnuts
- A pinch of cayenne pepper

Directions:
1. Preheat your oven to 425 ºF. Line a baking dish with waxed paper. Melt the butter and brush it over the fish. In a food processor, combine the rest of the ingredients. Coat the sea bass with the hazelnut mixture. Place in the oven and bake for about 15 minutes.

Nutrition Info:
- Per Servings 2.8g Carbs, 40g Protein, 31g Fat, 467 Calories

Steamed Chili-rubbed Tilapia

Servings: 4 | Cooking Time: 15 Minutes

Ingredients:
- 1 lb. tilapia fillet, skin removed
- 2 tbsp. chili powder
- 3 cloves garlic, peeled and minced
- 2 tbsp. extra virgin olive oil
- 2 tbsp soy sauce

Directions:
1. Place a trivet in a large saucepan and pour a cup or two of water into the pan. Bring it to a boil.
2. Place tilapia in a heatproof dish that fits inside a saucepan. Drizzle soy sauce and oil on the filet. Season with chili powder and garlic.

3. Seal dish with foil. Place the dish on the trivet inside the saucepan. Cover and steam for 15 minutes.
4. Serve and enjoy.

Nutrition Info:
- Per Servings 2g Carbs, 26g Protein, 10g Fat, 211 Calories

Shrimp Stuffed Zucchini

Servings: 4 | Cooking Time: 56 Minutes

Ingredients:
- 4 medium zucchinis
- 1 lb small shrimp, peeled, deveined
- 1 tbsp minced onion
- 2 tsp butter
- ¼ cup chopped tomatoes
- Salt and black pepper to taste
- 1 cup pork rinds, crushed
- 1 tbsp chopped basil leaves
- 2 tbsp melted butter

Directions:
1. Preheat the oven to 350ºF and trim off the top and bottom ends of the zucchinis. Lay them flat on a chopping board, and cut a ¼ -inch off the top to create a boat for the stuffing. Scoop out the seeds with a spoon and set the zucchinis aside.
2. Melt the firm butter in a small skillet and sauté the onion and tomato for 6 minutes. Transfer the mixture to a bowl and add the shrimp, half of the pork rinds, basil leaves, salt, and pepper.
3. Combine the ingredients and stuff the zucchini boats with the mixture. Sprinkle the top of the boats with the remaining pork rinds and drizzle the melted butter over them.
4. Place them on a baking sheet and bake them for 15 to 20 minutes. The shrimp should no longer be pink by this time. Remove the zucchinis after and serve with a tomato and mozzarella salad.

Nutrition Info:
- Per Servings 3.2g Carbs, 24.6g Protein, 14.4g Fat, 135 Calories

Bacon And Salmon Bites

Serves: 2 | Cooking Time: 15 Minutes

Ingredients:
- 1 salmon fillets
- 4 bacon slices, halved
- 2 tbsp chopped cilantro
- Seasoning:
- ¼ tsp salt
- 1/8 tsp ground black pepper

Directions:
1. Turn on the oven, then set it to 350 °F, and let it preheat. Meanwhile, cut salmon into bite-size pieces, then wrap each piece with a half slice of bacon, secure with a toothpick and season with salt and black pepper.Take a baking sheet, place prepared salmon pieces on it and bake for 13 to 15 minutes until nicely browned and thoroughly cooked.When done, sprinkle cilantro over salmon and serve.

Nutrition Info:
- 1 g Carbs; 10 g Protein; 9 g Fats; 120 Calories

Yummy Shrimp Fried Rice

Servings: 6 | Cooking Time: 20 Minutes

Ingredients:
- 4 tablespoons butter, divided
- 4 large eggs, lightly beaten
- 3 cups shredded cauliflower
- 1-pound uncooked medium shrimp, peeled and deveined
- 1/2 teaspoon salt
- 1/4 teaspoon pepper

Directions:
1. In a large skillet, melt 1 tablespoon butter over medium-high heat.
2. Pour eggs into skillet. As eggs set, lift edges, letting uncooked portion flow underneath. Remove eggs and keep warm.
3. Melt remaining butter in the skillet. Add the cauliflower, and shrimp; cook and stir for 5 minutes or until shrimp turn pink.
4. Meanwhile, chop eggs into small pieces. Return eggs to the pan; sprinkle with salt and pepper. Cook until heated through, stirring occasionally. Sprinkle with bacon if desired.

Nutrition Info:
- Per Servings 3.3g Carbs, 13g Protein, 11g Fat, 172 Calories

Cod With Balsamic Tomatoes

Servings: 4 | Cooking Time: 30 Minutes

Ingredients:
- 4 center-cut bacon strips, chopped
- 4 cod fillets
- 2 cups grape tomatoes, halved
- 2 tablespoons balsamic vinegar
- 4 tablespoons olive oil
- 1/2 teaspoon salt
- 1/4 teaspoon pepper

Directions:
1. In a large skillet, heat olive oil and cook bacon over medium heat until crisp, stirring occasionally.
2. Remove with a slotted spoon; drain on paper towels.
3. Sprinkle fillets with salt and pepper. Add fillets to bacon drippings; cook over medium-high heat until fish just begins to flake easily with a fork, 4-6 minutes on each side. Remove and keep warm.
4. Add tomatoes to skillet; cook and stir until tomatoes are softened, 2-4 minutes. Stir in vinegar; reduce heat to medium-low. Cook until sauce is thickened, 1-2 minutes longer.
5. Serve cod with tomato mixture and bacon.

Nutrition Info:
- Per Servings 5g Carbs, 26g Protein, 30.4g Fat, 442 Calories

Five-spice Steamed Tilapia

Servings: 4 | Cooking Time: 15 Minutes

Ingredients:
- 1 lb. Tilapia fillets,
- 1 tsp. Chinese five-spice powder
- 3 tablespoons coconut oil
- 3 scallions, sliced thinly
- Salt and pepper to taste

Directions:
1. Place a trivet in a large saucepan and pour a cup of water into the pan. Bring to a boil.
2. Place tilapia in a heatproof dish that fits inside a saucepan. Drizzle oil on tilapia. Season with salt, pepper, and Chinese five-spice powder. Garnish with scallions.
3. Seal dish with foil. Place the dish on the trivet inside the saucepan. Cover and steam for 15 minutes.
4. Serve and enjoy.

Nutrition Info:
- Per Servings 0.9g Carbs, 24g Protein, 12.3g Fat, 201 Calories

Blue Cheese Shrimps

Servings: 6 | Cooking Time: 15 Minutes

Ingredients:
- 3 ounces cream cheese, softened
- 2/3 cup minced fresh parsley, divided
- 1/4 cup crumbled blue cheese
- 1/2 teaspoon Creole mustard
- 24 cooked jumbo shrimp, peeled and deveined
- Pepper and salt to taste
- 5 tablespoon olive oil

Directions:
1. In a small bowl, beat cream cheese until smooth. Beat in 1/3 cup parsley, blue cheese, and mustard. Season with pepper and salt as desired. Refrigerate at least 1 hour.
2. Make a deep slit along the back of each shrimp to within 1/4-1/2 inch of the bottom. Stuff with cream cheese mixture; press remaining parsley onto cream cheese mixture.
3. Drizzle with olive oil last.

Nutrition Info:
- Per Servings 1.7g Carbs, 6g Protein, 17.8g Fat, 180 Calories

Coconut Milk Sauce Over Crabs

Servings: 6 | Cooking Time: 20 Minutes

Ingredients:
- 2-pounds crab quartered
- 1 can coconut milk
- 1 thumb-size ginger, sliced
- 1 onion, chopped
- 3 cloves of garlic, minced
- Pepper and salt to taste

Directions:
1. Place a heavy-bottomed pot on medium-high fire and add all ingredients.
2. Cover and bring to a boil, lower fire to a simmer, and simmer for 20 minutes.
3. Serve and enjoy.

Nutrition Info:
- Per Servings 6.3g Carbs, 29.3g Protein, 11.3g Fat, 244.1 Calories

Avocado And Salmon

Serves: 2 | Cooking Time: 0 Minutes

Ingredients:
- 1 avocado, halved, pitted
- 2 oz flaked salmon, packed in water
- 1 tbsp mayonnaise
- 1 tbsp grated cheddar cheese
- Seasoning:
- 1/8 tsp salt
- 2 tbsp coconut oil

Directions:
1. Prepare the avocado and for this, cut avocado in half and then remove its seed.Drain the salmon, add it in a bowl along with remaining ingredients, stir well and then scoop into the hollow on an avocado half.Serve.

Nutrition Info:
- 3 g Carbs; 19 g Protein; 48 g Fats; 525 Calories

Trout And Fennel Parcels

Servings: 4 | Cooking Time: 20 Minutes

Ingredients:
- ½ lb deboned trout, butterflied
- Salt and black pepper to season
- 3 tbsp olive oil + extra for tossing
- 4 sprigs rosemary
- 4 sprigs thyme
- 4 butter cubes
- 1 cup thinly sliced fennel
- 1 medium red onion, sliced
- 8 lemon slices
- 3 tsp capers to garnish

Directions:
1. Preheat the oven to 400ºF. Cut out parchment paper wide enough for each trout. In a bowl, toss the fennel and onion with a little bit of olive oil and share into the middle parts of the papers.
2. Place the fish on each veggie mound, top with a drizzle of olive oil each, salt and pepper, a sprig of rosemary and thyme, and 1 cube of butter. Also, lay the lemon slices on the fish. Wrap and close the fish packets securely, and place them on a baking sheet.
3. Bake in the oven for 15 minutes, and remove once ready. Plate them and garnish the fish with capers and serve with a squash mash.

Nutrition Info:
- Per Servings 2.8g Carbs, 17g Protein, 9.3g Fat, 234 Calories

Enchilada Sauce On Mahi Mahi

Servings: 2 | Cooking Time: 15 Minutes

Ingredients:
- 2 Mahi fillets, fresh
- ¼ cup commercial enchilada sauce
- Pepper to taste

Directions:
1. In a heat-proof dish that fits inside saucepan, place fish and top with enchilada sauce.
2. Place a large saucepan on the medium-high fire. Place a trivet inside the saucepan and fill the pan halfway with water. Cover and bring to a boil.
3. Cover dish with foil and place on a trivet.
4. Cover pan and steam for 10 minutes. Let it rest in pan for another 5 minutes.
5. Serve and enjoy topped with pepper.

Nutrition Info:
- Per Servings 8.9g Carbs, 19.8g Protein, 15.9g Fat, 257 Calories

Dilled Salmon In Creamy Sauce

Servings: 2 | Cooking Time: 20 Minutes

Ingredients:
- 2 salmon fillets
- ¾ tsp tarragon
- 1 tbsp duck fat
- ¾ tsp dill
- Sauce
- 2 tbsp butter
- ½ tsp dill
- ½ tsp tarragon
- ¼ cup heavy cream

Directions:
1. Season the salmon with dill and tarragon. Melt the duck fat in a pan over medium heat. Add salmon and cook for about 4 minutes on both sides. Set aside.
2. Melt the butter and add the dill and tarragon. Cook for 30 seconds to infuse the flavors. Whisk in the heavy cream and cook for one more minute. Serve the salmon topped with the sauce.

Nutrition Info:
- Per Servings 1.5g Carbs, 22g Protein, 40g Fat, 468 Calories

Simple Steamed Salmon Fillets

Servings: 3 | Cooking Time: 15 Minutes

Ingredients:
- 10 oz. salmon fillets
- 2 tbsp. coconut aminos
- 2 tbsp. lemon juice, freshly squeezed
- 1 tsp. sesame seeds, toasted
- 3 tbsp sesame oil
- Salt and pepper to taste

Directions:
1. Place a trivet in a large saucepan and pour a cup or two of water into the pan. Bring to a boil.
2. Place salmon in a heatproof dish that fits inside the saucepan. Season salmon with pepper and salt. Drizzle with coconut aminos, lemon juice, sesame oil, and sesame seeds.
3. Seal dish with foil. Place the dish on the trivet inside the saucepan. Cover and steam for 15 minutes.
4. Serve and enjoy.

Nutrition Info:
- Per Servings 2.6g Carbs, 20.1g Protein, 17.4g Fat, 210 Calories

Cedar Salmon With Green Onion

Servings: 5 | Cooking Time: 20 Mins

Ingredients:
- 3 untreated cedar planks
- 1/4 cup. chopped green onions
- 1 tablespoon. grated fresh ginger root
- 1 teaspoon. minced garlic
- 2 salmon fillets, skin removed
- 1/3 cup. olive oil
- 1/3 cup. mayo
- 1 1/2 tablespoons. rice vinegar

Directions:
1. Soak cedar planks in warm water for 1 hour more.
2. Whisk olive oil, rice vinegar, mayo, green onions, ginger, and garlic in a bowl. Marinade salmon fillets to coat completely. Cover the bowl with plastic wrap and marinate for 15 to 60 minutes.
3. Preheat an outdoor grill over medium heat. Lay planks on the center of hot grate Place the salmon fillets onto the planks and remove the marinade. Cover the grill and cook until cooked through, about 20 minutes, or until salmon is done to your liking. Serve the salmon on a platter right off the planks.

Nutrition Info:
- Per Servings 10g Carbs, 18g Protein, 27g Fat, 355 Calories

Mustard-crusted Salmon

Servings: 4 | Cooking Time: 15 Minutes

Ingredients:
- 1 ¼ lb. salmon fillets, cut into 4 portions
- 2 tsp. lemon juice
- 2 tbsp. stone-ground mustard
- Lemon wedges, for garnish
- 4 tbsp olive oil
- Salt and pepper to taste

Directions:
1. Place a trivet in a large saucepan and pour a cup of water into the pan. Bring to a boil.
2. Place salmon in a heatproof dish that fits inside saucepan and drizzle with olive oil. Season the salmon fillets with salt, pepper, and lemon juice. Sprinkle with mustard on top and garnish with lemon wedges on top. Seal dish with foil.
3. Place the dish on the trivet inside the saucepan. Cover and steam for 15 minutes.
4. Serve and enjoy.

Nutrition Info:
- Per Servings 2.9g Carbs, 29g Protein, 24.8g Fat, 360 Calories

Angel Hair Shirataki With Creamy Shrimp

Serves:4 | Cooking Time:25 Minutes

Ingredients:
- 2 (8 oz) packs angel hair shirataki noodles
- 1 tbsp olive oil
- 1 lb shrimp, deveined
- 2 tbsp unsalted butter
- 6 garlic cloves, minced
- ½ cup dry white wine
- 1 ½ cups heavy cream
- ½ cup grated Asiago cheese
- 2 tbsp chopped fresh parsley

Directions:
1. Heat olive oil in a skillet, season the shrimp with salt and pepper, and cook on both sides, 2 minutes; set aside. Melt butter in the skillet and sauté garlic. Stir in wine and cook until reduced by half, scraping the bottom of the pan to deglaze. Stir in heavy cream. Let simmer for 1 minute and stir in Asiago cheese to melt. Return the shrimp to the sauce and sprinkle the parsley on top. Bring 2 cups of water to a boi. Strain shirataki pasta and rinse under hot running water. Allow proper draining and pour the shirataki pasta into the boiling water. Cook for 3 minutes and strain again. Place a dry skillet and stir-fry the pasta until dry, 1-2 minutes. Season with salt and plate. Top with the shrimp sauce and serve.

Nutrition Info:
- Per Serves 6.3g Carbs; 33g Protein ; 32g Fats; 493 Calories

Asian-style Fish Salad

Serves: 2 | Cooking Time: 15 Minutes

Ingredients:
- Salad:
- 1/4 cup water
- 1/4 cup Sauvignon Blanc
- 1/2 pound salmon fillets
- 1 cup Chinese cabbage, sliced
- 1 tomato, sliced
- 2 radishes, sliced
- 1 bell pepper, sliced
- 1 medium-sized white onion, sliced
- Salad Dressing:
- 1/2 teaspoon fresh garlic, minced
- 1 fresh chili pepper, seeded and minced
- 1/2 teaspoon fresh ginger, peeled and grated
- 2 tablespoons fresh lime juice
- 1 tablespoon sesame oil
- 1 tablespoon tamari sauce
- 1 teaspoon xylitol
- 1 tablespoon fresh mint, roughly chopped
- Sea salt and freshly ground black pepper, to taste

Directions:
1. Place the water and Sauvignon Blanc in a sauté pan; bring to a simmer over moderate heat.
2. Place the salmon fillets, skin-side down in the pan and cover with the lid. Cook for 5 to 8 minutes or to your desired doneness; do not overcook the salmon; reserve.
3. Place the Chinese cabbage, tomato, radishes, bell pepper, and onion in a serving bowl.
4. Prepare the salad dressing by whisking all ingredients. Dress your salad, top with the salmon fillets and serve immediately!

Nutrition Info:
- Per Serves4.9g Carbs; 24.4g Protein; 15.1g Fat; 277 Calories

Tilapia With Olives & Tomato Sauce

Servings: 4 | Cooking Time: 30 Minutes

Ingredients:
- 4 tilapia fillets
- 2 garlic cloves, minced
- 2 tsp oregano
- 14 ounces diced tomatoes
- 1 tbsp olive oil
- ½ red onion, chopped
- 2 tbsp parsley
- ¼ cup kalamata olives

Directions:
1. Heat the olive oil in a skillet over medium heat and cook the onion for about 3 minutes. Add garlic and oregano and cook for 30 seconds. Stir in tomatoes and bring the mixture to a boil. Reduce the heat and simmer for 5 minutes. Add olives and tilapia, and cook for about 8 minutes. Serve the tilapia with tomato sauce.

Nutrition Info:
- Per Servings 6g Carbs, 23g Protein, 15g Fat, 282 Calories

Creamy Hoki With Almond Bread Crust

Servings: 4 | Cooking Time: 50 Minutes

Ingredients:
- 1 cup flaked smoked hoki, bones removed
- 1 cup cubed hoki fillets, cubed
- 4 eggs
- 1 cup water
- 3 tbsp almond flour
- 1 medium white onion, sliced
- 2 cups sour cream
- 1 tbsp chopped parsley
- 1 cup pork rinds, crushed
- 1 cup grated cheddar cheese
- Salt and black pepper to taste
- Cooking spray

Directions:
1. Preheat the oven to 360ºF and lightly grease a baking dish with cooking spray.
2. Then, boil the eggs in water in a pot over medium heat to be well done for 12 minutes, run the eggs under cold water and peel the shells. After, place on a cutting board and chop them.
3. Melt the butter in a saucepan over medium heat and sauté the onion for about 4 minutes. Turn the heat off and stir the almond flour into it to form a roux. Turn the heat back on and cook the roux to be golden brown and stir in the cream until the mixture is smooth. Season with salt and pepper, and stir in the parsley.
4. Spread the smoked and cubed fish in the baking dish, sprinkle the eggs on top, and spoon the sauce over. In a bowl, mix the pork rinds with the cheddar cheese, and sprinkle it over the sauce.
5. Bake the casserole in the oven for 20 minutes until the top is golden and the sauce and cheese are bubbly. Remove the bake after and serve with a steamed green vegetable mix.

Nutrition Info:
- Per Servings 3.5g Carbs, 28.5g Protein, 27g Fat, 386 Calories

Rosemary-lemon Shrimps

Servings: 4 | Cooking Time: 8 Minutes

Ingredients:
- 5 tablespoons butter
- ½ cup lemon juice, freshly squeezed
- 1 ½ lb. shrimps, peeled and deveined
- ¼ cup coconut aminos
- 1 tsp rosemary
- Pepper to taste

Directions:
1. Place all ingredients in a large pan on a high fire.
2. Boil for 8 minutes or until shrimps are pink.
3. Serve and enjoy.

Nutrition Info:
- Per Servings 3.7g Carbs, 35.8g Protein, 17.9g Fat, 315 Calories

Baked Fish With Feta And Tomato

Serves: 2 | Cooking Time: 15 Minutes

Ingredients:
- 2 pacific whitening fillets
- 1 scallion, chopped
- 1 Roma tomato, chopped
- 1 tsp fresh oregano
- 1-ounce feta cheese, crumbled
- Seasoning:
- 2 tbsp avocado oil
- 1/3 tsp salt
- 1/4 tsp ground black pepper
- ¼ crushed red pepper

Directions:
1. Turn on the oven, then set it to 400 °F and let it preheat. Take a medium skillet pan, place it over medium heat, add oil and when hot, add scallion and cook for 3 minutes. Add tomatoes, stir in ½ tsp oregano, 1/8 tsp salt, black pepper, red pepper, pour in ¼ cup water and bring it to simmer. Sprinkle remaining salt over fillets, add to the pan, drizzle with remaining oil, and then bake for 10 to 12 minutes until fillets are fork-tender. When done, top fish with remaining oregano and cheese and then serve.

Nutrition Info:
- 8 g Carbs; 26.7 g Protein; 29.5 g Fats; 427.5 Calories

Golden Pompano In Microwave

Servings: 2 | Cooking Time: 11 Minutes

Ingredients:
- ½-lb pompano
- 1 tbsp soy sauce, low sodium
- 1-inch thumb ginger, diced
- 1 lemon, halved
- 1 stalk green onions, chopped
- ¼ cup water
- 1 tsp pepper
- 4 tbsp olive oil

Directions:

1. In a microwavable casserole dish, mix well all ingredients except for pompano, green onions, and lemon.
2. Squeeze half of the lemon in dish and slice into thin circles the other half.
3. Place pompano in the dish and add lemon circles on top of the fish. Drizzle with pepper and olive oil.
4. Cover top of a casserole dish with a microwave-safe plate.
5. Microwave for 5 minutes.
6. Remove from microwave, turn over fish, sprinkle green onions, top with a microwavable plate.
7. Return to microwave and cook for another 3 minutes.
8. Let it rest for 3 minutes more.
9. Serve and enjoy.

Nutrition Info:
- Per Servings 6.3g Carbs, 22.2g Protein, 39.5g Fat, 464 Calories

Salmon And Cauliflower Rice Pilaf

Servings: 4 | Cooking Time: 25 Minutes

Ingredients:
- 1 cauliflower head, shredded
- ¼ cup dried vegetable soup mix
- 1 cup chicken broth
- 1 pinch saffron
- 1-lb wild salmon fillets
- 6 tbsp olive oil
- Pepper and salt to taste

Directions:
1. Place a heavy-bottomed pot on medium-high fire and add all ingredients and mix well.
2. Bring to a boil, lower fire to a simmer, and simmer for 10 minutes.
3. Turn off fire, shred salmon, adjust seasoning to taste.
4. Let it rest for 5 minutes.
5. Fluff again, serve, and enjoy.

Nutrition Info:
- Per Servings 4.7g Carbs, 31.8g Protein, 31.5g Fat, 429 Calories

Lemon Marinated Salmon With Spices

Servings: 2 | Cooking Time: 15 Minutes

Ingredients:
- 2 tablespoons. lemon juice
- 1 tablespoon. yellow miso paste
- 2 teaspoons. Dijon mustard
- 1 pinch cayenne pepper and sea salt to taste
- 2 center-cut salmon fillets, boned; skin on
- 1 1/2 tablespoons mayonnaise
- 1 tablespoon ground black pepper

Directions:
1. In a bowl, combine lemon juice with black pepper. Stir in mayonnaise, miso paste, Dijon mustard, and cayenne pepper, mix well. Pour over salmon fillets, reserve about a tablespoon marinade. Cover and marinate the fish in the refrigerator for 30 minutes.
2. Preheat oven to 450 degrees F. Line a baking sheet with parchment paper.

3. Lay fillets on the prepared baking sheet. Rub the reserved lemon-pepper marinade on fillets. Then season with cayenne pepper and sea salt to taste.
4. Bake in the oven for 10 to 15 minutes until cooked through.

Nutrition Info:
- Per Servings 7.1g Carbs, 20g Protein, 28.1g Fat, 361 Calories

Cod In Garlic Butter Sauce

Servings: 6 | Cooking Time: 20 Minutes

Ingredients:
- 2 tsp olive oil
- 6 Alaska cod fillets
- Salt and black pepper to taste
- 4 tbsp salted butter
- 4 cloves garlic, minced
- ⅓ cup lemon juice
- 3 tbsp white wine
- 2 tbsp chopped chives

Directions:
1. Heat the oil in a skillet over medium heat and season the cod with salt and black pepper. Fry the fillets in the oil for 4 minutes on one side, flip and cook for 1 minute. Take out, plate, and set aside.
2. In another skillet over low heat, melt the butter and sauté the garlic for 3 minutes. Add the lemon juice, wine, and chives. Season with salt, black pepper, and cook for 3 minutes until the wine slightly reduces. Put the fish in the skillet, spoon sauce over, cook for 30 seconds and turn the heat off.
3. Divide fish into 6 plates, top with sauce, and serve with buttered green beans.

Nutrition Info:
- Per Servings 2.3g Carbs, 20g Protein, 17.3g Fat, 264 Calories

Baked Cod And Tomato Capers Mix

Serves: 4 | Cooking Time: 25 Minutes

Ingredients:
- 4 cod fillets, boneless
- 2 tablespoons avocado oil
- 1 cup tomato passata
- 2 tablespoons capers, drained
- 2 tablespoons parsley, choppedA pinch of salt and black pepper

Directions:
1. In a roasting pan, combine the cod with the oil and the other ingredients, toss gently, introduce in the oven at 370 °F and bake for 25 minutes.
2. Divide between plates and serve.

Nutrition Info:
- 0.7g carbs; 2g fat; 5g protein; 150 calories

Red Cabbage Tilapia Taco Bowl

Servings: 4 | Cooking Time: 20 Minutes

Ingredients:
- 2 cups cauli rice
- Water for sprinkling
- 2 tsp ghee
- 4 tilapia fillets, cut into cubes
- ¼ tsp taco seasoning
- Pink salt and chili pepper to taste
- ¼ head red cabbage, shredded
- 1 ripe avocado, pitted and chopped

Directions:
1. Sprinkle cauli rice in a bowl with a little water and microwave for 3 minutes. Fluff after with a fork and set aside. Melt ghee in a skillet over medium heat, rub the tilapia with the taco seasoning, salt, and chili pepper, and fry until brown on all sides, for about 8 minutes in total.
2. Transfer to a plate and set aside. In 4 serving bowls, share the cauli rice, cabbage, fish, and avocado. Serve with chipotle lime sour cream dressing.

Nutrition Info:
- Per Servings 4g Carbs, 16.5g Protein, 23.4g Fat, 269 Calories

Asian-style Steamed Mussels

Serves:6 | Cooking Time:25 Minutes

Ingredients:
- 5 tbsp sesame oil
- 1 onion, chopped
- 3 lb mussels, cleaned
- 2 garlic cloves, minced
- 12 oz coconut milk
- 16 oz white wine
- 1 lime, juiced
- 2 tsp red curry powder
- 2 tbsp cilantro, chopped

Directions:
1. Warm the sesame oil in a saucepan over medium heat and cook onion and garlic cloves for 3 minutes. Pour in wine, coconut milk, and curry powder and cook for 5 minutes. Add mussels, turn off the heat, cover the saucepan, and steam the mussels until the shells open up, 5 minutes. Discard any closed mussels. Top with cilantro and serve.

Nutrition Info:
- Per Serves 5.4g Carbs ; 28.2g Protein ; 16g Fat ; 323 Calories

Shrimp Spread

Servings: 20 | Cooking Time: 0 Minutes

Ingredients:
- 1 package cream cheese, softened
- 1/2 cup sour cream
- 1 cup seafood cocktail sauce
- 12 ounces frozen cooked salad shrimp, thawed
- 1 medium green pepper, chopped
- Pepper

Directions:
1. In a large bowl, beat the cream cheese, and sour cream until smooth.
2. Spread mixture on a round 12-inch serving platter.
3. Top with seafood sauce.
4. Sprinkle with shrimp and green peppers. Cover and refrigerate.
5. Serve with crackers.

Nutrition Info:
- Per Servings 4g Carbs, 8g Protein, 10g Fat, 136 Calories

Salmon Panzanella

Servings: 4 | Cooking Time: 22 Minutes

Ingredients:
- 1 lb skinned salmon, cut into 4 steaks each
- 1 cucumber, peeled, seeded, cubed
- Salt and black pepper to taste
- 8 black olives, pitted and chopped
- 1 tbsp capers, rinsed
- 2 large tomatoes, diced
- 3 tbsp red wine vinegar
- ¼ cup thinly sliced red onion
- 3 tbsp olive oil
- 2 slices day-old zero carb bread, cubed
- ¼ cup thinly sliced basil leaves

Directions:
1. Preheat a grill to 350ºF and prepare the salad. In a bowl, mix the cucumbers, olives, pepper, capers, tomatoes, wine vinegar, onion, olive oil, bread, and basil leaves. Let sit for the flavors to incorporate.
2. Season the salmon steaks with salt and pepper; grill them on both sides for 8 minutes in total. Serve the salmon steaks warm on a bed of the veggies' salad.

Nutrition Info:
- Per Servings 3.1g Carbs, 28.5g Protein, 21.7g Fat, 338 Calories

Avocado Tuna Boats

Serves: 2 | Cooking Time: 10 Minutes

Ingredients:
- 4 oz tuna, packed in water, drained1 green onion sliced
- 1 avocado, halved, pitted
- 3 tbsp mayonnaise
- 1/3 tsp salt
- Seasoning:
- ¼ tsp ground black pepper
- ¼ tsp paprika

Directions:
1. Prepare the filling and for this, take a medium bowl, place tuna in it, add green onion, salt, black pepper, paprika and mayonnaise and then stir until well combined.Cut avocado in half lengthwise, then remove the pit and fill with prepared filling.Serve.

Nutrition Info:
- ; 7 g Carbs; 8 g Protein; 19 g Fats; 244 Calories

Halibut With Pesto

Servings: 4 | Cooking Time: 15 Minutes

Ingredients:
- 4 halibut fillets
- 1 cup basil leaves
- 2 cloves of garlic, minced
- 1 tbsp. lemon juice, freshly squeezed
- 2 tbsp pine nuts
- 2 tbsp. oil, preferably extra virgin olive oil
- Salt and pepper to taste

Directions:
1. In a food processor, pulse the basil, olive oil, pine nuts, garlic, and lemon juice until coarse. Season with salt and pepper to taste.
2. Place a trivet in a large saucepan and pour a cup or two of water into the pan. Bring to a boil.
3. Place salmon in a heatproof dish that fits inside a saucepan. Season salmon with pepper and salt. Drizzle with pesto sauce.
4. Seal dish with foil. Place the dish on the trivet inside the saucepan. Cover and steam for 15 minutes.
5. Serve and enjoy.

Nutrition Info:
- Per Servings 0.8g Carbs, 75.8g Protein, 8.4g Fat, 401 Calories

Grilled Shrimp With Chimichurri Sauce

Servings: 4 | Cooking Time: 55 Minutes

Ingredients:
- 1 pound shrimp, peeled and deveined
- 2 tbsp olive oil
- Juice of 1 lime
- Chimichurri
- ½ tsp salt
- ¼ cup olive oil
- 2 garlic cloves
- ¼ cup red onion, chopped
- ¼ cup red wine vinegar
- ½ tsp pepper
- 2 cups parsley
- ¼ tsp red pepper flakes

Directions:
1. Process the chimichurri ingredients in a blender until smooth; set aside. Combine shrimp, olive oil, and lime juice, in a bowl, and let marinate in the fridge for 30 minutes. Preheat your grill to medium. Add shrimp and cook about 2 minutes per side. Serve shrimp drizzled with the chimichurri sauce.

Nutrition Info:
- Per Servings 3.5g Carbs, 16g Protein, 20.3g Fat, 283 Calories

Lemon Chili Halibut

Servings: 2 | Cooking Time: 15 Minutes

Ingredients:
- 1-lb halibut fillets
- 1 lemon, sliced
- 1 tablespoon chili pepper flakes
- Pepper and salt to taste
- 4 tbsp olive oil

Directions:
1. In a heat-proof dish that fits inside saucepan, place fish. Top fish with chili flakes, lemon slices, salt, and pepper. Drizzle with olive oil. Cover dish with foil
2. Place a large saucepan on the medium-high fire. Place a trivet inside the saucepan and fill the pan halfway with water. Cover and bring to a boil.
3. Place dish on the trivet.
4. Cover pan and steam for 10 minutes. Let it rest in pan for another 5 minutes.
5. Serve and enjoy topped with pepper.

Nutrition Info:
- Per Servings 4.2g Carbs, 42.7g Protein, 58.4g Fat, 675 Calories

Tuna Steaks With Shirataki Noodles

Servings: 4 | Cooking Time: 30 Minutes

Ingredients:
- 1 pack miracle noodle angel hair
- 3 cups water
- Cooking spray
- 1 red bell pepper, seeded and halved
- 4 tuna steaks
- Salt and black pepper to taste
- Olive oil for brushing
- 2 tbsp pickled ginger
- 2 tbsp chopped cilantro

Directions:
1. Cook the shirataki rice as per package instructions: In a colander, rinse the shirataki noodles with running cold water. Bring a pot of salted water to a boil; blanch the noodles for 2 minutes. Drain and transfer to a dry skillet over medium heat. Dry roast for a minute until opaque.
2. Grease a grill's grate with cooking spray and preheat on medium heat. Season the red bell pepper and tuna with salt and black pepper, brush with olive oil, and grill covered. Cook both for 3 minutes on each side. Transfer to a plate to cool. Dice bell pepper with a knife.
3. Assemble the noodles, tuna, and bell pepper in serving plate. Top with pickled ginger and garnish with cilantro. Serve with roasted sesame sauce (low-carb).

Nutrition Info:
- Per Servings 2g Carbs, 22g Protein, 18.2g Fat, 310 Calories

Steamed Greek Snapper

Servings: 12 | Cooking Time: 15 Minutes

Ingredients:
- 6 tbsp. olive oil
- 1 clove of garlic, minced
- 2 tbsp. Greek yogurt
- 12 snapper fillets
- Salt and pepper to taste

Directions:
1. In a small bowl, combine the olive oil, garlic, and Greek yogurt. Season with salt and pepper to taste.
2. Place a trivet in a large saucepan and pour a cup or two of water into the pan. Bring to a boil.
3. Place snapper in a heatproof dish that fits inside a saucepan. If needed, cook in batches. Season snapper with pepper and salt and drizzle with olive oil. Slather with yogurt mixture.
4. Seal dish with foil. Place the dish on the trivet inside the saucepan. Cover and steam for 15 minutes.
5. Serve and enjoy.

Nutrition Info:
- Per Servings 0.4g Carbs, 44.8g Protein, 9.8g Fat, 280 Calories

Steamed Mustard Salmon

Servings: 4 | Cooking Time: 15 Minutes

Ingredients:
- 2 tbsp Dijon mustard
- 1 whole lemon
- 2 cloves of garlic, minced
- 4 salmon fillets, skin removed
- 1 tbsp dill weed
- Salt and pepper to taste

Directions:
1. Slice lemon in half. Slice one lemon in circles and juice the other half in a small bowl.
2. Whisk in mustard, garlic, and dill weed in a bowl of lemon. Season with pepper and salt.
3. Place a trivet in a large saucepan and pour a cup or two of water into the pan. Bring to a boil.
4. Place lemon slices in a heatproof dish that fits inside a saucepan. Season salmon with pepper and salt. Slather mustard mixture on top of salmon.
5. Seal dish with foil. Place the dish on the trivet inside the saucepan. Cover and steam for 15 minutes.
6. Serve and enjoy.

Nutrition Info:
- Per Servings 2.2g Carbs, 65.3g Protein, 14.8g Fat, 402 Calories

Chili-garlic Salmon

Servings: 4 | Cooking Time: 15 Minutes

Ingredients:
- 5 tbsp. sweet chili sauce
- ¼ cup coconut aminos
- 4 salmon fillets
- 3 tbsp. green onions, chopped
- 3 cloves garlic, peeled and minced
- Pepper to taste

Directions:
1. Place a trivet in a large saucepan and pour a cup or two of water into the pan. Bring to a boil.
2. In a small bowl, whisk well sweet chili sauce, garlic, and coconut aminos.
3. Place salmon in a heatproof dish that fits inside a saucepan. Season salmon with pepper. Drizzle with sweet chili sauce mixture. Sprinkle green onions on top of the filet.
4. Seal dish with foil. Place the dish on the trivet inside the saucepan. Cover and steam for 15 minutes.
5. Serve and enjoy.

Nutrition Info:
- Per Servings 0.9g Carbs, 65.4g Protein, 14.4g Fat, 409 Calories

Parmesan Fish Bake

Servings: 4 | Cooking Time: 40 Minutes

Ingredients:
- Cooking spray
- 2 salmon fillets, cubed
- 3 white fish, cubed
- 1 broccoli, cut into florets
- 1 tbsp butter, melted
- Pink salt and black pepper to taste
- 1 cup crème fraiche
- ¼ cup grated Parmesan cheese
- Grated Parmesan cheese for topping

Directions:
1. Preheat oven to 400ºF and grease an 8 x 8 inches casserole dish with cooking spray. Toss the fish cubes and broccoli in butter and season with salt and pepper to taste. Spread in the greased dish.
2. Mix the crème fraiche with Parmesan cheese, pour and smear the cream on the fish, and sprinkle with some more Parmesan. Bake for 25 to 30 minutes until golden brown on top, take the dish out, sit for 5 minutes and spoon into plates. Serve with lemon-mustard asparagus.

Nutrition Info:
- Per Servings 4g Carbs, 28g Protein, 17g Fat, 354 Calories

Pistachio-crusted Salmon

Servings: 4 | Cooking Time: 35 Minutes

Ingredients:
- 4 salmon fillets
- ½ tsp pepper
- 1 tsp salt
- ¼ cup mayonnaise
- ½ cup chopped pistachios
- Sauce
- 1 chopped shallot
- 2 tsp lemon zest
- 1 tbsp olive oil
- A pinch of pepper
- 1 cup heavy cream

Directions:
1. Preheat the oven to 370ºF.
2. Brush the salmon with mayonnaise and season with salt and pepper. Coat with pistachios, place in a lined baking dish and bake for 15 minutes.
3. Heat the olive oil in a saucepan and sauté the shallot for 3 minutes. Stir in the rest of the sauce ingredients. Bring the mixture to a boil and cook until thickened. Serve the fish with the sauce.

Nutrition Info:
• Per Servings 6g Carbs, 34g Protein, 47g Fat, 563 Calories

Boiled Garlic Clams

Servings: 6 | Cooking Time: 10 Minutes

Ingredients:
• 3 tbsp butter
• 6 cloves of garlic
• 50 small clams in the shell, scrubbed
• ½ cup fresh parsley, chopped
• 4 tbsp. extra virgin olive oil
• 1 cup water
• Salt and pepper to taste

Directions:
1. Heat the olive oil and butter in a large pot placed on medium-high fire for a minute.
2. Stir in the garlic and cook until fragrant and slightly browned.
3. Stir in the clams, water, and parsley. Season with salt and pepper to taste.
4. Cover and cook for 5 minutes or until clams have opened.
5. Discard unopened clams and serve.

Nutrition Info:
• Per Servings 0.9g Carbs, 11.3g Protein, 12.8g Fat, 159 Calories

Seared Scallops With Chorizo And Asiago Cheese

Servings: 4 | Cooking Time: 15 Minutes

Ingredients:
• 2 tbsp ghee
• 16 fresh scallops
• 8 ounces chorizo, chopped
• 1 red bell pepper, seeds removed, sliced
• 1 cup red onions, finely chopped
• 1 cup asiago cheese, grated
• Salt and black pepper to taste

Directions:
1. Melt half of the ghee in a skillet over medium heat, and cook the onion and bell pepper for 5 minutes until tender. Add the chorizo and stir-fry for another 3 minutes. Remove and set aside.
2. Pat dry the scallops with paper towels, and season with salt and pepper. Add the remaining ghee to the skillet and sear the scallops for 2 minutes on each side to have a golden brown color. Add the chorizo mixture back and warm through. Transfer to serving platter and top with asiago cheese.

Nutrition Info:
• Per Servings 5g Carbs, 36g Protein, 32g Fat, 491 Calories

Asian Seafood Stir-fry

Serves: 4 | Cooking Time: 15 Minutes

Ingredients:
• 4 teaspoons sesame oil
• 1/2 cup yellow onion, sliced
• 1 cup asparagus spears, sliced
• 1/2 cup celery, chopped
• 1/2 cup enoki mushrooms
• 1 pound bay scallops
• 1 tablespoon fresh parsley, chopped
• Kosher salt and ground black pepper, to taste
• 1/2 teaspoon red pepper flakes, crushed
• 1 tablespoon coconut aminos
• 2 tablespoons rice wine
• 1/2 cup dry roasted peanuts, roughly chopped

Directions:
1. Heat 1 teaspoon of the sesame oil in a wok over a medium-high flame. Now, fry the onion until crisp-tender and translucent; reserve.
2. Heat another teaspoon of the sesame oil and fry the asparagus and celery for about 3 minutes until crisp-tender; reserve.
3. Then, heat another teaspoon of the sesame oil and cook the mushrooms for 2 minutes more or until they start to soften; reserve.
4. Lastly, heat the remaining teaspoon of sesame oil and cook the bay scallops just until they are opaque.
5. Return all reserved vegetables to the wok. Add in the remaining ingredients and toss to combine. Serve warm and enjoy!

Nutrition Info:
• Per Serves 5.9g Carbs; 27g Protein; 12.5g Fat; 236 Calories

Steamed Asparagus And Shrimps

Servings: 6 | Cooking Time: 15 Minutes

Ingredients:
• 1-pound shrimps, peeled and deveined
• 1 bunch asparagus, trimmed
• ½ tablespoon Cajun seasoning
• 2 tablespoons butter
• 5 tablespoons oil
• Salt and pepper to taste

Directions:
1. In a heat-proof dish that fits inside the saucepan, add all ingredients. Mix well.
2. Place a large saucepan on the medium-high fire. Place a trivet inside the saucepan and fill the pan halfway with water. Cover and bring to a boil.
3. Cover dish with foil and place on a trivet.
4. Cover pan and steam for 10 minutes. Let it rest in pan for another 5 minutes.
5. Serve and enjoy.

Nutrition Info:
• Per Servings 1.1g Carbs, 15.5g Protein, 15.8g Fat, 204.8 Calories

Chapter 5 Poultry Recipes

Chapter 5 Poultry Recipes

Chicken And Zucchini Bake

Servings: 4 | Cooking Time: 45 Minutes

Ingredients:
- 1 zucchini, chopped
- Salt and black pepper, to taste
- 1 tsp garlic powder
- 1 tbsp avocado oil
- 2 chicken breasts, skinless, boneless, sliced
- 1 tomato, cored and chopped
- ½ tsp dried oregano
- ½ tsp dried basil
- ½ cup mozzarella cheese, shredded

Directions:
1. Apply pepper, garlic powder and salt to the chicken. Set a pan over medium heat and warm avocado oil, add in the chicken slices, cook until golden; remove to a baking dish. To the same pan add the zucchini, tomato, pepper, basil, oregano, and salt, cook for 2 minutes, and spread over chicken.
2. Bake in the oven at 330ºF for 20 minutes. Sprinkle the mozzarella over the chicken, return to the oven, and bake for 5 minutes until the cheese is melted and bubbling. Serve with green salad.

Nutrition Info:
- Per Servings 2g Carbs, 35g Protein, 11g Fat, 235 Calories

Easy Chicken Meatloaf

Servings: 8 | Cooking Time: 50 Minutes

Ingredients:
- 1 cup sugar-free marinara sauce
- 2 lb ground chicken
- 2 tbsp fresh parsley, chopped
- 3 garlic cloves, minced
- 2 tsp onion powder
- 2 tsp Italian seasoning
- Salt and ground black pepper, to taste
- For the filling
- ½ cup ricotta cheese
- 1 cup Grana Padano cheese, grated
- 1 cup Colby cheese, shredded
- 2 tsp fresh chives, chopped
- 2 tbsp fresh parsley, chopped
- 1 garlic clove, minced

Directions:
1. Using a bowl, combine the chicken with half of the marinara sauce, pepper, onion powder, Italian seasoning, salt, and 2 garlic cloves. In a separate bowl, combine the ricotta cheese with half of the Grana Padano cheese, chives, pepper, 1 garlic clove, half of the Colby cheese, salt, and 2 tablespoons parsley. Place half of the chicken mixture into a loaf pan, and spread evenly.
2. Place in cheese filling and spread evenly. Top with the rest of the meat mixture and spread again. Set the meatloaf in the oven at 380ºF and bake for 25 minutes. Remove meatloaf from oven, spread the rest of the marinara sauce, Grana Padano cheese and Colby cheese, and bake for 18 minutes. Allow meatloaf cooling and serve in slices sprinkled with 2 tbsp of chopped parsley.

Nutrition Info:
- Per Servings 4g Carbs, 28g Protein, 14g Fat, 273 Calories

Chicken Garam Masala

Servings: 4 | Cooking Time: 45 Minutes

Ingredients:
- 1 lb chicken breasts, sliced lengthwise
- 2 tbsp butter
- 1 tbsp olive oil
- 1 yellow bell pepper, finely chopped
- 1 ¼ cups heavy whipping cream
- 1 tbsp fresh cilantro, finely chopped
- Salt and pepper, to taste
- For the garam masala
- 1 tsp ground cumin
- 2 tsp ground coriander
- 1 tsp ground cardamom
- 1 tsp turmeric
- 1 tsp ginger
- 1 tsp paprika
- 1 tsp cayenne, ground
- 1 pinch ground nutmeg

Directions:
1. Set your oven to 400ºF. In a bowl, mix the garam masala spices. Coat the chicken with half of the masala mixture. Heat the olive oil and butter in a frying pan over medium-high heat, and brown the chicken for 3-5 minutes per side. Transfer to a baking dish.
2. To the remaining masala, add heavy cream and bell pepper. Season with salt and pepper and pour over the chicken. Bake in the oven for 20 minutes until the mixture starts to bubble. Garnish with chopped cilantro to serve.

Nutrition Info:
- Per Servings 5g Carbs, 33g Protein, 50g Fat, 564 Calories

Fried Chicken Breasts

Servings: 4 | Cooking Time: 20 Minutes

Ingredients:
- 2 chicken breasts, cut into strips
- 4 ounces pork rinds, crushed
- 2 cups coconut oil
- 16 ounces jarred pickle juice
- 2 eggs, whisked

Directions:
1. Using a bowl, combine the chicken breast pieces with pickle juice and refrigerate for 12 hours while covered. Set the

eggs in a bowl, and pork rinds in a separate one. Dip the chicken pieces in the eggs, and then in pork rinds, and ensure they are well coated.

2. Set a pan over medium-high heat and warm oil, fry the chicken for 3 minutes on each side, remove to paper towels, drain the excess grease, and enjoy.

Nutrition Info:
- Per Servings 2.5g Carbs, 23g Protein, 16g Fat, 387 Calories

Sticky Cranberry Chicken Wings

Servings: 6 | Cooking Time: 50 Minutes

Ingredients:
- 2 lb chicken wings
- 4 tbsp unsweetened cranberry puree
- 2 tbsp olive oil
- Salt to taste
- Sweet chili sauce to taste
- Lemon juice from 1 lemon

Directions:
1. Preheat the oven (broiler side) to 400ºF. Then, in a bowl, mix the cranberry puree, olive oil, salt, sweet chili sauce, and lemon juice. After, add in the wings and toss to coat.
2. Place the chicken under the broiler, and cook for 45 minutes, turning once halfway.
3. Remove the chicken after and serve warm with a cranberry and cheese dipping sauce.

Nutrition Info:
- Per Servings 1.6g Carbs, 17.6g Protein, 8.5g Fat, 152 Calories

Easy Chicken Vindaloo

Servings: 5 | Cooking Time: 30 Minutes

Ingredients:
- 1 lb. chicken thighs, skin and bones not removed
- 2 tbsp. garam masala
- 6 whole red dried chilies
- 1 onion, sliced
- 5 cloves of garlic, crushed
- Pepper and salt to taste
- 1 tsp oil
- 1 cup water

Directions:
1. On high fire, heat a saucepan for 2 minutes. Add oil to the pan and swirl to coat bottom and sides. Heat oil for a minute.
2. Add chicken with skin side touching pan and sear for 5 minutes. Turn chicken over and sear the other side for 3 minutes. Transfer chicken to a plate.
3. In the same pan, sauté garlic for a minute. Add onion and sauté for 3 minutes. Stir in garam masala and chilies.
4. Return chicken to the pot and mix well. Add water and season with pepper and salt.
5. Cover and lower fire to simmer and cook for 15 minutes.
6. Serve and enjoy.

Nutrition Info:
- Per Servings 1.4g Carbs, 15.2g Protein, 15.1g Fat, 206 Calories

Turkey Stew With Salsa Verde

Servings: 6 | Cooking Time: 30 Minutes

Ingredients:
- 4 cups leftover turkey meat, chopped
- 2 cups green beans
- 6 cups chicken stock
- Salt and ground black pepper, to taste
- 1 tbsp canned chipotle peppers, chopped
- ½ tsp garlic powder
- ½ cup salsa verde
- 1 tsp ground coriander
- 2 tsp cumin
- ¼ cup sour cream
- 1 tbsp fresh cilantro, chopped

Directions:
1. Set a pan over medium heat. Add in the stock and heat. Stir in the green beans, and cook for 10 minutes. Place in the turkey, garlic powder, ground coriander, salt, salsa verde, chipotles, cumin, and pepper, and cook for 10 minutes.
2. Stir in the sour cream, kill the heat, and separate into bowls. Top with chopped cilantro and enjoy.

Nutrition Info:
- Per Servings 2g Carbs, 27g Protein, 11g Fat, 193 Calories

Basil Turkey Meatballs

Servings: 4 | Cooking Time: 15 Minutes

Ingredients:
- 1 pound ground turkey
- 2 tbsp chopped sun-dried tomatoes
- 2 tbsp chopped basil
- ½ tsp garlic powder
- 1 egg
- ½ tsp salt
- ¼ cup almond flour
- 2 tbsp olive oil
- ½ cup shredded mozzarella
- ¼ tsp pepper

Directions:
1. Place everything except the oil in a bowl. Mix with your hands until combined. Form 16 meatballs out of the mixture. Heat the olive oil in a skillet over medium heat. Cook the meatballs for 3 minutes per each side.

Nutrition Info:
- Per Servings 2g Carbs, 22g Protein, 26g Fat, 310 Calories

Broccoli Chicken Stew

Servings: 4 | Cooking Time: 30 Minutes

Ingredients:
- 1 package frozen chopped broccoli
- 1 cup shredded sharp cheddar cheese
- ½ cup sour cream
- ¾ cup Campbell's broccoli cheese soup
- 4 boneless skinless chicken breasts, thawed
- ½ cup water

Directions:

1. Add all ingredients, except for broccoli in a pot on high fire and bring to a boil.
2. Once boiling, lower fire to a simmer and cook for 20 minutes, stirring frequently.
3. Adjust seasoning to taste. Add broccoli and continue cooking and stirring for another 5 minutes.
4. Serve and enjoy.

Nutrition Info:
• Per Servings 9.7g Carbs, 63.9g Protein, 22.1g Fat, 511 Calories

Spicy Chicken Kabobs

Servings: 6 | Cooking Time: 1 Hour And 20 Minutes

Ingredients:
• 2 pounds chicken breasts, cubed
• 1 tsp sesame oil
• 1 tbsp olive oil
• 1 cup red bell pepper pieces
• 2 tbsp five spice powder
• 2 tbsp granulated sweetener
• 1 tbsp fish sauce

Directions:
1. Combine the sauces and seasonings in a bowl. Add the chicken, and let marinate for 1 hour in the fridge. Preheat the grill. Take 12 skewers and thread the chicken and bell peppers. Grill for 3 minutes per side.

Nutrition Info:
• Per Servings 3.1g Carbs, 17.5g Protein, 13.5g Fat, 198 Calories

Chicken And Spinach Stir Fry

Servings: 4 | Cooking Time: 10 Minutes

Ingredients:
• 2 cloves of garlic, minced
• 1 tablespoon fresh ginger, grated
• 1 ¼ pounds boneless chicken breasts, cut into strips
• 2 tablespoons yellow miso, diluted in water
• 2 cups baby spinach
• 2 tablespoons olive oil
• Pepper and salt to taste

Directions:
1. Heat oil in a skillet over medium-high heat and sauté the garlic for 30 seconds until fragrant.
2. Stir in the ginger and chicken breasts. Season lightly with pepper and salt.
3. Cook for 5 minutes while stirring constantly.
4. Stir in the diluted miso paste.
5. Continue cooking for 3 more minutes before adding spinach.
6. Cook for another minute or until the spinach leaves have wilted.

Nutrition Info:
• Per Servings 1.3g Carbs, 32.5g Protein, 10.5g Fat, 237 Calories

Chicken Stew With Sun-dried Tomatoes

Servings: 4 | Cooking Time: 60 Minutes

Ingredients:
• 2 carrots, chopped
• 2 tbsp olive oil
• 2 celery stalks, chopped
• 2 cups chicken stock
• 1 shallot, chopped
• 28 oz chicken thighs, skinless, boneless
• 3 garlic cloves, peeled and minced
• ½ tsp dried rosemary
• 2 oz sun-dried tomatoes, chopped
• 1 cup spinach
• ¼ tsp dried thyme
• ½ cup heavy cream
• Salt and ground black pepper, to taste
• A pinch of xanthan gum

Directions:
1. In a pot, heat the olive oil over medium heat and add garlic, carrots, celery, and shallot; season with salt and pepper and sauté for 5-6 minutes until tender. Stir in the chicken and cook for 5 minutes.
2. Pour in the stock, tomatoes, rosemary, and thyme, and cook for 30 minutes covered. Stir in xanthan gum, cream, and spinach; cook for 5 minutes. Adjust the seasonings and separate into bowls.

Nutrition Info:
• Per Servings 6g Carbs, 23g Protein, 11g Fat, 224 Calories

Buttered Duck Breast

Servings: 1 | Cooking Time: 30 Minutes

Ingredients:
• 1 medium duck breast, skin scored
• 1 tbsp heavy cream
• 2 tbsp butter
• Salt and black pepper, to taste
• 1 cup kale
• ¼ tsp fresh sage

Directions:
1. Set the pan over medium-high heat and warm half of the butter. Place in sage and heavy cream, and cook for 2 minutes. Set another pan over medium-high heat. Place in the remaining butter and duck breast as the skin side faces down, cook for 4 minutes, flip, and cook for 3 more minutes.
2. Place the kale to the pan containing the sauce, cook for 1 minute. Set the duck breast on a flat surface and slice. Arrange the duck slices on a platter and drizzle over the sauce.

Nutrition Info:
• Per Servings 2g Carbs, 35g Protein, 46g Fat, 547 Calories

Chicken Stroganoff

Servings: 4 | Cooking Time: 4 Hours 15 Minutes

Ingredients:
- 2 garlic cloves, minced
- 8 oz mushrooms, chopped
- ¼ tsp celery seeds, ground
- 1 cup chicken stock
- 1 cup sour cream
- 1 cup leeks, chopped
- 1 pound chicken breasts
- 1½ tsp dried thyme
- 2 tbsp fresh parsley, chopped
- Salt and black pepper, to taste
- 4 zucchinis, spiralized

Directions:
1. Place the chicken in a slow cooker. Place in the salt, leeks, sour cream, half of the parsley, celery seeds, garlic, pepper, mushrooms, stock, and thyme. Cook on high for 4 hours while covered.
2. Uncover the pot, add more pepper and salt if desired, and the rest of the parsley. Heat a pan with water over medium heat, place in some salt, bring to a boil, stir in the zucchini pasta, cook for 1 minute, and drain. Place in serving bowls, top with the chicken mixture, and serve.

Nutrition Info:
- Per Servings 4g Carbs, 26g Protein, 22g Fat, 365 Calories

Baked Pecorino Toscano Chicken

Servings: 4 | Cooking Time: 60 Minutes

Ingredients:
- 4 chicken breasts, skinless and boneless
- ½ cup mayonnaise
- ½ cup buttermilk
- Salt and ground black pepper, to taste
- ¾ cup Pecorino Toscano cheese, grated
- Cooking spray
- 8 mozzarella cheese slices
- 1 tsp garlic powder

Directions:
1. Spray a baking dish, add in the chicken breasts, and top 2 mozzarella cheese slices to each piece. Using a bowl, combine the Pecorino cheese, pepper, buttermilk, mayonnaise, salt, and garlic. Sprinkle this over the chicken, set the dish in the oven at 370ºF, and bake for 1 hour.

Nutrition Info:
- Per Servings 6g Carbs, 20g Protein, 24g Fat, 346 Calories

Herby Chicken Meatballs

Servings: 3 | Cooking Time: 25 Minutes

Ingredients:
- 1 pound ground chicken
- Salt and black pepper, to taste
- 2 tbsp ranch dressing
- ½ cup almond flour
- ¼ cup mozzarella cheese, grated
- 1 tbsp dry Italian seasoning
- ¼ cup hot sauce + more for serving
- 1 egg

Directions:
1. Using a bowl, combine chicken meat, pepper, ranch dressing, Italian seasoning, flour, hot sauce, mozzarella cheese, salt, and the egg. Form 9 meatballs, arrange them on a lined baking tray and cook for 16 minutes at 480ºF. Place the chicken meatballs in a bowl and serve along with hot sauce.

Nutrition Info:
- Per Servings 2.1g Carbs, 32g Protein, 31g Fat, 456 Calories

Paprika Chicken With Cream Sauce

Servings: 4 | Cooking Time: 50 Minutes

Ingredients:
- 1 pound chicken thighs
- Salt and black pepper, to taste
- 1 tsp onion powder
- ¼ cup heavy cream
- 2 tbsp butter
- 2 tbsp sweet paprika

Directions:
1. Using a bowl, combine the paprika with onion powder, pepper, and salt. Season chicken pieces with this mixture and lay on a lined baking sheet; bake for 40 minutes in the oven at 400ºF. Split the chicken in serving plates, and set aside.
2. Add the cooking juices to a skillet over medium heat, and mix with the heavy cream and butter. Cook for 5-6 minutes until the sauce is thickened. Sprinkle the sauce over the chicken and serve.

Nutrition Info:
- Per Servings 2.6g Carbs, 31.3g Protein, 33g Fat, 381 Calories

Chicken Paella With Chorizo

Servings: 6 | Cooking Time: 63 Minutes

Ingredients:
- 18 chicken drumsticks
- 12 oz chorizo, chopped
- 1 white onion, chopped
- 4 oz jarred piquillo peppers, finely diced
- 2 tbsp olive oil
- ½ cup chopped parsley
- 1 tsp smoked paprika
- 2 tbsp tomato puree
- ½ cup white wine
- 1 cup chicken broth
- 2 cups cauli rice
- 1 cup chopped green beans
- 1 lemon, cut in wedges
- Salt and pepper, to taste

Directions:
1. Preheat the oven to 350ºF.
2. Heat the olive oil in a cast iron pan over medium heat, meanwhile season the chicken with salt and pepper, and fry in the hot oil on both sides for 10 minutes to lightly brown. After, remove onto a plate with a perforated spoon.

3. Then, add the chorizo and onion to the hot oil, and sauté for 4 minutes. Include the tomato puree, piquillo peppers, and paprika, and let simmer for 2 minutes. Add the broth, and bring the ingredients to boil for 6 minutes until slightly reduced.
4. Stir in the cauli rice, white wine, green beans, half of the parsley, and lay the chicken on top. Transfer the pan to the oven and continue cooking for 20-25 minutes. Let the paella sit to cool for 10 minutes before serving garnished with the remaining parsley and lemon wedges.

Nutrition Info:
- Per Servings 3g Carbs, 22g Protein, 28g Fat, 440 Calories

Oregano & Chili Flattened Chicken

Servings: 6 | Cooking Time: 5 Minutes

Ingredients:
- 6 chicken breasts
- 4 cloves garlic, minced
- ½ cup oregano leaves, chopped
- ½ cup lemon juice
- 2/3 cup olive oil
- ¼ cup erythritol
- Salt and black pepper to taste
- 3 small chilies, minced

Directions:
1. Preheat a grill to 350ºF.
2. In a bowl, mix the garlic, oregano, lemon Juice, olive oil, and erythritol. Set aside.
3. While the spices incorporate in flavor, cover the chicken with plastic wraps, and use the rolling pin to pound to ½ -inch thickness. Remove the wrap afterward, and brush the mixture on the chicken on both sides. Place on the grill, cover the lid and cook for 15 minutes.
4. Then, baste the chicken with more of the spice mixture, and continue cooking for 15 more minutes.

Nutrition Info:
- Per Servings 3g Carbs, 26g Protein, 9g Fat, 265 Calories

Quattro Formaggi Chicken

Servings: 8 | Cooking Time: 40 Minutes

Ingredients:
- 3 pounds chicken breasts
- 2 ounces mozzarella cheese, cubed
- 2 ounces mascarpone cheese
- 4 ounces cheddar cheese, cubed
- 2 ounces provolone cheese, cubed
- 1 zucchini, shredded
- Salt and ground black pepper, to taste
- 1 tsp garlic, minced
- ½ cup pancetta, cooked and crumbled

Directions:
1. Sprinkle pepper and salt to the zucchini, squeeze well, and place to a bowl. Stir in the pancetta, mascarpone, cheddar cheese, provolone cheese, mozzarella, pepper, and garlic.
2. Cut slits into chicken breasts, apply pepper and salt, and stuff with the zucchini and cheese mixture. Set on a lined baking sheet, place in the oven at 400ºF, and bake for 45 minutes.

Nutrition Info:
- Per Servings 2g Carbs, 51g Protein, 37g Fat, 565 Calories

Easy Chicken Chili

Servings: 4 | Cooking Time: 30 Minutes

Ingredients:
- 4 chicken breasts, skinless, boneless, cubed
- 1 tbsp butter
- ½ onion, choppde
- 2 cups chicken broth
- 8 oz diced tomatoes
- 2 oz tomato puree
- 1 tbsp chili powder
- 1 tbsp cumin
- ½ tbsp garlic powder
- 1 serrano pepper, minced
- ½ cup shredded cheddar cheese
- Salt and black pepper to taste

Directions:
1. Set a large pan over medium-high heat and add the chicken. Cover with water and bring to a boil. Cook until no longer pink, for 10 minutes. Transfer the chicken to a flat surface to shred with forks.
2. In a large pot, pour in the butter and set over medium heat. Sauté onion until transparent for 5 minutes.
3. Stir in the chicken, tomatoes, cumin, serrano pepper, garlic powder, tomato puree, broth, and chili powder. Adjust the seasoning and let the mixture boil. Reduce heat to simmer for about 10 minutes.
4. Divide chili among bowls and top with shredded cheese to serve.

Nutrition Info:
- Per Servings 5.6g Carbs, 45g Protein, 21g Fat, 421 Calories

Greek Chicken Stew

Servings: 4 | Cooking Time: 30 Minutes

Ingredients:
- ¼ cup feta cheese
- Sliced and pitted Kalamata olives
- 1 bottle ken's steak house Greek dressing with Feta cheese, olive oil, and black olives
- 4 boneless and skinless thawed chicken breasts
- 1 cup water

Directions:
1. Add all ingredients in a pot, except for feta, on high fire, and bring to a boil.
2. Once boiling, lower fire to a simmer and cook for 25 minutes.
3. Adjust seasoning to taste and stir in feta.
4. Serve and enjoy.

Nutrition Info:
- Per Servings 3.2g Carbs, 54.4g Protein, 65.1g Fat, 818 Calories

Greek Chicken With Capers

Servings: 4 | Cooking Time: 30 Minutes

Ingredients:
- ¼ cup olive oil
- 1 onion, chopped
- 4 chicken breasts, skinless and boneless
- 4 garlic cloves, minced
- Salt and ground black pepper, to taste
- ½ cup kalamata olives, pitted and chopped
- 1 tbsp capers
- 1 pound tomatoes, chopped
- ½ tsp red chili flakes

Directions:
1. Sprinkle pepper and salt on the chicken, and rub with half of the oil. Add the chicken to a pan set over high heat, cook for 2 minutes, flip to the other side, and cook for 2 more minutes. Set the chicken breasts in the oven at 450°F and bake for 8 minutes. Split the chicken into serving plates.
2. Set the same pan over medium heat and warm the remaining oil, place in the onion, olives, capers, garlic, and chili flakes, and cook for 1 minute. Stir in the tomatoes, pepper, and salt, and cook for 2 minutes. Sprinkle over the chicken breasts and enjoy.

Nutrition Info:
- Per Servings 2.2g Carbs, 25g Protein, 21g Fat, 387 Calories

Chicken Gumbo

Servings: 5 | Cooking Time: 40 Minutes

Ingredients:
- 2 sausages, sliced
- 3 chicken breasts, cubed
- 1 cup celery, chopped
- 2 tbsp dried oregano
- 2 bell peppers, seeded and chopped
- 1 onion, peeled and chopped
- 2 cups tomatoes, chopped
- 4 cups chicken broth
- 3 tbsp dried thyme
- 2 tbsp garlic powder
- 2 tbsp dry mustard
- 1 tsp cayenne powder
- 1 tbsp chili powder
- Salt and black pepper, to taste
- 6 tbsp cajun seasoning
- 3 tbsp olive oil

Directions:
1. In a pot over medium heat warm olive oil. Add the sausages, chicken, pepper, onion, dry mustard, chili, tomatoes, thyme, bell peppers, salt, oregano, garlic powder, cayenne, and cajun seasoning.
2. Cook for 10 minutes. Add the remaining ingredients and bring to a boil. Reduce the heat and simmer for 20 minutes covered. Serve hot divided between bowls.

Nutrition Info:
- Per Servings 6g Carbs, 26g Protein, 22g Fat, 361 Calories

Stir Fried Broccoli 'n Chicken

Servings: 5 | Cooking Time: 20 Minutes

Ingredients:
- 1 tbsp. coconut oil
- 3 cloves of garlic, minced
- 1 ½ lb. chicken breasts, cut into strips
- ¼ cup coconut aminos
- 1 head broccoli, cut into florets
- Pepper to taste

Directions:
1. On medium fire, heat a saucepan for 2 minutes. Add oil to the pan and swirl to coat bottom and sides. Heat oil for a minute.
2. Add garlic and sauté for a minute. Stir in chicken and stir fry for 5 minutes.
3. Add remaining ingredients. Season generously with pepper.
4. Increase fire to high and stir fry for 3 minutes.
5. Lower fire to low, cover, and cook for 5 minutes.
6. Serve and enjoy.

Nutrition Info:
- Per Servings 1.8g Carbs, 28.6g Protein, 15.4g Fat, 263 Calories

Fried Chicken With Coconut Sauce

Servings: 6 | Cooking Time: 35 Minutes

Ingredients:
- 1 tbsp coconut oil
- 3 ½ pounds chicken breasts
- 1 cup chicken stock
- 1¼ cups leeks, chopped
- 1 tbsp lime juice
- ¼ cup coconut cream
- 2 tsp paprika
- 1 tsp red pepper flakes
- 2 tbsp green onions, chopped
- Salt and ground black pepper, to taste

Directions:
1. Set a pan over medium-high heat and warm oil, place in the chicken, cook each side for 2 minutes, set to a plate, and set aside. Set heat to medium, place the leeks to the pan and cook for 4 minutes.
2. Stir in the pepper, stock, pepper flakes, salt, paprika, coconut cream, and lime juice. Take the chicken back to the pan, place in more pepper and salt, cook while covered for 15 minutes.

Nutrition Info:
- Per Servings 3.2g Carbs, 58g Protein, 35g Fat, 491 Calories

Pesto Chicken

Servings: 4 | Cooking Time: 30 Minutes

Ingredients:
- 2 cups basil leaves
- ¼ cup + 1 tbsp extra virgin olive oil, divided
- 5 sun-dried tomatoes
- 4 chicken breasts
- 6 cloves garlic, smashed, peeled, and minced
- What you'll need from the store cupboard:
- Salt and pepper to taste
- Water

Directions:
1. Put in the food processor the basil leaves, ¼ cup olive oil, and tomatoes. Season with salt and pepper to taste. Add a cup of water if needed.
2. Season chicken breasts with pepper and salt generously.
3. On medium fire, heat a saucepan for 2 minutes. Add a tbsp of olive oil to the pan and swirl to coat bottom and sides. Heat oil for a minute.
4. Add chicken and sear for 5 minutes per side.
5. Add pesto sauce, cover, and cook on low fire for 15 minutes or until chicken is cooked thoroughly.
6. Serve and enjoy.

Nutrition Info:
- Per Servings 1.1g Carbs, 60.8g Protein, 32.7g Fat, 556 Calories

Chicken And Green Cabbage Casserole

Servings: 4 | Cooking Time: 55 Minutes

Ingredients:
- 3 cups cheddar cheese, grated
- 10 ounces green cabbage, shredded
- 3 chicken breasts, skinless, boneless, cooked, cubed
- 1 cup mayonnaise
- 1 tbsp coconut oil, melted
- ⅓ cup chicken stock
- Salt and ground black pepper, to taste
- Juice of 1 lemon

Directions:
1. Apply oil to a baking dish, and set chicken pieces to the bottom. Spread green cabbage, followed by half of the cheese. Using a bowl, combine the mayonnaise with pepper, stock, lemon juice, and salt.
2. Pour this mixture over the chicken, spread the rest of the cheese, cover with aluminum foil, and bake for 30 minutes in the oven at 350ºF. Open the aluminum foil, and cook for 20 more minutes.

Nutrition Info:
- Per Servings 6g Carbs, 25g Protein, 15g Fat, 231 Calories

Stewed Chicken Salsa

Servings: 4 | Cooking Time: 25 Minutes

Ingredients:
- 1 cup shredded cheddar cheese
- 8-ounces cream cheese
- 16-ounces salsa
- 4 skinless and boneless thawed chicken breasts
- 4 tablespoons butter
- 1 cup water

Directions:
1. Add all ingredients in a pot, except for sour cream, on high fire, and bring to a boil.
2. Once boiling, lower fire to a simmer and cook for 20 minutes.
3. Adjust seasoning to taste and stir in sour cream.
4. Serve and enjoy.

Nutrition Info:
- Per Servings 9.6g Carbs, 67.8g Protein, 32.6g Fat, 658 Calories

Chicken Curry

Servings: 6 | Cooking Time: 30 Minutes

Ingredients:
- 1 ½ lb. boneless chicken breasts
- 2 tbsp. curry powder
- 2 cups chopped tomatoes
- 2 cups coconut milk, freshly squeezed
- 1 thumb-size ginger, peeled and sliced
- Pepper and salt to taste
- 2 tsp oil, divided

Directions:
1. On high fire, heat a saucepan for 2 minutes. Add 1 tsp oil to the pan and swirl to coat bottom and sides. Heat oil for a minute.
2. Sear chicken breasts for 4 minutes per side. Transfer to a chopping board and chop into bite-sized pieces.
3. Meanwhile, in the same pan, add remaining oil and heat for a minute. Add ginger sauté for a minute. Stir in tomatoes and curry powder. Crumble and wilt tomatoes for 5 minutes.
4. Add chopped chicken and continue sautéing for 7 minutes.
5. Deglaze the pot with 1 cup of coconut milk. Season with pepper and salt. Cover and simmer for 15 minutes.
6. Stir in remaining coconut milk and cook until heated through, around 3 minutes.

Nutrition Info:
- Per Servings 7.4g Carbs, 28.1g Protein, 22.4g Fat, 336 Calories

Poulet En Papiotte

Servings: 4 | Cooking Time: 48 Minutes

Ingredients:
- 4 chicken breasts, skinless, scored
- 4 tbsp white wine
- 2 tbsp olive oil + extra for drizzling
- 4 tbsp butter
- 3 cups mixed mushrooms, teared up
- 3 medium celeriac, peeled, chopped
- 2 cups water
- 3 cloves garlic, minced
- 4 sprigs thyme, chopped
- 3 lemons, juiced
- Salt and black pepper to taste
- 2 tbsp Dijon mustard

Directions:
1. Preheat the oven to 450ºF.
2. Arrange the celeriac on a baking sheet, drizzle it with a little oil, and bake for 20 minutes; set aside.
3. In a bowl, evenly mix the chicken, roasted celeriac, mushrooms, garlic, thyme, lemon juice, salt, pepper, and mustard. Make 4 large cuts of foil, fold them in half, and then fold them in half again. Tightly fold the two open edges together to create a bag.
4. Now, share the chicken mixture into each bag, top with the white wine, olive oil, and a tablespoon each of butter on each. Seal the last open end securely making sure not to pierce the bag. Put the bag on a baking tray and bake the chicken in the middle of the oven for 25 minutes.

Nutrition Info:
- Per Servings 4.8g Carbs, 25g Protein, 16.5g Fat, 364 Calories

Chicken With Parmesan Topping

Servings: 4 | Cooking Time: 45 Minutes

Ingredients:
- 4 chicken breast halves, skinless and boneless
- Salt and black pepper, to taste
- ¼ cup green chilies, chopped
- 5 bacon slices, chopped
- 8 ounces cream cheese
- ¼ cup onion, peeled and chopped
- ½ cup mayonnaise
- ½ cup Grana Padano cheese, grated
- 1 cup cheddar cheese, grated
- 2 ounces pork skins, crushed
- 4 tbsp melted butter
- ½ cup Parmesan cheese

Directions:
1. Lay the chicken breasts in a baking dish, season with pepper, and salt, place in the oven at 420ºF and bake for 30 minutes. Set a pan over medium heat, add in the bacon, cook until crispy and remove to a plate. Stir in the onion, and cook for 3 minutes.
2. Remove from heat, add in bacon, cream cheese, ½ cup Grana Padano, mayonnaise, chilies, and cheddar cheese, and spread over the chicken. In a bowl, combine the pork skin with

½ cup Parmesan cheese, and butter. Spread over the chicken as well, place in an oven, and bake for 10 minutes.

Nutrition Info:
- Per Servings 5g Carbs, 25g Protein, 15g Fat, 361 Calories

Bacon Chicken Alfredo

Servings: 4 | Cooking Time: 35 Minutes

Ingredients:
- 4-ounces mushrooms drained and sliced
- 1 cup shredded mozzarella cheese
- 1 jar Classico creamy alfredo sauce
- 6 slices chopped hickory bacon
- 4 boneless skinless chicken breasts thawed or fresh
- Pepper and salt to taste
- ½ cup water

Directions:
1. Add all ingredients in a pot on high fire and bring it to a boil.
2. Once boiling, lower fire to a simmer and cook for 30 minutes, stirring every now and then.
3. Adjust seasoning to taste.
4. Serve and enjoy.

Nutrition Info:
- Per Servings 7.7g Carbs, 75.8g Protein, 70.8g Fat, 976 Calories

Turkey, Coconut And Kale Chili

Servings: 5 | Cooking Time: 30 Minutes

Ingredients:
- 18 ounces turkey breasts, cubed
- 1 cup kale, chopped
- 20 ounces canned diced tomatoes
- 2 tbsp coconut oil
- 2 tbsp coconut cream
- 2 garlic cloves, peeled and minced
- 2 onions, and sliced
- 1 tbsp ground coriander
- 2 tbsp fresh ginger, grated
- 1 tbsp turmeric
- 1 tbsp cumin
- Salt and ground black pepper, to taste
- 2 tbsp chili powder

Directions:
1. Set a pan over medium-high heat and warm the coconut oil, stir in the turkey and onion, and cook for 5 minutes. Place in garlic and ginger, and cook for 1 minute. Stir in the tomatoes, pepper, turmeric, coriander, salt, cumin, and chili powder. Place in the coconut cream, and cook for 10 minutes.
2. Transfer to an immersion blender alongside kale; blend well. Allow simmering, cook for 15 minutes.

Nutrition Info:
- Per Servings 4.2g Carbs, 25g Protein, 15.2g Fat, 295 Calories

Oven-baked Skillet Lemon Chicken

Servings: 4 | Cooking Time: 60 Minutes

Ingredients:
- 6 small chicken thighs
- 1 medium onion
- 1 lemon
- ¼ cup lemon juice, freshly squeezed
- Salt and pepper to taste

Directions:
1. Place all ingredients in a Ziploc bag and allow to marinate for at least 6 hours in the fridge.
2. Preheat the oven to 350F.
3. Place the chicken–sauce and all–into a skillet.
4. Put the skillet in the oven and bake for 1 hour or until the chicken is tender.

Nutrition Info:
- Per Servings 6.2g Carbs, 48.2g Protein, 42.4g Fat, 610 Calories

Smoky Paprika Chicken

Servings: 8 | Cooking Time: 10 Minutes

Ingredients:
- 2 lb. chicken breasts, sliced into strips
- 2 tbsp. smoked paprika
- 1 tsp Cajun seasoning
- 1 tbsp minced garlic
- 1 large onion, sliced thinly
- Salt and pepper to taste
- 1 tbsp. olive oil

Directions:
1. In a large bowl, marinate chicken strips in paprika, Cajun, pepper, salt, and minced garlic for at least 30 minutes.
2. On high fire, heat a saucepan for 2 minutes. Add oil to the pan and swirl to coat bottom and sides. Heat oil for a minute.
3. Stir fry chicken and onion for 7 minutes or until chicken is cooked.
4. Serve and enjoy.

Nutrition Info:
- Per Servings 1.5g Carbs, 34g Protein, 12.4g Fat, 217 Calories

Chili Lime Chicken

Servings: 5 | Cooking Time: 30 Minutes

Ingredients:
- 1 lb. chicken breasts, skin and bones removed
- Juice from 1 ½ limes, freshly squeezed
- 1 tbsp. chili powder
- 1 tsp. cumin
- 6 cloves garlic, minced
- Pepper and salt to taste
- 1 cup water
- 4 tablespoon olive oil

Directions:
1. Place all ingredients in a heavy-bottomed pot and give a good stir.

2. Place on high fire and bring it to a boil. Cover, lower fire to a simmer, and cook for 20 minutes.
3. Remove chicken and place in a bowl. Shred using two forks. Return shredded chicken to the pot.
4. Boil for 10 minutes or until sauce is rendered.
5. Serve and enjoy.

Nutrition Info:
- Per Servings 1.5g Carbs, 19.3g Protein, 19.5g Fat, 265 Calories

Parmesan Wings With Yogurt Sauce

Servings: 6 | Cooking Time: 25 Minutes

Ingredients:
- For the Dipping Sauce
- 1 cup plain yogurt
- 1 tsp fresh lemon juice
- Salt and black pepper to taste
- For the Wings
- 2 lb chicken wings
- Salt and black pepper to taste
- Cooking spray
- ½ cup melted butter
- ½ cup Hot sauce
- ¼ cup grated Parmesan cheese

Directions:
1. Mix the yogurt, lemon juice, salt, and black pepper in a bowl. Chill while making the chicken.
2. Preheat oven to 400ºF and season wings with salt and black pepper. Line them on a baking sheet and grease lightly with cooking spray. Bake for 20 minutes until golden brown. Mix butter, hot sauce, and parmesan in a bowl. Toss chicken in the sauce to evenly coat and plate. Serve with yogurt dipping sauce and celery strips.

Nutrition Info:
- Per Servings 4g Carbs, 24g Protein, 36.4g Fat, 452 Calories

Baked Chicken Pesto

Servings: 4 | Cooking Time:20 Minutes

Ingredients:
- 2 tsp grated parmesan cheese
- 6 tbsp shredded reduced-fat mozzarella cheese
- 1 medium tomato (thinly sliced)
- 4 tsp basil pesto
- 2 boneless, skinless chicken breasts around 1-lb
- Salt and pepper to taste

Directions:
1. In cool water, wash chicken and dry using a paper towel. Create 4 thin slices of chicken breasts by slicing horizontally.
2. Preheat oven to 400oF and then line a baking sheet with parchment or foil.
3. Put into the baking sheet the slices of chicken. Season with pepper and salt. And spread at least 1 teaspoon of pesto on each chicken slice.
4. For 15 minutes, bake the chicken and ensure that the center is no longer pink. After which remove baking sheet and top chicken with parmesan cheese, mozzarella, and tomatoes.

5. Put into the oven once again and heat for another 3 to 5 minutes to melt the cheese, then ready to serve.

Nutrition Info:
• Per Servings 2.0g Carbs, 40.0g Protein, 8.0g Fat, 238 Calories

Chicken With Green Sauce

Servings: 4 | Cooking Time: 35 Minutes

Ingredients:
• 2 tbsp butter
• 4 scallions, chopped
• 4 chicken breasts, skinless and boneless
• Salt and black pepper, to taste
• 6 ounces sour cream
• 2 tbsp fresh dill, chopped

Directions:
1. Heat a pan with the butter over medium-high heat, add in the chicken, season with pepper and salt, and fry for 2-3 per side until golden. Transfer to a baking dish and cook in the oven for 15 minutes at 390°F, until no longer pink.
2. To the pan add scallions, and cook for 2 minutes. Pour in the sour cream, warm through without boil. Slice the chicken and serve on a platter with green sauce spooned over and fresh dill.

Nutrition Info:
• Per Servings 2.3g Carbs, 18g Protein, 9g Fat, 236 Calories

Chicken Country Style

Servings: 4 | Cooking Time: 25 Minutes

Ingredients:
• 3 tablespoons butter
• 1 packet dry Lipton's onion soup mix
• 1 can Campbell's chicken gravy
• 4 skinless and boneless chicken breasts
• 1/3 teaspoon pepper
• 1 cup water

Directions:
1. Add all ingredients in a pot on high fire and bring it to a boil.
2. Once boiling, lower fire to a simmer and cook for 25 minutes.
3. Adjust seasoning to taste.
4. Serve and enjoy.

Nutrition Info:
• Per Servings 6.8g Carbs, 53.7g Protein, 16.9g Fat, 380 Calories

Cheesy Turkey And Broccoli Traybake

Servings: 4 | Cooking Time: 30 Minutes

Ingredients:
• 1 lb turkey breasts, cooked
• 2 tbsp olive oil
• 1 head broccoli, cut into florets
• ½ cup sour cream
• ½ cup heavy cream
• 1 cup Monterrey Jack cheese, grated
• 4 tbsp pork rinds, crushed
• Salt and black pepper, to taste
• ½ tsp paprika
• 1 tsp oregano

Directions:
1. Set oven to 450ºF and grease and line a baking tray. Boil water in a pan. Add in broccoli and cook for 8 minutes. Use two forks to shred the turkey.
2. Place the turkey into a large bowl together with sour cream, olive oil, and broccoli and stir to combine. Transfer the mixture to the baking tray, firmly press down. Sprinkle heavy cream over the dish, top with seasonings; and coat with grated cheese. Cover with the pork rinds.
3. Place in the oven and cook until bubbling for 20-25 minutes. Ladle to a serving plate and enjoy!

Nutrition Info:
• Per Servings 2.6g Carbs, 29g Protein, 28g Fat, 365 Calories

Spinach Chicken Cheesy Bake

Servings: 6 | Cooking Time: 45 Minutes

Ingredients:
• 6 chicken breasts, skinless and boneless
• 1 tsp mixed spice seasoning
• Pink salt and black pepper to season
• 2 loose cups baby spinach
• 3 tsp olive oil
• 4 oz cream cheese, cubed
• 1 ¼ cups shredded mozzarella cheese
• 4 tbsp water

Directions:
1. Preheat oven to 370ºF.
2. Season chicken with spice mix, salt, and black pepper. Pat with your hands to have the seasoning stick on the chicken. Put in the casserole dish and layer spinach over the chicken. Mix the oil with cream cheese, mozzarella, salt, and black pepper and stir in water a tablespoon at a time. Pour the mixture over the chicken and cover the pot with aluminium foil.
3. Bake for 20 minutes, remove foil and continue cooking for 15 minutes until a nice golden brown color is formed on top. Take out and allow sitting for 5 minutes.
4. Serve warm with braised asparagus.

Nutrition Info:
• Per Servings 3.1g Carbs, 15g Protein, 30.2g Fat, 340 Calories

Slow-cooked Mexican Turkey Soup

Servings: 4 | Cooking Time: 4 Hours 15 Minutes

Ingredients:
- 1 ½ lb turkey breasts, skinless, boneless, cubed
- 4 cups chicken stock
- 1 chopped onion
- 1 cup canned chunky salsa
- 8 ounces cheddar cheese, into chunks
- ¼ tsp cayenne red pepper
- 4 oz canned diced green chilies
- 1 tsp fresh cilantro, chopped

Directions:
1. In a slow cooker, combine the turkey with salsa, onion, green chilies, cayenne pepper, chicken stock, and cheese, and cook for 4 hours on high while covered. Open the slow cooker, sprinkle with fresh cilantro and ladle in bowls to serve.

Nutrition Info:
- Per Servings 6g Carbs, 38g Protein, 24g Fat, 387 Calories

Homemade Chicken Pizza Calzone

Servings: 4 | Cooking Time: 60 Minutes

Ingredients:
- 2 eggs
- 1 low carb pizza crust
- ½ cup Pecorino cheese, grated
- 1 lb chicken breasts, skinless, boneless, halved
- ½ cup sugar-free marinara sauce
- 1 tsp Italian seasoning
- 1 tsp onion powder
- 1 tsp garlic powder
- Salt and black pepper, to taste
- ¼ cup flax seed, ground
- 6 ounces provolone cheese

Directions:
1. Using a bowl, combine the Italian seasoning with onion powder, salt, Pecorino cheese, pepper, garlic powder, and flax seed. In a separate bowl, combine the eggs with pepper and salt.
2. Dip the chicken pieces in eggs, and then in seasoning mixture, lay all parts on a lined baking sheet, and bake for 25 minutes in the oven at 390º F.
3. Place the pizza crust dough on a lined baking sheet and spread half of the provolone cheese on half. Remove chicken from oven, chop it, and scatter it over the provolone cheese. Spread over the marinara sauce and top with the remaining cheese.
4. Cover with the other half of the dough and shape the pizza in a calzone. Seal the edges, set in the oven and bake for 20 minutes. Allow the calzone to cool down before slicing and enjoy.

Nutrition Info:
- Per Servings 4.6g Carbs, 28g Protein, 15g Fat, 425 Calories

Broccoli And Turkey Bacon Crepes

Servings: 8 | Cooking Time: 40 Minutes

Ingredients:
- 6 eggs
- 1 cup cream cheese
- 1 tsp erythritol
- 1½ tbsp coconut flour
- ⅓ cup Parmesan cheese, grated
- A pinch of xanthan gum
- Cooking spray
- 1 cup broccoli florets
- 1 cup mushrooms, sliced
- 8 ounces turkey bacon, cubed
- 8 ounces cheese blend
- 1 garlic clove, minced
- 1 onion, chopped
- 2 tbsp red wine vinegar
- 2 tbsp butter
- ½ cup heavy cream
- 1 tsp Worcestershire sauce
- ¼ cup chicken stock
- A pinch of nutmeg
- Fresh parsley, chopped
- Salt and black pepper, to taste

Directions:
1. Using a bowl, combine 3/4 cup of cream cheese, eggs, erythritol, coconut flour, xanthan, Parmesan cheese to obtain a crepe batter. Set a pan sprayed with cooking spray over medium heat, pour some of the batter, spread well into the pan, cook for 2 minutes, flip to the other side, and cook for 40 seconds more or until golden. Do the same with the rest of the batter, greasing the pan with cooking spray between each one. Stack all the crepes on a serving plate.
2. In the same pan, melt the butter and stir in the onion and garlic; sauté for 3 minutes, until tender. Stir in the mushrooms and cook for 5 minutes.
3. Add in the turkey bacon, salt, vinegar, heavy cream, 6 ounces of the cheese blend, remaining cream cheese, nutmeg, pepper, broccoli, stock, and Worcestershire sauce, and cook for 7 minutes. Fill each crepe with this mixture, roll up each one, and arrange on a baking dish. Scatter over the remaining cheese blend, set under a preheated broiler for 5 minutes. Set the crepes on serving plates, garnish with chopped parsley, and enjoy.

Nutrition Info:
- Per Servings 7g Carbs, 25g Protein, 32g Fat, 371 Calories

Chicken Breasts With Cheddar & Pepperoni

Servings: 4 | Cooking Time: 40 Minutes

Ingredients:
- 12 oz canned tomato sauce
- 1 tbsp olive oil
- 4 chicken breast halves, skinless and boneless
- Salt and ground black pepper, to taste
- 1 tsp dried oregano
- 4 oz cheddar cheese, sliced

- 1 tsp garlic powder
- 2 oz pepperoni, sliced

Directions:

1. Preheat your oven to 390ºF. Using a bowl, combine chicken with oregano, salt, garlic, and pepper.

2. Heat a pan with the olive oil over medium-high heat, add in the chicken, cook each side for 2 minutes, and remove to a baking dish. Top with the cheddar cheese slices spread the sauce, then cover with pepperoni slices. Bake for 30 minutes. Serve warm garnished with fresh oregano if desired

Nutrition Info:

- Per Servings 4.5g Carbs, 32g Protein, 21g Fat, 387 Calories

Grilled Chicken Wings

Servings: 4 | Cooking Time: 2 Hours 25 Minutes

Ingredients:

- 2 pounds wings
- Juice from 1 lemon
- ½ cup fresh parsley, chopped
- 2 garlic cloves, peeled and minced
- 1 Serrano pepper, chopped
- 3 tbsp olive oil
- ½ tsp cilantro
- Salt and ground black pepper, to taste
- Lemon wedges, for serving
- Ranch dip, for serving

Directions:

1. Using a bowl, stir together lemon juice, garlic, salt, serrano pepper, cilantro, olive oil, and pepper. Place in the chicken wings and toss well to coat. Refrigerate for 2 hours. Set a grill over high heat and add on the chicken wings; cook each side for 6 minutes. Set the chicken wings on a plate and serve alongside lemon wedges and ranch dip.

Nutrition Info:

- Per Servings 4.3g Carbs, 18.5g Protein, 11.5g Fat, 216 Calories

Chicken & Squash Traybake

Servings: 4 | Cooking Time: 60 Minutes

Ingredients:

- 2 lb chicken thighs
- 1 pound butternut squash, cubed
- ½ cup black olives, pitted
- ¼ cup olive oil
- 5 garlic cloves, sliced
- 1 tbsp dried oregano
- Salt and black pepper, to taste

Directions:

1. Set oven to 400ºF and grease a baking dish. Place in the chicken with the skin down. Set the garlic, olives and butternut squash around the chicken then drizzle with oil.

2. Spread pepper, salt, and oregano over the mixture then add into the oven. Cook for 45 minutes.

Nutrition Info:

- Per Servings 5.5g Carbs, 31g Protein, 15g Fat, 411 Calories

Roasted Chicken With Tarragon

Servings: 4 | Cooking Time: 50 Minutes

Ingredients:

- 2 lb chicken thighs
- 2 lb radishes, sliced
- 4 ¼ oz butter
- 1 tbsp tarragon
- Salt and black pepper, to taste
- 1 cup mayonnaise

Directions:

1. Set an oven to 400ºF and grease a baking dish. Add in the chicken, radishes, tarragon, pepper, and salt. Place in butter then set into the oven and cook for 40 minutes. Kill the heat, set on a serving plate and enjoy alongside mayonnaise.

Nutrition Info:

- Per Servings 5.5g Carbs, 42g Protein, 23g Fat, 415 Calories

Spanish Chicken

Servings: 4 | Cooking Time: 60 Minutes

Ingredients:

- 1/2 cup mushrooms, chopped
- 1 pound chorizo sausages, chopped
- 2 tbsp avocado oil
- 4 cherry peppers, chopped
- 1 red bell pepper, seeded, chopped
- 1 onion, peeled and sliced
- 2 tbsp garlic, minced
- 2 cups tomatoes, chopped
- 4 chicken thighs
- Salt and black pepper, to taste
- ½ cup chicken stock
- 1 tsp turmeric
- 1 tbsp vinegar
- 2 tsp dried oregano
- Fresh parsley, chopped, for serving

Directions:

1. Set a pan over medium heat and warm half of the avocado oil, stir in the chorizo sausages, and cook for 5-6 minutes until browned; remove to a bowl. Heat the rest of the oil, place in the chicken thighs, and apply pepper and salt for seasoning. Cook each side for 3 minutes and set aside on a bowl.

2. In the same pan, add the onion, bell pepper, cherry peppers, and mushrooms, and cook for 4 minutes. Stir in the garlic and cook for 2 minutes. Pour in the stock, turmeric, salt, tomatoes, pepper, vinegar, and oregano. Stir in the chorizo sausages and chicken, place everything to the oven at 400ºF, and bake for 30 minutes. Ladle into serving bowls and garnish with chopped parsley to serve.

Nutrition Info:

- Per Servings 4g Carbs, 25g Protein, 33g Fat, 415 Calories

Chicken Drumsticks In Tomato Sauce

Servings: 4 | Cooking Time: 1 Hour 35 Minutes

Ingredients:
- 8 chicken drumsticks
- 1 ½ tbsp olive oil
- 1 medium white onion, diced
- 3 medium turnips, peeled and diced
- 2 medium carrots, chopped in 1-inch pieces
- 2 green bell peppers, seeded, cut into chunks
- 2 cloves garlic, minced
- ¼ cup coconut flour
- 1 cup chicken broth
- 1 can sugar-free tomato sauce
- 2 tbsp dried Italian herbs
- Salt and black pepper to taste

Directions:
1. Preheat oven to 400°F.
2. Heat the oil in a large skillet over medium heat, meanwhile season the drumsticks with salt and pepper, and fry them in the oil to brown on both sides for 10 minutes. Remove to a baking dish.
3. Next, sauté the onion, turnips, bell peppers, carrots, and garlic in the same oil and for 10 minutes with continuous stirring.
4. Then, in a bowl, evenly combine the broth, coconut flour, tomato paste, and Italian herbs together, and pour it over the vegetables in the pan. Stir and cook to thicken for 4 minutes.
5. Turn the heat off and pour the mixture on the chicken in the baking dish. Bake the chicken and vegetables in the oven for around 1 hour. Remove from the oven and serve with steamed cauli rice.

Nutrition Info:
- Per Servings 7.3g Carbs, 50.8g Protein, 34.2g Fat, 515 Calories

Zucchini Spaghetti With Turkey Bolognese Sauce

Servings: 6 | Cooking Time: 30 Minutes

Ingredients:
- 2 cups sliced mushrooms
- 2 tsp olive oil
- 1 pound ground turkey
- 3 tbsp pesto sauce
- 1 cup diced onion
- 2 cups broccoli florets
- 6 cups zucchini, spiralized

Directions:
1. Heat the oil in a skillet. Add zucchini and cook for 2-3 minutes, stirring continuously; set aside.
2. Add turkey to the skillet and cook until browned, about 7-8 minutes. Transfer to a plate. Add onion and cook until translucent, about 3 minutes. Add broccoli and mushrooms, and cook for 7 more minutes. Return the turkey to the skillet. Stir in the pesto sauce. Cover the pan, lower the heat, and simmer for 15 minutes. Stir in zucchini pasta and serve immediately.

Nutrition Info:
- Per Servings 3.8g Carbs, 19g Protein, 16g Fat, 273 Calories

Turkey Burgers With Fried Brussels Sprouts

Servings: 4 | Cooking Time: 30 Minutes

Ingredients:
- For the burgers
- 1 pound ground turkey
- 1 free-range egg
- ½ onion, chopped
- 1 tsp salt
- ½ tsp ground black pepper
- 1 tsp dried thyme
- 2 oz butter
- For the fried Brussels sprouts
- 1 ½ lb Brussels sprouts, halved
- 3 oz butter
- 1 tsp salt
- ½ tsp ground black pepper

Directions:
1. Combine the burger ingredients in a mixing bowl. Create patties from the mixture. Set a large pan over medium-high heat, warm butter, and fry the patties until cooked completely.
2. Place on a plate and cover with aluminium foil to keep warm. Fry brussels sprouts in butter, season to your preference, then set to a bowl. Plate the burgers and brussels sprouts and serve.

Nutrition Info:
- Per Servings 5.8g Carbs, 31g Protein, 25g Fat, 443 Calories

Spinach Artichoke Heart Chicken

Servings: 4 | Cooking Time: 30 Minutes

Ingredients:
- 4 chicken breasts
- 1 package frozen spinach
- 1 package cream cheese, softened
- ½ can quartered artichoke hearts, drained and chopped
- ¼ cup. shredded Parmesan cheese
- ¼ cup. mayonnaise
- 2 tbsp. olive oil
- 2 tbsps. grated mozzarella cheese
- ½ teaspoon. garlic powder
- Salt to taste

Directions:
1. Place the spinach in a bowl and microwave for 2 to 3 minutes. Let chill and drain.
2. Stir in cream cheese, artichoke hearts, Parmesan cheese, mayonnaise, garlic powder, and salt, whisk together. Cut chicken breasts to an even thickness. Spread salt and pepper over chicken breasts per side.
3. Preheat oven to 375 degrees F.
4. In a large skillet over medium-high, heat olive oil for 2 to 3 minutes. Lay chicken breasts in a large baking dish, pour spinach-artichoke mixture over chicken breasts. Place in the oven and bake at least 165 degrees F.
5. Sprinkle with mozzarella cheese and bake for 1 to 2 minutes more. Serve and enjoy.

Nutrition Info:
- Per Servings 5.4g Carbs, 56g Protein, 33.3g Fat, 554 Calories

Bacon And Chicken Cottage Pie

Servings: 4 | Cooking Time: 55 Minutes

Ingredients:
- ½ cup onion, chopped
- 4 bacon slices
- 3 tbsp butter
- 1 carrot, chopped
- 3 garlic cloves, minced
- Salt and ground black pepper, to taste
- ¾ cup crème fraîche
- ½ cup chicken stock
- 12 ounces chicken breasts, cubed
- 2 tbsp Dijon mustard
- ¾ cup cheddar cheese, shredded
- For the dough
- ¾ cup almond flour
- 3 tbsp cream cheese
- 1½ cup mozzarella cheese, shredded
- 1 egg
- 1 tsp onion powder
- 1 tsp garlic powder
- 1 tsp Italian seasoning
- Salt and ground black pepper, to taste

Directions:
1. Set a pan over medium heat and warm butter and sauté the onion, garlic, pepper, bacon, salt, and carrot, for 5 minutes. Add in the chicken, and cook for 3 minutes. Stir in the crème fraîche, salt, mustard, pepper, and stock, cook for 7 minutes. Add in the cheddar and set aside.
2. Using a bowl, combine the mozzarella cheese with the cream cheese, and heat in a microwave for 1 minute. Stir in the garlic powder, salt, flour, pepper, Italian seasoning, onion powder, and egg. Knead the dough well, split into 4 pieces, and flatten each into a circle. Set the chicken mixture into 4 ramekins, top each with a dough circle, place in an oven at 370º F for 25 minutes.

Nutrition Info:
- Per Servings 8.2g Carbs, 41g Protein, 45g Fat, 571 Calories

Avocado Cheese Pepper Chicken

Servings: 5 | Cooking Time: 20 Minutes

Ingredients:
- ¼ tsp. cayenne pepper
- 1½ cup. cooked and shredded chicken
- 2 tbsps. cream cheese
- 2 tbsps. lemon juice
- 2 large avocados, diced
- Black pepper and salt to taste
- ¼ cup. mayonnaise
- 1 tsp. dried thyme
- ½ tsp. onion powder
- ½ tsp. garlic powder

Directions:
1. Remove the insides of your avocado halves and set them in a bowl.
2. Stir all ingredients to avocado flesh.
3. Fill avocados with chicken mix.

4. Serve and enjoy.

Nutrition Info:
- Per Servings 5g Carbs, 24g Protein, 40g Fat, 476 Calories

Yummy Chicken Nuggets

Servings: 2 | Cooking Time: 25 Minutes

Ingredients:
- ½ cup almond flour
- 1 egg
- 2 tbsp garlic powder
- 2 chicken breasts, cubed
- Salt and black pepper, to taste
- ½ cup butter

Directions:
1. Using a bowl, combine salt, garlic powder, flour, and pepper, and stir. In a separate bowl, beat the egg. Add the chicken breast cubes in egg mixture, then in the flour mixture. Set a pan over medium-high heat and warm butter, add in the chicken nuggets, and cook for 6 minutes on each side. Remove to paper towels, drain the excess grease and serve.

Nutrition Info:
- Per Servings 4.3g Carbs, 35g Protein, 37g Fat, 417 Calories

Yummy Chicken Queso

Servings: 4 | Cooking Time: 25 Minutes

Ingredients:
- ½ teaspoon garlic salt
- 4-ounce can diced drained green chiles
- 10-ounce can mild rotel drained
- ¾ cup medium queso dip
- 4 boneless skinless boneless fresh or thawed chicken breasts
- 5 tablespoons olive oil
- 1 cup water

Directions:
1. Add all ingredients in a pot on high fire and bring it to a boil.
2. Once boiling, lower fire to a simmer and cook for 20 minutes. Stir frequently.
3. Adjust seasoning to taste.
4. Serve and enjoy.

Nutrition Info:
- Per Servings 7.2g Carbs, 56.6g Protein, 21.7g Fat, 500 Calories

One Pot Chicken Alfredo

Servings: 4 | Cooking Time: 20 Minutes

Ingredients:
- 1-pound cooked chicken breasts, chopped
- 1 jar Prego Alfredo Sauce
- ¼ cup mozzarella cheese
- ½ cup bacon bits, fried and crumbled
- Pepper and salt to taste
- 2 tbsp water

Directions:
1. Add all ingredients in a pot.
2. Close the lid and bring to a boil over medium flame.

3. Allow simmering for 20 minutes.
4. Serve and enjoy.

Nutrition Info:
- Per Servings 6.5g Carbs, 53.4g Protein, 64.5g Fat, 899 Calories

Rosemary Turkey Pie

Servings: 4 | Cooking Time: 40 Minutes

Ingredients:
- 2 cups chicken stock
- 1 cup turkey meat, cooked and chopped
- Salt and ground black pepper, to taste
- 1 tsp fresh rosemary, chopped
- ½ cup kale, chopped
- ½ cup butternut squash, chopped
- ½ cup Monterey jack cheese, shredded
- ¼ tsp smoked paprika
- ¼ tsp garlic powder
- ¼ tsp xanthan gum
- Cooking spray
- For the crust:
- ¼ cup butter
- ¼ tsp xanthan gum
- 2 cups almond flour
- A pinch of salt
- 1 egg
- ¼ cup cheddar cheese

Directions:
1. Set a greased pot over medium-high heat. Place in turkey and squash, and cook for 10 minutes. Stir in stock, Monterey Jack cheese, garlic powder, rosemary, pepper, smoked paprika, kale, and salt.
2. In a bowl, combine ½ cup stock from the pot with ¼ teaspoon xanthan gum, and transfer everything to the pot; set aside. In a separate bowl, stir together salt, ¼ teaspoon xanthan gum, and flour.
3. Stir in the butter, cheddar cheese, egg, until a pie crust dough forms. Form into a ball and refrigerate. Spray a baking dish with cooking spray and sprinkle pie filling on the bottom. Set the dough on a working surface, roll into a circle, and top filling with this. Ensure well pressed and seal edges, set in an oven at 350ºF, and bake for 35 minutes. Allow the pie to cool, and enjoy.

Nutrition Info:
- Per Servings 5.6g Carbs, 21g Protein, 23g Fat, 325 Calories

Duck & Vegetable Casserole

Servings: 2 | Cooking Time: 20 Minutes

Ingredients:
- 2 duck breasts, skin on and sliced
- 2 zucchinis, sliced
- 1 tbsp coconut oil
- 1 green onion bunch, chopped
- 1 carrot, chopped
- 2 green bell peppers, seeded and chopped
- Salt and ground black pepper, to taste

Directions:

1. Set a pan over medium-high heat and warm oil, stir in the green onions, and cook for 2 minutes. Place in the zucchini, bell peppers, pepper, salt, and carrot, and cook for 10 minutes.
2. Set another pan over medium-high heat, add in duck slices and cook each side for 3 minutes. Pour the mixture into the vegetable pan. Cook for 3 minutes. Set in bowls and enjoy.

Nutrition Info:
- Per Servings 8g Carbs, 53g Protein, 21g Fat, 433 Calories

Stuffed Chicken Breasts With Cucumber Noodle Salad

Servings: 4 | Cooking Time: 60 Minutes

Ingredients:
- For the chicken
- 4 chicken breasts
- 1/3 cup baby spinach
- 1/4 cup goat cheese
- 1/4 cup shredded cheddar cheese
- 4 tbsp butter
- Salt and black pepper, to taste
- For the tomato sauce
- 1 tbsp butter
- 1 shallot, chopped
- 2 garlic cloves, chopped
- ½ tbsp red wine vinegar
- 2 tbsp tomato paste
- 14 oz canned crushed tomatoes
- ½ tsp salt
- 1 tsp dried basil
- 1 tsp dried oregano
- Black pepper, to taste
- For the salad
- 2 cucumbers, spiralized
- 2 tbsp olive oil
- 1 tbsp rice vinegar

Directions:
1. Set oven to 400ºF and grease a baking dish. Set aside.
2. Place a pan over medium heat. Melt 2 tbsp of butter and sauté spinach until it shrinks; season with salt and pepper. Transfer into a medium bowl containing the goat cheese, stir and set to one side. Cut the chicken breasts lengthwise and stuff with the cheese mixture and set into the baking dish. On top, spread the grated cheddar cheese, add 2 tbsp of butter then set into the oven. Bake until cooked through for 20-30 minutes.
3. Set a pan over medium-high heat and warm 1 tbsp of butter. Add in garlic and shallot and cook until soft. Place in herbs, tomato paste, vinegar, tomatoes, salt, and pepper. Bring the mixture to a boil. Set heat to low and simmer for 15 minutes.
4. Arrange the cucumbers on a serving platter, season with salt, pepper, olive oil, and vinegar, Top with the chicken and pour over the sauce.

Nutrition Info:
- Per Servings 6g Carbs, 43g Protein, 31g Fat, 453 Calories

Chicken Skewers With Celery Fries

Servings: 4 | Cooking Time: 60 Minutes

Ingredients:
- 2 chicken breasts
- ½ tsp salt
- ¼ tsp ground black pepper
- 2 tbsp olive oil
- 1/4 chicken broth
- For the fries
- 1 lb celery root
- 2 tbsp olive oil
- ½ tsp salt
- ¼ tsp ground black pepper

Directions:
1. Set an oven to 400ºF. Grease and line a baking sheet. In a large bowl, mix oil, spices and the chicken; set in the fridge for 10 minutes while covered. Peel and chop celery root to form fry shapes and place into a separate bowl. Apply oil to coat and add pepper and salt for seasoning. Arrange to the baking tray in an even layer and bake for 10 minutes.
2. Take the chicken from the refrigerator and thread onto the skewers. Place over the celery, pour in the chicken broth, then set in the oven for 30 minutes. Serve with lemon wedges.

Nutrition Info:
- Per Servings 6g Carbs, 39g Protein, 43g Fat, 579 Calories

Easy Bbq Chicken And Cheese

Servings: 4 | Cooking Time: 40 Minutes

Ingredients:
- 1-pound chicken tenders, boneless
- ½ cup commercial BBQ sauce, keto-friendly
- 1 teaspoon liquid smoke
- 1 cup mozzarella cheese, grated
- ½ pound bacon, fried and crumbled
- Pepper and salt to taste

Directions:
1. With paper towels, dry chicken tenders. Season with pepper and salt.
2. Place chicken tenders on an oven-safe dish.
3. Whisk well BBQ sauce and liquid smoke in a bowl and pour over chicken tenders. Coat well in the sauce.
4. Bake in a preheated 400oF oven for 30 minutes.
5. Remove from oven, turnover chicken tenders, sprinkle cheese on top.
6. Return to the oven and continue baking for 10 minutes more.
7. Serve and enjoy with a sprinkle of bacon bits.

Nutrition Info:
- Per Servings 6.7g Carbs, 34.6g Protein, 31.5g Fat, 351 Calories

Chicken With Anchovy Tapenade

Servings: 2 | Cooking Time: 30 Minutes

Ingredients:
- 1 chicken breast, cut into 4 pieces
- 2 tbsp coconut oil
- 3 garlic cloves, and crushed
- For the tapenade
- 1 cup black olives, pitted
- 1 oz anchovy fillets, rinsed
- 1 garlic clove, crushed
- Salt and ground black pepper, to taste
- 2 tbsp olive oil
- ¼ cup fresh basil, chopped
- 1 tbsp lemon juice

Directions:
1. Using a food processor, combine the olives, salt, olive oil, basil, lemon juice, anchovy fillets, and pepper, blend well. Set a pan over medium-high heat and warm coconut oil, stir in the garlic, and cook for 2 minutes.
2. Place in the chicken pieces and cook each side for 4 minutes. Split the chicken among plates and apply a topping of the anchovy tapenade.

Nutrition Info:
- Per Servings 3g Carbs, 25g Protein, 13g Fat, 155 Calories

Baked Chicken With Acorn Squash And Goat's Cheese

Servings: 6 | Cooking Time: 1 Hour 15 Minutes

Ingredients:
- 6 chicken breasts, skinless and boneless
- 1 lb acorn squash, peeled and sliced
- Salt and ground black pepper, to taste
- 1 cup goat's cheese, shredded
- Cooking spray

Directions:
1. Take cooking oil and spray on a baking dish, add in chicken breasts, pepper, squash, and salt and drizzle with olive. Transfer in the oven set at 420ºF, and bake for 1 hour. Scatter goat's cheese, and bake for 15 minutes. Remove to a serving plate and enjoy.

Nutrition Info:
- Per Servings 5g Carbs, 12g Protein, 16g Fat, 235 Calories

Heart Healthy Chicken Salad

Servings: 4 | Cooking Time: 45 Minutes

Ingredients:
- 3 tbsp mayonnaise, low-fat
- ½ tsp onion powder
- 1 tbsp lemon juice
- ¼ cup celery (chopped)
- 3 ¼ cups chicken breast (cooked, cubed, and skinless)
- Salt and pepper to taste

Directions:
1. Bake chicken breasts for 45 minutes at 350oF. Let it cool and cut them into cubes and place them in the refrigerator.

2. Combine all other ingredients in a large bowl then add the chilled chicken.
3. Mix well and ready to serve.
4. Enjoy!

Nutrition Info:
• Per Servings 1.0g Carbs, 50.0g Protein, 22.0g Fat, 408 Calories

Chicken In Creamy Spinach Sauce

Servings: 4 | Cooking Time: 20 Minutes

Ingredients:
• 1 pound chicken thighs
• 2 tbsp coconut oil
• 2 tbsp coconut flour
• 2 cups spinach, chopped
• 1 tsp oregano
• 1 cup heavy cream
• 1 cup chicken broth
• 2 tbsp butter

Directions:
1. Warm the coconut oil in a skillet and brown the chicken on all sides, about 6-8 minutes. Set aside.
2. Melt the butter and whisk in the flour over medium heat. Whisk in the heavy cream and chicken broth and bring to a boil. Stir in oregano. Add the spinach to the skillet and cook until wilted.
3. Add the thighs in the skillet and cook for an additional 5 minutes.

Nutrition Info:
• Per Servings 2.6g Carbs, 18g Protein, 38g Fat, 446 Calories

Chicken In Creamy Mushroom Sauce

Servings: 4 | Cooking Time: 36 Minutes

Ingredients:
• 1 tbsp ghee
• 4 chicken breasts, cut into chunks
• Salt and black pepper to taste
• 1 packet white onion soup mix
• 2 cups chicken broth
• 15 baby bella mushrooms, sliced
• 1 cup heavy cream
• 1 small bunch parsley, chopped

Directions:
1. Melt ghee in a saucepan over medium heat, season the chicken with salt and black pepper, and brown on all sides for 6 minutes in total. Put in a plate.
2. In a bowl, stir the onion soup mix with chicken broth and add to the saucepan. Simmer for 3 minutes and add the mushrooms and chicken. Cover and simmer for another 20 minutes.
3. Stir in heavy cream and parsley, cook on low heat for 3 minutes, and season with salt and pepper.
4. Ladle the chicken with creamy sauce and mushrooms over beds of cauli mash. Garnish with parsley.

Nutrition Info:
• Per Servings 2g Carbs, 22g Protein, 38.2g Fat, 448 Calories

Turkey Enchilada Bowl

Servings: 4 | Cooking Time: 30 Minutes

Ingredients:
• 2 tbsp coconut oil
• 1 lb boneless, skinless turkey thighs, cut into pieces
• ¾ cup red enchilada sauce (sugar-free)
• ¼ cup water
• ¼ cup chopped onion
• 3 oz canned diced green chilis
• 1 avocado, diced
• 1 cup shredded mozzarella cheese
• ¼ cup chopped pickled jalapeños
• ½ cup sour cream
• 1 tomato, diced

Directions:
1. Set a large pan over medium-high heat. Add coconut oil and warm. Place in the turkey and cook until browned on the outside. Stir in onion, chillis, water, and enchilada sauce, then close with a lid.
2. Allow simmering for 20 minutes until the turkey is cooked through. Spoon the turkey on a serving bowl and top with the sauce, cheese, sour cream, tomato, and avocado.

Nutrition Info:
• Per Servings 5.9g Carbs, 38g Protein, 40.2g Fat, 568 Calories

Stewed Italian Chicken

Servings: 4 | Cooking Time: 25 Minutes

Ingredients:
• 3 ounces Italian dressing
• 4 boneless skinless chicken breasts thawed
• 5 tablespoons olive oil
• ½ cup water
• Salt and pepper to taste

Directions:
1. Add all ingredients in a pot on high fire and bring it to a boil.
2. Once boiling, lower fire to a simmer and cook for 20 minutes.
3. Adjust seasoning to taste.
4. Serve and enjoy.

Nutrition Info:
• Per Servings 3.6g Carbs, 53.6g Protein, 31.0g Fat, 545 Calories

Turkey & Mushroom Bake

Servings: 8 | Cooking Time: 55 Minutes

Ingredients:
• 4 cups mushrooms, sliced
• 1 egg, whisked
• 3 cups green cabbage, shredded
• 3 cups turkey meat, cooked and chopped
• ½ cup chicken stock
• ½ cup cream cheese
• 1 tsp poultry seasoning
• 2 cup cheddar cheese, grated

- ½ cup Parmesan cheese, grated
- Salt and ground black pepper, to taste
- ¼ tsp garlic powder

Directions:

1. Set a pan over medium-low heat. Stir in chicken broth, egg, Parmesan cheese, pepper, garlic powder, poultry seasoning, cheddar cheese, cream cheese, and salt, and simmer.
2. Place in the cabbage and turkey meat, and set away from the heat.
3. Add the mushrooms, pepper, turkey mixture and salt in a baking dish and spread. Place aluminum foil to cover, set in an oven at 390ºF, and bake for 35 minutes. Allow cooling and enjoy.

Nutrition Info:

- Per Servings 3g Carbs, 25g Protein, 15g Fat, 245 Calories

Grilled Paprika Chicken With Steamed Broccoli

Servings: 6 | Cooking Time: 17 Minutes

Ingredients:

- Cooking spray
- 3 tbsp smoked paprika
- Salt and black pepper to taste
- 2 tsp garlic powder
- 1 tbsp olive oil
- 6 chicken breasts
- 1 head broccoli, cut into florets

Directions:

1. Place broccoli florets onto the steamer basket over the boiling water; steam approximately 8 minutes or until crisp-tender. Set aside. Grease grill grate with cooking spray and preheat to 400ºF.
2. Combine paprika, salt, black pepper, and garlic powder in a bowl. Brush chicken with olive oil and sprinkle spice mixture over and massage with hands.
3. Grill chicken for 7 minutes per side until well-cooked, and plate. Serve warm with steamed broccoli.

Nutrition Info:

- Per Servings 2g Carbs, 26g Protein, 35.3g Fat, 422 Calories

Chicken With Asparagus & Root Vegetables

Servings: 4 | Cooking Time: 35 Minutes

Ingredients:

- 2 cups whipping cream
- 3 chicken breasts, boneless, skinless, chopped
- 3 tbsp butter
- ½ cup onion, chopped
- ¾ cup carrot, chopped
- 5 cups chicken stock
- Salt and black pepper, to taste
- 1 bay leaf
- 1 turnip, chopped
- 1 parsnip, chopped
- 17 ounces asparagus, trimmed
- 3 tsp fresh thyme, chopped

Directions:

1. Set a pan over medium heat and add whipping cream, allow simmering, and cook until it's reduced by half for about 7 minutes. Set another pan over medium heat and warm butter, sauté the onion for 3 minutes. Pour in the chicken stock, carrots, turnip, and parsnip, chicken, and bay leaf, bring to a boil, and simmer for 20 minutes.
2. Add in the asparagus and cook for 7 minutes. Discard the bay leaf, stir in the reduced whipping cream, adjust the seasoning and ladle the stew into serving bowls. Scatter with fresh thyme.

Nutrition Info:

- Per Servings 7.4g Carbs, 37g Protein, 31g Fat, 497 Calories

Stuffed Mushrooms With Chicken

Servings: 5 | Cooking Time: 40 Minutes

Ingredients:

- 3 cups cauliflower florets
- Salt and black pepper, to taste
- 1 onion, chopped
- 1½ pounds ground chicken
- 3 tsp fajita seasoning
- 2 tbsp butter
- 10 portobello mushrooms, stems removed
- ½ cup vegetable broth

Directions:

1. In a food processor, add the cauliflower florets, pepper and salt, blend for a few times, and transfer to a plate. Set a pan over medium heat and warm butter, stir in onion and cook for 3 minutes. Add in the cauliflower rice, and cook for 3 minutes.
2. Stir in the seasoning, pepper, chicken, broth, and salt and cook for a further 2 minutes. Arrange the mushrooms on a lined baking sheet, stuff each one with chicken mixture, put in the oven at 350ºF, and bake for 30 minutes. Serve in serving plates and enjoy.

Nutrition Info:

- Per Servings 6g Carbs, 14g Protein, 16g Fat, 261 Calories

Cheddar Chicken Tenders

Servings: 4 | Cooking Time: 40 Minutes

Ingredients:

- 2 eggs
- 3 tbsp butter, melted
- 3 cups coarsely crushed cheddar cheese
- ½ cup pork rinds, crushed
- 1 lb chicken tenders
- Pink salt to taste

Directions:

1. Preheat oven to 350ºF and line a baking sheet with parchment paper. Whisk the eggs with the butter in one bowl and mix the cheese and pork rinds in another bowl.
2. Season chicken with salt, dip in egg mixture, and coat generously in cheddar mixture. Place on baking sheet, cover with aluminium foil and bake for 25 minutes. Remove foil and bake further for 12 minutes to golden brown. Serve chicken with mustard dip.

Nutrition Info:

- Per Servings 1.3g Carbs, 42g Protein, 54g Fat, 507 Calories

Easy Asian Chicken

Servings: 5 | Cooking Time: 16 Minutes

Ingredients:
- 1 ½ lb. boneless chicken breasts, sliced into strips
- 1 tbsp ginger slices
- 3 tbsp coconut aminos
- ¼ cup organic chicken broth
- 3 cloves of garlic, minced
- 5 tablespoons sesame oil

Directions:
1. On high fire, heat a heavy-bottomed pot for 2 minutes. Add oil to a pan and swirl to coat bottom and sides. Heat oil for a minute.
2. Add garlic and ginger sauté for a minute.
3. Stir in chicken breast and sauté for 5 minutes. Season with coconut aminos and sauté for another 2 minutes.
4. Add remaining ingredients and bring to a boil.
5. Let it boil for 5 minutes.
6. Serve and enjoy.

Nutrition Info:
- Per Servings 1.2g Carbs, 30.9g Protein, 17.6g Fat, 299 Calories

Roasted Stuffed Chicken With Tomato Basil Sauce

Servings: 6 | Cooking Time: 35 Minutes

Ingredients:
- 4 ounces cream cheese
- 3 ounces mozzarella slices
- 10 ounces spinach
- ⅓ cup shredded mozzarella
- 1 tbsp olive oil
- 1 cup tomato basil sauce
- 3 whole chicken breasts

Directions:
1. Preheat your oven to 400ºF. Combine the cream cheese, shredded mozzarella, and spinach in the microwave.
2. Cut the chicken with the knife a couple of times horizontally. Stuff with the spinach mixture. Brush the top with olive oil. Place on a lined baking dish and bake in the oven for 25 minutes.
3. Pour the tomato basil sauce over and top with mozzarella slices. Return to the oven and cook for an additional 5 minutes.

Nutrition Info:
- Per Servings 2.5g Carbs, 37g Protein, 28g Fat, 338 Calories

Stuffed Avocados With Chicken

Servings: 2 | Cooking Time: 10 Minutes

Ingredients:
- 2 avocados, cut in half and pitted
- ¼ cup pesto
- 1 tsp dried thyme
- 2 tbsp cream cheese
- 1½ cups chicken, cooked and shredded
- Salt and ground black pepper, to taste
- ¼ tsp cayenne pepper
- ½ tsp onion powder
- ½ tsp garlic powder
- 1 tsp paprika
- Salt and black pepper, to taste
- 2 tbsp lemon juice

Directions:
1. Scoop the insides of the avocado halves, and place the flesh in a bowl. Add in the chicken. Stir in the remaining ingredients. Stuff the avocado cups with chicken mixture and enjoy.

Nutrition Info:
- Per Servings 5g Carbs, 24g Protein, 40g Fat, 511 Calories

Chapter 6 Pork, Beef & Lamb Recipes

Chapter 6 Pork, Beef & Lamb Recipes

Pork Osso Bucco

Servings: 6 | Cooking Time: 1 Hour 55 Minutes

Ingredients:
- 4 tbsp butter, softened
- 6 pork shanks
- 2 tbsp olive oil
- 3 cloves garlic, minced
- 1 cup diced tomatoes
- Salt and black pepper to taste
- ½ cup chopped onions
- ½ cup chopped celery
- ½ cup chopped carrots
- 2 cups Cabernet Sauvignon
- 5 cups beef broth
- ½ cup chopped parsley + extra to garnish
- 2 tsp lemon zest

Directions:
1. Melt the butter in a large saucepan over medium heat. Season the pork with salt and pepper and brown it for 12 minutes; remove to a plate.
2. In the same pan, sauté 2 cloves of garlic and onions in the oil, for 3 minutes then return the pork shanks. Stir in the Cabernet, carrots, celery, tomatoes, and beef broth with a season of salt and pepper. Cover the pan and let it simmer on low heat for 1 ½ hours basting the pork every 15 minutes with the sauce.
3. In a bowl, mix the remaining garlic, parsley, and lemon zest to make a gremolata, and stir the mixture into the sauce when it is ready. Turn the heat off and dish the Osso Bucco. Garnish with parsley and serve with a creamy turnip mash.

Nutrition Info:
- Per Servings 6.1g Carbs, 34g Protein, 40g Fat, 590 Calories

Bbq Pork Pizza With Goat Cheese

Servings: 4 | Cooking Time: 30 Minutes

Ingredients:
- 1 low carb pizza bread
- Olive oil for brushing
- 1 cup grated manchego cheese
- 2 cups leftover pulled pork
- ½ cup sugar-free BBQ sauce
- 1 cup crumbled goat cheese

Directions:
1. Preheat oven to 400ºF and put pizza bread on a pizza pan. Brush with olive oil and sprinkle the manchego cheese all over. Mix the pork with BBQ sauce and spread over the cheese. Drop goat cheese on top and bake for 25 minutes until the cheese has melted and golden brown on top. Slice the pizza with a cutter and serve warm.

Nutrition Info:
- Per Servings 6g Carbs, 5g Protein, 24g Fat, 344 Calories

Pork Nachos

Servings: 4 | Cooking Time: 15 Minutes

Ingredients:
- 1 bag low carb tortilla chips
- 2 cups leftover pulled pork
- 1 red bell pepper, seeded and chopped
- 1 red onion, diced
- 2 cups shredded Monterey Jack cheese

Directions:
1. Preheat oven to 350ºF. Arrange the chips in a medium cast iron pan, scatter pork over, followed by red bell pepper, and onion, and sprinkle with cheese. Place the pan in the oven and cook for 10 minutes until the cheese has melted. Allow cooling for 3 minutes and serve.

Nutrition Info:
- Per Servings 9.3g Carbs, 22g Protein, 25g Fat, 452 Calories

Moroccan Style Beef Stew

Servings: 8 | Cooking Time: 45 Minutes

Ingredients:
- ½ cup sliced onions
- 4 tablespoons garam masala
- 2 pounds beef roast
- 5 tablespoons butter
- 1 large bell pepper, seeded and chopped
- 2 cups water
- Salt and pepper to taste
- 1 tablespoon oil

Directions:
1. Heat the oil in a heavy-bottomed pot over a high flame and sauté the onions for 10 minutes until lightly golden.
2. Stir in the garam masala and sear the beef roast on all sides.
3. Add remaining ingredients and bring to a boil.
4. Once boiling, lower fire to a simmer, cover, and cook for 30 minutes.
5. Serve and enjoy.

Nutrition Info:
- Per Servings 1.2g Carbs, 25.1g Protein, 30.8g Fat, 350 Calories

Italian Shredded Beef

Servings: 6 | Cooking Time: 42 Minutes

Ingredients:
- 3 pounds chuck roast, trimmed from excess fat and cut into chunks
- 1 packet Italian salad dressing mix
- 8 ounces pepperoncini pepper slices
- 1 can beef broth
- Salt and pepper to taste
- 1 cup water

- 1 tsp oil

Directions:

1. Place a heavy-bottomed pot on medium-high fire and heat for 2 minutes. Add oil and swirl to coat the bottom and sides of pot and heat for a minute.
2. Season roast with pepper and salt. Brown roast for 4 minutes per side. Transfer to a chopping board and chop into 4 equal pieces.
3. Add remaining ingredients to the pot along with sliced beef.
4. Cover and simmer for 30 minutes or until beef is fork-tender. Stir the bottom of the pot now and then. Turn off the fire.
5. With two forks, shred beef.
6. Turn on fire to high and boil uncovered until sauce is rendered, around 5 minutes.

Nutrition Info:

- Per Servings 6.6g Carbs, 61.5g Protein, 20.5g Fat, 455 Calories

Slow Cooker Pork

Servings: 10 | Cooking Time: 10 Hours

Ingredients:

- 3 lb. boneless pork loin roast
- ¼ cup Dijon mustard
- 1 tsp. dried thyme leaves
- 2 bay leaves
- 5 tablespoons olive oil
- Salt and pepper to taste
- 1 ½ cups water

Directions:

1. Place all ingredients in the slow cooker.
2. Season with salt and pepper and give a good stir.
3. Cover and cook on low for 10 hours.
4. Serve and enjoy.

Nutrition Info:

- Per Servings 0.4g Carbs, 30.7g Protein, 15.7g Fat, 245 Calories

Garlic Pork Chops

Servings: 4 | Cooking Time: 30 Minutes

Ingredients:

- 1 ½ cups chicken broth
- 1 tablespoon butter
- 2 lemons, juiced
- 4 ¾ inch boneless pork chops
- 6 cloves garlic, minced
- Salt and pepper to taste
- 1 tablespoon olive oil

Directions:

1. Heat the olive oil in a large pot on medium-high fire.
2. Season the pork with salt, pepper, and garlic powder.
3. Place the pork in the Instant Pot and brown the sides. Set aside.
4. Add the garlic and sauté for a minute. Add the lemon juice and chicken broth. Stir in the butter.
5. Add the pork chops back to the pan. Cover the lid and simmer for 20 minutes.
6. Serve and enjoy.

Nutrition Info:

- Per Servings 4.8g Carbs, 50.2g Protein, 14.0g Fat, 355 Calories

Pork Wraps

Servings: 6 | Cooking Time: 40 Minutes

Ingredients:

- 6 bacon slices
- 2 tbsp fresh parsley, chopped
- 1 pound pork cutlets, sliced
- ⅓ cup ricotta cheese
- 1 tbsp coconut oil
- ¼ cup onion, chopped
- 3 garlic cloves, peeled and minced
- 2 tbsp Parmesan cheese, grated
- 15 ounces canned diced tomatoes
- ⅓ cup vegetable stock
- Salt and ground black pepper, to taste
- ½ tsp Italian seasoning

Directions:

1. Use a meat pounder to flatten the pork pieces. Set the bacon slices on top of each piece, then divide the parsley, ricotta cheese, and Parmesan cheese. Roll each pork piece and secure with a toothpick. Set a pan over medium heat and warm oil, cook the pork rolls until browned, and remove to a plate.
2. Add in the onion and garlic, and cook for 5 minutes. Place in the stock and cook for 3 minutes. Get rid of the toothpicks from the rolls and return them to the pan. Stir in the pepper, salt, tomatoes, and Italian seasoning, bring to a boil, set heat to medium-low, and cook for 20 minutes while covered. Split among bowls and enjoy.

Nutrition Info:

- Per Servings 2g Carbs, 34g Protein, 37g Fat, 435 Calories

Spiced Pork Roast With Collard Greens

Servings: 4 | Cooking Time: 40 Minutes

Ingredients:

- 2 tbsp olive oil
- Salt and black pepper, to taste
- 1 ½ pounds pork loin
- A pinch of dry mustard
- 1 tsp hot red pepper flakes
- ½ tsp ginger, minced
- 1 cup collard greens, chopped
- 2 garlic cloves, minced
- ½ lemon sliced
- ¼ cup water

Directions:

1. Using a bowl, combine the ginger with salt, mustard, and pepper. Add in the meat, toss to coat. Heat the oil in a saucepan over medium-high heat, brown the pork on all sides, for 10 minutes.
2. Transfer to the oven and roast for 1 hour at 390 F. To the saucepan, add collard greens, lemon slices, garlic, and water; cook for 10 minutes. Serve on a platter, sprinkle pan juices on

top and enjoy.

Nutrition Info:
• Per Servings 3g Carbs, 45g Protein, 23g Fat, 430 Calories

Garlic Beef & Egg Frittata

Servings: 4 | Cooking Time: 30 Minutes

Ingredients:
• 3 eggs, beaten
• 3 cloves of garlic, minced
• 1 onion, chopped
• ½ pound lean ground beef
• 1 stalk green onion, sliced
• 2 tablespoons olive oil
• A dash of salt
• ¼ tsp pepper

Directions:
1. Place a small cast iron pan on medium fire and heat for 2 minutes.
2. Add beef and crumble. Cook for 5 minutes.
3. Add onion and garlic, continue cooking beef until browned, around 5 minutes more. Discard any fat.
4. Season with pepper and salt.
5. Spread beef in the pan and lower fire to low.
6. Meanwhile, whisk eggs in a bowl. Pour over meat, cover, and cook for 10 minutes on low.
7. Place pan in the oven and broil on low for 3 minutes. Let it set for 5 minutes.
8. Serve and enjoy topped with green onions.

Nutrition Info:
• Per Servings 3.8g Carbs, 22.7g Protein, 20.5g Fat, 294 Calories

Parsley Beef Burgers

Servings: 6 | Cooking Time: 25 Minutes

Ingredients:
• 2 pounds ground beef
• 1 tbsp onion flakes
• ¾ almond flour
• ¼ cup beef broth
• 1 tbsp chopped parsley
• 1 tbsp Worcestershire sauce

Directions:
1. Combine all ingredients in a bowl. Mix well with your hands and make 6 patties out of the mixture. Arrange on a lined baking sheet. Bake at 370ºF, for about 18 minutes, until nice and crispy.

Nutrition Info:
• Per Servings 2.5g Carbs, 27g Protein, 28g Fat, 354 Calories

Grilled Fennel Cumin Lamb Chops

Servings: 6 | Cooking Time: 20 Minutes

Ingredients:
• 6 lamb rib chops
• 1 clove of garlic, minced
• ¾ teaspoon fennel seeds, crushed
• ¼ teaspoon ground coriander
• 5 tablespoons olive oil
• 1/8 teaspoon cracked black pepper
• Salt to taste

Directions:
1. Place the lamb rib chops in a shallow dish and rub onto the surface the garlic, fennel seeds, coriander, salt, and black pepper. Drizzle with olive oil. Allow to marinate in the fridge for 4 hours.
2. Heat the grill to medium and place the grill rack 6 inches above the heat source.
3. Grill the lamb chops for 10 minutes on each side or until well-done. For medium-rare lamb chops, cook for 6 to 8 minutes on each side.

Nutrition Info:
• Per Servings 0.5g Carbs, 17.0g Protein, 14.1g Fat, 190 Calories

Keto Beefy Burritos

Servings: 6 | Cooking Time: 25 Minutes

Ingredients:
• 1-pound lean ground beef
• 6 large kale leaves
• 1/4 cup onion
• 1/4 cup low-sodium tomato puree
• 1/4 teaspoon ground cumin
• What you'll need from the store cupboard:
• 1/4 teaspoon black pepper
• ½ tsp salt

Directions:
1. In a medium skillet, brown ground beef for 15 minutes; drain oil on paper towels.
2. Spray skillet with non-stick cooking spray; add onion to cook for 3-5 minutes, until vegetables are softened.
3. Add beef, tomato puree, black pepper, and cumin to onion/pepper mixture.
4. Mix well and cook for 3 to 5 minutes on low heat.
5. Divide the beef mixture among kale leaves.
6. Roll the kale leaves over burrito style, making sure that both ends are folded first, so the mixture does not fall out. Secure with a toothpick.

Nutrition Info:
• Per Servings 6.0g Carbs, 25.0g Protein, 32.0g Fat, 412 Calories

Beef Stovies

Servings: 4 | Cooking Time: 60 Minutes

Ingredients:
- 1 lb ground beef
- 1 large onion, chopped
- 6 parsnips, peeled and chopped
- 1 large carrot, chopped
- 1 tbsp olive oil
- 1 clove garlic, minced
- Salt and black pepper to taste
- 1 cup chicken broth
- ¼ tsp allspice
- 2 tsp rosemary leaves
- 1 tbsp sugar-free Worcestershire sauce
- ½ small cabbage, shredded

Directions:
1. Heat the oil in a skillet over medium heat and cook the beef for 4 minutes. Season with salt and pepper, and occasionally stir while breaking the lumps in it.
2. Add the onion, garlic, carrots, rosemary, and parsnips. Stir and cook for a minute, and pour the chicken broth, allspice, and Worcestershire sauce in it. Stir the mixture and cook the ingredients on low heat for 40 minutes.
3. Stir in the cabbage, season with salt and pepper, and cook the ingredients further for 2 minutes. After, turn the heat off, plate the stovies, and serve with wilted spinach and collards.

Nutrition Info:
- Per Servings 3g Carbs, 14g Protein, 18g Fat, 316 Calories

Roast Rack Of Lamb

Servings: 8 | Cooking Time: 30 Minutes

Ingredients:
- 2 1-pound French-style lamb rib roast, trimmed from fat
- 1 cup dry red wine
- 2 cloves of garlic, minced
- 1 tablespoon chopped rosemary
- 3 tablespoons dried cranberries, chopped
- 5 tablespoons olive oil
- Pepper and salt to taste

Directions:
1. In a resealable plastic, place the lamb and add in red wine, garlic, olive oil, and rosemary. Seal the bag and turn it to coat the lamb with the spices. Marinate inside the fridge for at least 4 hours while turning the bag occasionally.
2. Preheat the oven to 45000F and remove the lamb from the marinade. Reserve the juices.
3. Place the lamb bone side down on a roasting pan lined with foil.
4. Pour the reserved marinade over the roasting pan.
5. Roast for 30 minutes until the lamb turns slightly golden. Turn the lamb every 10 minutes and baste with the sauce.
6. Once cooked, take out the lamb from the oven and slice.
7. Serve with chopped cranberries on top.

Nutrition Info:
- Per Servings 1.7g Carbs, 27.8g Protein, 20.5g Fat, 306 Calories

Pork Chops And Peppers

Servings: 4 | Cooking Time: 20 Minutes

Ingredients:
- 4 thick pork chops
- 1 onion, chopped
- 2 cloves of garlic, minced
- 2 red and yellow bell peppers, seeded and julienned
- Salt and pepper to taste
- 5 tablespoons oil

Directions:
1. In a large saucepan, place on medium fire and heat 1 tsp oil for 3 minutes.
2. Add pork chop and cook for 5 minutes per side. Season pork chops with salt and pepper.
3. Transfer pork chops to a plate and let it rest.
4. In the same pan, add remaining oil. Increase fire to medium-high and sauté garlic. Stir in onions and bell peppers. Sauté until tender and crisp around 5 minutes.
5. Serve pork chops topped with bell pepper mixture.

Nutrition Info:
- Per Servings 4.3g Carbs, 23.9g Protein, 16.3g Fat, 245 Calories

Pork In White Wine

Servings: 6 | Cooking Time: 1 Hour 25 Minutes

Ingredients:
- 2 tbsp olive oil
- 2 pounds pork stew meat, cubed
- Salt and black pepper, to taste
- 2 tbsp butter
- 4 garlic cloves, minced
- ¾ cup beef stock
- ½ cup white wine
- 3 carrots, chopped
- 1 cabbage head, shredded
- ½ cup scallions, chopped
- 1 cup heavy cream

Directions:
1. Set a pan over medium-high heat and warm butter and oil. Sear the pork until brown. Add garlic, scallions and carrots; sauté for 5 minutes. Pour in the cabbage, stock and wine, and bring to a boil.
2. Reduce the heat and cook for 1 hour while covered. Add in the heavy cream as you stir for 1 minute, adjust the seasonings and serve in bowls.

Nutrition Info:
- Per Servings 6g Carbs, 43g Protein, 32.5g Fat, 514 Calories

Pork And Cabbage Soup

Servings: 10 | Cooking Time: 50 Minutes

Ingredients:
- 3 lb. pork butt, cut into chunks
- 1 thumb-size ginger, sliced
- 1 head cabbage, cut into quarters
- 1 scallion, green part only
- 1 small onion, chopped

- Pepper and salt to taste
- 3 cups water

Directions:

1. Place all ingredients in a heavy-bottomed pot except for cabbage. Give a good stir and season with salt and pepper to taste.
2. Cover and bring to a boil. Once boiling, lower fire to a simmer and simmer for 30 minutes.
3. Add cabbage and simmer for another 10 minutes.
4. Adjust seasoning to taste.
5. Serve and enjoy.

Nutrition Info:

- Per Servings 4.6g Carbs, 35.2g Protein, 24.7g Fat, 383 Calories

Ribeye Steak With Shitake Mushrooms

Servings: 1 | Cooking Time: 25 Minutes

Ingredients:

- 6 ounces ribeye steak
- 2 tbsp butter
- 1 tsp olive oil
- ½ cup shitake mushrooms, sliced
- Salt and ground pepper, to taste

Directions:

1. Heat the olive oil in a pan over medium heat. Rub the steak with salt and pepper and cook about 4 minutes per side; set aside. Melt the butter in the pan and cook the shitakes for 4 minutes. Pour the butter and mushrooms over the steak to serve.

Nutrition Info:

- Per Servings 3g Carbs, 33g Protein, 31g Fat, 478 Calories

Beef Meatballs With Onion Sauce

Servings: 5 | Cooking Time: 35 Minutes

Ingredients:

- 2 pounds ground beef
- Salt and black pepper, to taste
- ½ tsp garlic powder
- 1 ¼ tbsp coconut aminos
- 1 cup beef stock
- ¾ cup almond flour
- 1 tbsp fresh parsley, chopped
- 1 tbsp dried onion flakes
- 1 onion, sliced
- 2 tbsp butter
- ¼ cup sour cream

Directions:

1. Using a bowl, combine the beef with salt, garlic powder, almond flour, onion flakes, parsley, 1 tablespoon coconut aminos, black pepper, ¼ cup of beef stock. Form 6 patties, place them on a baking sheet, put in the oven at 370ºF, and bake for 18 minutes.
2. Set a pan with the butter over medium heat, stir in the onion, and cook for 3 minutes. Stir in the remaining beef stock, sour cream, and remaining coconut aminos, and bring to a simmer.

3. Remove from heat, adjust the seasoning with black pepper and salt. Serve the meatballs topped with onion sauce.

Nutrition Info:

- Per Servings 6g Carbs, 32g Protein, 23g Fat, 435 Calories

Mushroom Beef Stew

Servings: 5 | Cooking Time: 1h 30mins

Ingredients:

- 2 pounds beef chuck roast, cut into 1/2-inch thick strips
- 1/2 medium onion, sliced or diced
- 8 ounces sliced mushrooms
- 2 cups beef broth, divided
- Salt and pepper to taste
- 1 tablespoon butter
- 2 cloves garlic, minced
- 1 tablespoon fresh chopped chives
- 1 tablespoon olive oil

Directions:

1. Heat olive oil in a large skillet over high heat. Stir in beef with salt and pepper; cook, stirring constantly, for 6-7 minutes. Remove beef from the pan and set aside.
2. Add butter, mushrooms and onions into the pan; cook and stir over medium heat.
3. Add garlic and stir for 30 seconds. Stir in 1 cup. broth and simmer 3-4 minutes.
4. Return beef to the pan. Stir in remaining broth and chives; bring to a simmer and cook on low heat for about 1 hour, covered, stirring every 20 minutes.
5. Season with salt and pepper to taste. Serve.

Nutrition Info:

- Per Servings 4.1g Carbs, 15.8g Protein, 24.5g Fat, 307 Calories

Venison Tenderloin With Cheese Stuffing

Servings: 8 | Cooking Time: 30 Minutes

Ingredients:

- 2 pounds venison tenderloin
- 2 garlic cloves, minced
- 2 tbsp chopped almonds
- ½ cup gorgonzola
- ½ cup feta cheese
- 1 tsp chopped onion
- ½ tsp Sea salt

Directions:

1. Preheat your grill to medium. Slice the tenderloin lengthwise to make a pocket for the filling. Combine the rest of the ingredients in a bowl. Stuff the tenderloin with the filling. Shut the meat with skewers and grill for as long as it takes to reach your desired density.

Nutrition Info:

- Per Servings 1.7g Carbs, 25g Protein, 12g Fat, 194 Calories

Herb Pork Chops With Raspberry Sauce

Servings: 4 | Cooking Time: 17 Minutes

Ingredients:
- 1 tbsp olive oil + extra for brushing
- 2 lb pork chops
- Pink salt and black pepper to taste
- 2 cups raspberries
- ¼ cup water
- 1 ½ tbsp Italian Herb mix
- 3 tbsp balsamic vinegar
- 2 tsp sugar-free Worcestershire sauce

Directions:
1. Heat oil in a skillet over medium heat, season the pork with salt and black pepper and cook for 5 minutes on each side. Put on serving plates and reserve the pork drippings.
2. Mash the raspberries with a fork in a bowl until jam-like. Pour into a saucepan, add the water, and herb mix. Bring to boil on low heat for 4 minutes. Stir in pork drippings, vinegar, and Worcestershire sauce. Simmer for 1 minute. Spoon sauce over the pork chops and serve with braised rapini.

Nutrition Info:
- Per Servings 1.1g Carbs, 26.3g Protein, 32.5g Fat, 413 Calories

Simple Pulled Pork

Servings: 4 | Cooking Time: 25 Minutes

Ingredients:
- 4 pork chops, deboned
- 1 onion, sliced
- 5 cloves of garlic, minced
- 1 tbsp soy sauce
- 1 ½ cups water
- Salt and pepper to taste

Directions:
1. In a heavy-bottomed pot, add all ingredients and mix well.
2. Cover and cook on medium-high fire until boiling. Lower fire to a simmer and cook for 25 minutes undisturbed.
3. Turn off fire and let it cool a bit.
4. With two forks, shred meat.
5. Serve and enjoy.

Nutrition Info:
- Per Servings 2.4g Carbs, 40.7g Protein, 17.4g Fat, 339 Calories

Beef Enchilada Stew

Servings: 4 | Cooking Time: 40 Minutes

Ingredients:
- 1 cup Mexican cheese, shredded
- 1 can mild green chilies, drained
- 2 teaspoons garlic salt
- 1 10-ounce can La Victoria mild red enchilada sauce
- 2-lbs London broil beef, sliced into 2-inch cubes
- Pepper and salt to taste

Directions:
1. Add all ingredients in a pot on high fire and bring to a boil.

2. Once boiling, lower fire to a simmer and cook for 25 minutes.
3. Adjust seasoning to taste.
4. Serve and enjoy.

Nutrition Info:
- Per Servings 10.1g Carbs, 64.2g Protein, 47.4g Fat, 764 Calories

Caribbean Beef

Servings: 8 | Cooking Time: 1 Hour 10 Minutes

Ingredients:
- 2 onions, chopped
- 2 tbsp avocado oil
- 2 pounds beef stew meat, cubed
- 2 red bell peppers, seeded and chopped
- 1 habanero pepper, chopped
- 4 green chilies, chopped
- 14.5 ounces canned diced tomatoes
- 2 tbsp fresh cilantro, chopped
- 4 garlic cloves, minced
- ½ cup vegetable broth
- Salt and black pepper, to taste
- 1 ½ tsp cumin
- ½ cup black olives, chopped
- 1 tsp dried oregano

Directions:
1. Set a pan over medium-high heat and warm avocado oil. Brown the beef on all sides; remove and set aside. Stir-fry in the red bell peppers, green chilies, oregano, garlic, habanero pepper, onions, and cumin, for about 5-6 minutes. Pour in the tomatoes and broth, and cook for 1 hour. Stir in the olives, adjust the seasonings and serve in bowls sprinkled with fresh cilantro.

Nutrition Info:
- Per Servings 8g Carbs, 25g Protein, 14g Fat, 305 Calories

Cranberry Gravy Brisket

Servings: 7 | Cooking Time: 25 Minutes

Ingredients:
- 1 tablespoon prepared mustard
- ½ cup chopped onion
- 1 can tomato sauce
- ½ cup cranberries, pitted
- 1 fresh beef brisket
- 5 tablespoons olive oil
- ½ teaspoon salt
- ¼ teaspoon pepper

Directions:
1. Add all ingredients in a pot on high fire and bring to a boil.
2. Once boiling, lower fire to a simmer and cook for 25 minutes.
3. Adjust seasoning to taste.
4. Serve and enjoy.

Nutrition Info:
- Per Servings 9.7g Carbs, 24.9g Protein, 24.4g Fat, 364 Calories

Pork Lettuce Cups

Servings: 6 | Cooking Time: 20 Minutes

Ingredients:
- 2 lb ground pork
- 1 tbsp ginger- garlic paste
- Pink salt and chili pepper to taste
- 1 tsp ghee
- 1 head Iceberg lettuce
- 2 sprigs green onion, chopped
- 1 red bell pepper, seeded and chopped
- ½ cucumber, finely chopped

Directions:
1. Put the pork with ginger-garlic paste, salt, and chili pepper seasoning in a saucepan. Cook for 10 minutes over medium heat while breaking any lumps until the pork is no longer pink. Drain liquid and add the ghee, melt and brown the meat for 4 minutes, continuously stirring. Turn the heat off.
2. Pat the lettuce dry with paper towel and in each leaf, spoon two to three tablespoons of pork, top with green onions, bell pepper, and cucumber. Serve with soy drizzling sauce.

Nutrition Info:
- Per Servings 1g Carbs, 19g Protein, 24.3g Fat, 311 Calories

Pork Pie With Cauliflower

Servings: 8 | Cooking Time: 1 Hour And 30 Minutes

Ingredients:
- Crust:
- 1 egg
- ¼ cup butter
- 2 cups almond flour
- ¼ tsp xanthan gum
- ¼ cup shredded mozzarella
- A pinch of salt
- Filling:
- 2 pounds ground pork
- ½ cup water
- ⅓ cup pureed onion
- ¾ tsp allspice
- 1 cup cooked and mashed cauliflower
- 1 tbsp ground sage
- 2 tbsp butter

Directions:
1. Preheat your oven to 350ºF.
2. Whisk together all crust ingredients in a bowl. Make two balls out of the mixture and refrigerate for 10 minutes. Combine the water, meat, and salt, in a pot over medium heat. Cook for about 15 minutes, place the meat along with the other ingredients in a bowl. Mix with your hands to combine.
3. Roll out the pie crusts and place one at the bottom of a greased pie pan. Spread the filling over the crust. Top with the other coat. Bake in the oven for 50 minutes then serve.

Nutrition Info:
- Per Servings 4g Carbs, 29g Protein, 41g Fat, 485 Calories

Baked Pork Meatballs In Pasta Sauce

Servings: 6 | Cooking Time: 45 Minutes

Ingredients:
- 2 lb ground pork
- 1 tbsp olive oil
- 1 cup pork rinds, crushed
- 3 cloves garlic, minced
- ½ cup coconut milk
- 2 eggs, beaten
- ½ cup grated Parmesan cheese
- ½ cup grated asiago cheese
- Salt and black pepper to taste
- ¼ cup chopped parsley
- 2 jars sugar-free marinara sauce
- ½ tsp Italian seasoning
- 1 cup Italian blend kinds of cheeses
- Chopped basil to garnish
- Cooking spray

Directions:
1. Preheat the oven to 400ºF, line a cast iron pan with foil and oil it with cooking spray. Set aside.
2. Combine the coconut milk and pork rinds in a bowl. Mix in the ground pork, garlic, Asiago cheese, Parmesan cheese, eggs, salt, and pepper, just until combined. Form balls of the mixture and place them in the prepared pan. Bake in the oven for 20 minutes at a reduced temperature of 370ºF.
3. Transfer the meatballs to a plate. Remove the foil and pour in half of the marinara sauce. Place the meatballs back in the pan and pour the remaining marinara sauce all over them. Sprinkle all over with the Italian blend cheeses, drizzle the olive oil on them, and then sprinkle with Italian seasoning.
4. Cover the pan with foil and put it back in the oven to bake for 10 minutes. After, remove the foil, and continue cooking for 5 minutes. Once ready, take out the pan and garnish with basil. Serve on a bed of squash spaghetti.

Nutrition Info:
- Per Servings 4.1g Carbs, 46.2g Protein, 46.8g Fat, 590 Calories

Pork And Mushroom Bake

Servings: 6 | Cooking Time: 1 Hour And 15 Minutes

Ingredients:
- 1 onion, chopped
- 2 cans mushroom soup
- 6 pork chops
- ½ cup sliced mushrooms
- Salt and ground pepper, to taste

Directions:
1. Preheat the oven to 370ºF.
2. Season the pork chops with salt and pepper, and place in a baking dish. Combine the mushroom soup, mushrooms, and onion, in a bowl. Pour this mixture over the pork chops. Bake for 45 minutes.

Nutrition Info:
- Per Servings 8g Carbs, 19.4g Protein, 32.6g Fat, 403 Calories

Simple Corned Beef

Servings: 6 | Cooking Time: 1 Hour And 30 Minutes

Ingredients:
- 2 pounds corned beef brisket, cut into 1-inch cubes
- 2 cups water
- 2 onions, chopped
- 6 garlic cloves, smashed
- 1 cup olive oil
- 1 tbsp peppercorns
- 1 tsp salt

Directions:
1. Place all ingredients in a heavy-bottomed pot on high fire and bring to a boil.
2. Once boiling, lower fire to a simmer.
3. Simmer for 60 minutes.
4. Turn off fire and shred beef with two forks.
5. Turn on fire and continue cooking until sauce is reduced.
6. Serve and enjoy.

Nutrition Info:
- Per Servings 0.6g Carbs, 12.1g Protein, 30.2g Fat, 314 Calories

Rib Roast With Roasted Red Shallots And Garlic

Servings: 6 | Cooking Time: 55 Minutes

Ingredients:
- 5 lb rib roast, on the bone
- 3 heads garlic, cut in half
- 3 tbsp olive oil
- 6 shallots, peeled and halved
- 2 lemons, zested and juiced
- 3 tbsp mustard seeds
- 3 tbsp swerve
- Salt and black pepper to taste
- 3 tbsp thyme leaves

Directions:
1. Preheat the oven to 450°F. Place the garlic heads and shallots in the roasting dish, toss them with olive oil, and cook in the oven for 15 minutes. Pour the lemon juice on them and set aside. Score shallow crisscrosses patterns on the meat and set aside.
2. Mix the swerve, mustard seeds, thyme, salt, pepper, and lemon zest to make a rub; and apply it all over the beef with your hands particularly into the cuts. Place the beef on the shallots and garlic; cook it in the oven for 15 minutes. Reduce the heat to 400°F, cover the top of the dish with foil, and continue cooking for 5 minutes.
3. Once ready, remove the dish, and let the meat sit covered for 15 minutes before slicing. Use the beef pieces in salads or sandwiches.

Nutrition Info:
- Per Servings 2.5g Carbs, 58.4g Protein, 38.6g Fat, 556 Calories

Pork Sausage With Spinach

Servings: 6 | Cooking Time: 35 Minutes

Ingredients:
- 1 onion, chopped
- 2 tbsp olive oil
- 1½ pound Italian pork sausage, sliced
- 1 red bell pepper, seeded and chopped
- Salt and black pepper, to taste
- 4 pounds spinach, chopped
- 1 garlic, minced
- ¼ cup green chili pepper, chopped
- 1 cup water

Directions:
1. Set a pan over medium-high heat, warm oil and cook the sausage for 10 minutes. Stir in the onion, garlic and bell pepper, and fry for 3-4 minutes. Place in the spinach, salt, water, black pepper, chili pepper, and cook for 10 minutes. Split among serving bowls and enjoy.

Nutrition Info:
- Per Servings 6.2g Carbs, 29g Protein, 28g Fat, 352 Calories

Adobo Beef Fajitas

Servings: 4 | Cooking Time: 35 Minutes

Ingredients:
- 2 lb skirt steak, cut in halves
- 2 tbsp Adobo seasoning
- Pink salt to taste
- 2 tbsp olive oil
- 2 large white onion, chopped
- 1 cup sliced mixed bell peppers, chopped
- 12 low carb tortillas

Directions:
1. Season the steak with adobo and marinate in the fridge for one hour.
2. Preheat grill to 425°F and cook steak for 6 minutes on each side, flipping once until lightly browned. Remove from heat and wrap in foil and let sit for 10 minutes. This allows the meat to cook in its heat for a few more minutes before slicing.
3. Heat the olive oil in a skillet over medium heat and sauté the onion and bell peppers for 5 minutes or until soft. Cut steak against the grain into strips and share on the tortillas. Top with the veggies and serve with guacamole.

Nutrition Info:
- Per Servings 5g Carbs, 18g Protein, 25g Fat, 348 Calories

Balsamic Grilled Pork Chops

Servings: 6 | Cooking Time: 2 Hours 20 Minutes

Ingredients:
- 6 pork loin chops, boneless
- 2 tbsp erythritol
- ¼ cup balsamic vinegar
- 3 cloves garlic, minced
- ¼ cup olive oil
- ⅓ tsp salt
- Black pepper to taste

Directions:

1. Put the pork in a plastic bag. In a bowl, mix the erythritol, balsamic vinegar, garlic, olive oil, salt, pepper, and pour the sauce over the pork. Seal the bag, shake it, and place in the refrigerator.

2. Marinate the pork for 1 to 2 hours. Preheat the grill on medium-high heat, remove the pork when ready, and grill covered for 10 to 12 minutes on each side. Remove the pork chops, let them sit for 4 minutes, and serve with a syrupy parsnip sauté.

Nutrition Info:
- Per Servings 1.5g Carbs, 38.1g Protein, 26.8g Fat, 418 Calories

Italian Sausage Stew

Servings: 6 | Cooking Time: 35 Minutes

Ingredients:
- 1 pound Italian sausage, sliced
- 1 red bell pepper, seeded and chopped
- 2 onions, chopped
- Salt and black pepper, to taste
- 1 cup fresh parsley, chopped
- 6 green onions, chopped
- ¼ cup avocado oil
- 1 cup beef stock
- 4 garlic cloves
- 24 ounces canned diced tomatoes
- 16 ounces okra, trimmed and sliced
- 6 ounces tomato sauce
- 2 tbsp coconut aminos
- 1 tbsp hot sauce

Directions:

1. Set a pot over medium-high heat and warm oil, place in the sausages, and cook for 2 minutes. Stir in the onion, green onions, garlic, pepper, bell pepper, and salt, and cook for 5 minutes.

2. Add in the hot sauce, stock, tomatoes, coconut aminos, okra, and tomato sauce, bring to a simmer and cook for 15 minutes. Adjust the seasoning with salt and pepper. Share into serving bowls and sprinkle with fresh parsley to serve.

Nutrition Info:
- Per Servings 7g Carbs, 16g Protein, 25g Fat, 314 Calories

Classic Italian Bolognese Sauce

Servings: 5 | Cooking Time: 35 Minutes

Ingredients:
- 1 pound ground beef
- 2 garlic cloves
- 1 onion, chopped
- 1 tsp oregano
- 1 tsp sage
- 1 tsp marjoram
- 1 tsp rosemary
- 7 oz canned chopped tomatoes
- 1 tbsp olive oil

Directions:

1. Heat olive oil in a saucepan. Add onion and garlic and cook for 3 minutes. Add beef and cook until browned, about 4-5

minutes. Stir in the herbs and tomatoes. Cook for 15 minutes. Serve with zoodles.

Nutrition Info:
- Per Servings 5.9g Carbs, 26g Protein, 20g Fat, 318 Calories

Simple Beef Curry

Servings: 6 | Cooking Time:30 Minutes

Ingredients:
- 2 pounds boneless beef chuck
- 1 tbsp ground turmeric
- 1 tsp ginger paste
- 6 cloves garlic, minced
- 1 onion, chopped
- 3 tbsp olive oil
- 1 cup water
- Pepper and salt to taste

Directions:

1. In a saucepan, heat the olive oil over medium heat then add onion and garlic for 5 minutes.

2. Stir in beef and sauté for 10 minutes.

3. Add remaining ingredients, cover, and simmer for 20 minutes.

4. Adjust seasoning if needed.

5. Serve and enjoy.

Nutrition Info:
- Per Servings 5.0g Carbs, 33.0g Protein, 16.0g Fat, 287 Calories

Cherry-balsamic Sauced Beef

Servings: 4 | Cooking Time: 40 Minutes

Ingredients:
- 2-lbs London broil beef, sliced into 2-inch cubes
- 1/3 cup balsamic vinegar
- ½ cup dried cherries
- ½ teaspoon pepper
- 1 teaspoon salt
- 1 tablespoon canola oil
- ½ cup water

Directions:

1. Add all ingredients in a pot on high fire and bring to a boil.

2. Once boiling, lower fire to a simmer and cook for 35 minutes.

3. Adjust seasoning to taste.

4. Serve and enjoy.

Nutrition Info:
- Per Servings 4.6g Carbs, 82.2g Protein, 17.2g Fat, 525 Calories

Garlic Crispy Pork Loin

Servings: 4 | Cooking Time: 1h 5 Minutes

Ingredients:
- 1 quart cold water
- 3 cloves garlic, crushed
- 3 tablespoons. chopped fresh ginger
- 1 boneless pork loin roast
- 2 tablespoons. Dijon mustard
- Salt and freshly ground black pepper to taste
- 2 teaspoons. dried rosemary
- 1 tablespoon olive oil
- 2 tablespoons stevia
- 1/2 teaspoon red pepper flakes

Directions:
1. Mix water, salt, 1 tbsp. stevia, garlic, ginger, rosemary and red pepper flakes in a large bowl.
2. Place pork loin in brine mixture and refrigerate for 8 to 10 hours. Remove pork from brine, pat dry, and season all sides with salt and black pepper.
3. Preheat oven to 325 degrees F.
4. Heat olive oil in a skillet over high heat. Cook pork for about 10 minutes.
5. Transfer skillet to the oven and roast for about 40 minutes.
6. Mix 2 tablespoons stevia and Dijon mustard together in a small bowl.
7. Remove pork roast from the oven and spread stevia mixture on all sides. Cook for an additional 15 minutes at 145 degrees F. Serve and enjoy.

Nutrition Info:
- Per Servings 19.3g Carbs, 30.7g Protein, 18.9g Fat, 376 Calories

Zoodle, Bacon, Spinach, And Halloumi Gratin

Servings: 4 | Cooking Time: 35 Minutes

Ingredients:
- 2 large zucchinis, spiralized
- 4 slices bacon, chopped
- 2 cups baby spinach
- 4 oz halloumi cheese, cut into cubes
- 2 cloves garlic, minced
- 1 cup heavy cream
- ½ cup sugar-free tomato sauce
- 1/6 cup water
- 1 cup grated mozzarella cheese
- ½ tsp dried Italian mixed herbs
- Salt and black pepper to taste

Directions:
1. Preheat the oven to 350ºF. Place the cast iron pan over medium heat and fry the bacon for 4 minutes, then add garlic and cook for 1 minute.
2. In a bowl, mix the heavy cream, tomato sauce, and water, and add it to the pan. Stir in the zucchini, spinach, halloumi, Italian herbs, salt, and pepper to taste.
3. Turn the heat off, sprinkle the mozzarella cheese on top, and transfer the pan to the oven. Bake for 20 minutes or until the cheese is golden.

4. When ready, remove the pan and serve the gratin warm with a low carb baguette.

Nutrition Info:
- Per Servings 5.3g Carbs, 16g Protein, 27g Fat, 350 Calories

Spicy Mesquite Ribs

Servings: 6 | Cooking Time: 8 Hours 45 Minutes

Ingredients:
- 3 racks pork ribs, silver lining removed
- 2 cups sugar-free BBQ sauce
- 2 tbsp erythritol
- 2 tsp chili powder
- 2 tsp cumin powder
- 2 tsp onion powder
- 2 tsp smoked paprika
- 2 tsp garlic powder
- Salt and black pepper to taste
- 1 tsp mustard powder

Directions:
1. Preheat a smoker to 400ºF using mesquite wood to create flavor in the smoker.
2. In a bowl, mix the erythritol, chili powder, cumin powder, black pepper, onion powder, smoked paprika, garlic powder, salt, and mustard powder. Rub the ribs and let marinate for 30 minutes.
3. Place on the grill grate, and cook at reduced heat of 225ºF for 4 hours. Flip the ribs after and continue cooking for 4 hours. Brush the ribs with bbq sauce on both sides and sear them in increased heat for 3 minutes per side. Remove the ribs and let sit for 4 minutes before slicing. Serve with red cabbage coleslaw.

Nutrition Info:
- Per Servings 0g Carbs, 44.5g Protein, 36.6g Fat, 580 Calories

Mustardy Pork Chops

Servings: 4 | Cooking Time: 15 Minutes

Ingredients:
- 4 pork loin chops
- 1 tsp Dijon mustard
- 1 tbsp soy sauce
- 1 tsp lemon juice
- 1 tbsp water
- Salt and black pepper, to taste
- 1 tbsp butter
- A bunch of scallions, chopped

Directions:
1. Using a bowl, combine the water with lemon juice, mustard and soy sauce. Set a pan over medium heat and warm butter, add in the pork chops, season with salt, and pepper, cook for 4 minutes, turn, and cook for additional 4 minutes. Remove the pork chops to a plate and keep warm.
2. In the same pan, pour in the mustard sauce, and simmer for 5 minutes. Spread this over pork, top with scallions, and enjoy.

Nutrition Info:
- Per Servings 1.2g Carbs, 38g Protein, 21.5g Fat, 382 Calories

Pulled Pork With Avocado

Servings: 12 | Cooking Time: 2 Hours 55 Minutes

Ingredients:
- 4 pounds pork shoulder
- 1 tbsp avocado oil
- ½ cup beef stock
- ¼ cup jerk seasoning
- 6 avocado, sliced

Directions:
1. Rub the pork shoulder with jerk seasoning, and set in a greased baking dish. Pour in the stock, and cook for 1 hour 45 minutes in your oven at 350ºF covered with aluminium foil.
2. Discard the foil and cook for another 20 minutes. Leave to rest for 30 minutes, and shred it with 2 forks. Serve topped with avocado slices.

Nutrition Info:
- Per Servings 4.1g Carbs, 42g Protein, 42.6g Fat, 567 Calories

Garlic Pork Chops With Mint Pesto

Servings: 4 | Cooking Time: 3 Hours 10 Minutes

Ingredients:
- 1 cup parsley
- 1 cup mint
- 1½ onions, chopped
- ⅓ cup pistachios
- 1 tsp lemon zest
- 5 tbsp avocado oil
- Salt, to taste
- 4 pork chops
- 5 garlic cloves, minced
- Juice from 1 lemon

Directions:
1. In a food processor, combine the parsley with avocado oil, mint, pistachios, salt, lemon zest, and 1 onion. Rub the pork with this mixture, place in a bowl, and refrigerate for 1 hour while covered.
2. Remove the chops and set to a baking dish, place in ½ onion, and garlic; sprinkle with lemon juice, and bake for 2 hours in the oven at 250ºF. Split amongst plates and enjoy.

Nutrition Info:
- Per Servings 5.5g Carbs, 37g Protein, 40g Fat, 567 Calories

Beef And Egg Rice Bowls

Servings: 4 | Cooking Time: 22 Minutes

Ingredients:
- 2 cups cauli rice
- 3 cups frozen mixed vegetables
- 3 tbsp ghee
- 1 lb skirt steak
- Salt and black pepper to taste
- 4 fresh eggs
- Hot sauce (sugar-free) for topping

Directions:
1. Mix the cauli rice and mixed vegetables in a bowl, sprinkle with a little water, and steam in the microwave for 1 minute to be tender. Share into 4 serving bowls.
2. Melt the ghee in a skillet, season the beef with salt and pepper, and brown for 5 minutes on each side. Use a perforated spoon to ladle the meat onto the vegetables.
3. Wipe out the skillet and return to medium heat, crack in an egg, season with salt and pepper and cook until the egg white has set, but the yolk is still runny 3 minutes. Remove egg onto the vegetable bowl and fry the remaining 3 eggs. Add to the other bowls.
4. Drizzle the beef bowls with hot sauce and serve.

Nutrition Info:
- Per Servings 4g Carbs, 15g Protein, 26g Fat, 320 Calories

Peanut Butter Pork Stir-fry

Servings: 4 | Cooking Time: 23 Minutes

Ingredients:
- 1 ½ tbsp ghee
- 2 lb pork loin, cut into strips
- Pink salt and chili pepper to taste
- 2 tsp ginger- garlic paste
- ¼ cup chicken broth
- 5 tbsp peanut butter
- 2 cups mixed stir-fry vegetables

Directions:
1. Melt the ghee in a wok and mix the pork with salt, chili pepper, and ginger-garlic paste. Pour the pork into the wok and cook for 6 minutes until no longer pink.
2. Mix the peanut butter with some broth to be smooth, add to the pork and stir; cook for 2 minutes. Pour in the remaining broth, cook for 4 minutes, and add the mixed veggies. Simmer for 5 minutes.
3. Adjust the taste with salt and black pepper, and spoon the stir-fry to a side of cilantro cauli rice.

Nutrition Info:
- Per Servings 1g Carbs, 22.5g Protein, 49g Fat, 571 Calories

Rolled Shoulder With Basil And Pine Nuts

Servings: 4 | Cooking Time: 1 Hour 20 Minutes

Ingredients:
- 1 lb rolled lamb shoulder, boneless
- 1 ½ cups basil leaves, chopped
- 5 tbsp pine nuts, chopped
- ½ cup green olives, pitted and chopped
- 3 cloves garlic, minced
- Salt and black pepper to taste

Directions:
1. Preheat the oven to 450ºF. In a bowl, combine the basil, pine nuts, olives, and garlic. Season with salt and black pepper.
2. Untie the lamb flat onto a chopping board, spread the basil mixture all over, and rub the spice onto the meat. Roll the lamb over the spice mixture and tie it together using 3 to 4 strings of butcher's twine. Place the lamb onto a baking dish and cook in the oven for 10 minutes. Reduce the heat to 350ºF and continue cooking for 40 minutes.

3. When ready, transfer the meat to a cleaned chopping board; let it rest for 10 minutes before slicing. Serve with a side of equally roasted capsicums and root vegetables.

Nutrition Info:
• Per Servings 2.2g Carbs, 42.7g Protein, 37.7g Fat, 547 Calories

Beefy Bbq Ranch

Servings: 4 | Cooking Time: 40 Minutes

Ingredients:
• 2-lbs London broil roast, sliced into 2-inch cubes
• 1 Hidden Valley Ranch seasoning mix packet
• 1-pound bacon
• 1 tablespoon barbecue powder
• 1 cup water
• Pepper and salt to taste

Directions:
1. Add all ingredients in a pot on high fire and bring to a boil.
2. Once boiling, lower fire to a simmer and cook for 35 minutes.
3. Adjust seasoning to taste.
4. Serve and enjoy.

Nutrition Info:
• Per Servings 8.4g Carbs, 65.3g Protein, 39.7g Fat, 642 Calories

Greek Pork With Olives

Servings: 4 | Cooking Time: 45 Minutes

Ingredients:
• 4 pork chops, bone-in
• Salt and ground black pepper, to taste
• 1 tsp dried rosemary
• 3 garlic cloves, peeled and minced
• ½ cup kalamata olives, pitted and sliced
• 2 tbsp olive oil
• ¼ cup vegetable broth

Directions:
1. Season pork chops with pepper and salt, and add in a roasting pan. Stir in the garlic, olives, olive oil, broth, and rosemary, set in the oven at 425°F, and bake for 10 minutes. Reduce heat to 350°F and roast for 25 minutes. Slice the pork, split among plates, and sprinkle with pan juices all over.

Nutrition Info:
• Per Servings 2.2g Carbs, 36g Protein, 25.2g Fat, 415 Calories

Beef Cotija Cheeseburger

Servings: 4 | Cooking Time: 15 Minutes

Ingredients:
• 1 lb ground beef
• 1 tsp dried parsley
• ½ tsp sugar-free Worcestershire sauce
• Salt and black pepper to taste
• 1 cup cotija cheese, shredded
• 4 low carb buns, halved

Directions:
1. Preheat a grill to 400°F and grease the grate with cooking spray.
2. Mix the beef, parsley, Worcestershire sauce, salt, and black pepper with your hands until evenly combined. Make medium sized patties out of the mixture, about 4 patties. Cook on the grill for 7 minutes one side to be cooked through and no longer pink.
3. Flip the patties and top with cheese. Cook for another 7 minutes to be well done while the cheese melts onto the meat. Remove the patties and sandwich into two halves of a bun each. Serve with a tomato dipping sauce and zucchini fries.

Nutrition Info:
• Per Servings 2g Carbs, 21g Protein, 32g Fat, 386 Calories

Garlic Lime Marinated Pork Chops

Servings: 4 | Cooking Time: 10 Minutes

Ingredients:
• 4 6-ounce lean boneless pork chops, trimmed from fat
• 4 cloves of garlic, crushed
• 1 teaspoon cumin
• 1 teaspoon paprika
• ½ lime, juiced and zested
• 1 tsp black pepper
• ½ tsp salt
• 5 tablespoons olive oil

Directions:
1. In a bowl, season the pork with the rest of the ingredients.
2. Allow marinating inside the fridge for at least 2 hours.
3. Place the pork chops in a baking dish or broiler pan and grill for 5 minutes on each side until golden brown.
4. Serve with salad if desired.

Nutrition Info:
• Per Servings 2.4g Carbs, 38.5g Protein, 22.9g Fat, 376 Calories

Beef Provençal

Servings: 4 | Cooking Time: 50 Minutes

Ingredients:
• 12 ounces beef steak racks
• 2 fennel bulbs, sliced
• Salt and black pepper, to taste
• 3 tbsp olive oil
• ½ cup apple cider vinegar
• 1 tsp herbs de Provence
• 1 tbsp swerve

Directions:
1. In a bowl, mix the fennel with 2 tbsp of oil, swerve, and vinegar, toss to coat well, and set to a baking dish. Season with herbs de Provence, pepper and salt, and cook in the oven at 400°F for 15 minutes.
2. Sprinkle pepper and salt to the beef, place into an oiled pan over medium-high heat, and cook for a couple of minutes. Place the beef to the baking dish with the fennel, and bake for 20 minutes. Split everything among plates and enjoy.

Nutrition Info:
• Per Servings 5.2g Carbs, 19g Protein, 11.3g Fat, 230 Calories

Seasoned Garlic Pork Chops

Servings: 8 | Cooking Time: 10 Mins

Ingredients:
- 1/2 cup water
- 1/3 cup mayo
- 3 tablespoons lemon pepper seasoning
- 2 teaspoons minced garlic
- 6 boneless pork loin chops, trimmed of fat
- 1/4 cup olive oil

Directions:
1. Mix water, mayo, olive oil, lemon pepper seasoning, and minced garlic in a deep bowl.
2. Add pork chops and marinate in refrigerator at least 2 hours.
3. Preheat an outdoor grill at medium-high heat and lightly oil the grate.
4. Remove pork chops and cook on the preheated grill for 5 to 6 minutes per side at 145 degrees F.
5. Serve and enjoy.

Nutrition Info:
- Per Servings 2.1g Carbs, 40.7g Protein, 22g Fat, 380 Calories

Beef And Butternut Squash Stew

Servings: 4 | Cooking Time: 40 Minutes

Ingredients:
- 3 tsp olive oil
- 1 pound ground beef
- 1 cup beef stock
- 14 ounces canned tomatoes with juice
- 1 tbsp stevia
- 1 pound butternut squash, chopped
- 1 tbsp Worcestershire sauce
- 2 bay leaves
- Salt and ground black pepper, to taste
- 3 tbsp fresh parsley, chopped
- 1 onion, chopped
- 1 tsp dried sage
- 1 tbsp garlic, minced

Directions:
1. Set a pan over medium heat and heat olive oil, stir in the onion, garlic, and beef, and cook for 10 minutes. Add in butternut squash, Worcestershire sauce, bay leaves, stevia, beef stock, canned tomatoes, and sage, and bring to a boil. Reduce heat, and simmer for 20 minutes.
2. Adjust the seasonings. Split into bowls and enjoy.

Nutrition Info:
- Per Servings 7.3g Carbs, 32g Protein, 17g Fat, 343 Calories

Beef And Feta Salad

Servings: 4 | Cooking Time: 35 Minutes

Ingredients:
- 3 tbsp olive oil
- ½ pound beef rump steak, cut into strips
- Salt and ground black pepper, to taste
- 1 tsp cumin
- A pinch of dried thyme
- 2 garlic cloves, minced
- 4 ounces feta cheese, crumbled
- ½ cup pecans, toasted
- 2 cups spinach
- 1½ tbsp lemon juice
- ¼ cup fresh mint, chopped

Directions:
1. Season the beef with salt, 1 tbsp of olive oil, garlic, thyme, black pepper, and cumin. Place on preheated grill over medium-high heat, and cook for 10 minutes, flip once. Sprinkle the pecans on a lined baking sheet, place in the oven at 350ºF, and toast for 10 minutes.
2. Remove the grilled beef to a cutting board, leave to cool, and slice into strips.
3. In a salad bowl, combine the spinach with pepper, mint, remaining olive oil, salt, lemon juice, feta cheese, and pecans, and toss well to coat. Top with the beef slices and enjoy.

Nutrition Info:
- Per Servings 3.5g Carbs, 17g Protein, 43g Fat, 434 Calories

Garlicky Beef Stew

Servings: 5 | Cooking Time: 2h 30mins

Ingredients:
- 4 slices bacon, cut into small pieces
- 2 1/2 pounds boneless beef chuck, cut into 2-inch pieces
- 2 onions, coarsely chopped
- 2 1/2 cups chicken stock, or as needed to cover
- 4 sprigs fresh thyme
- 4 cloves garlic, minced
- 1 1/2 teaspoon salt
- 1/2 teaspoon freshly ground black pepper, or to taste

Directions:
1. In a skillet over medium-high heat, cook bacon for 3 to 4 minutes. Turn off heat and transfer bacon into a stew pot.
2. Season beef chuck cubes with 1 teaspoon salt and black pepper to taste. Then broil beef pieces for 5 minutes on High.
3. Add beef in stew pot with bacon. Lower the heat to medium; cook and stir onions for 5 to 8 minutes; season with a large pinch of salt. Mix in the garlic, saute for 1 minute; stir in tomato paste, thyme sprigs, 1/2 teaspoon black pepper, and enough chicken broth in a skillet. Reduce heat to low and cover. Simmer stew about 2 hours.
4. Remove cover and bring stew to a boil on Medium and cook for 15 to 20 minutes.
5. Remove and discard thyme sprigs and sprinkle salt and pepper to taste.

Nutrition Info:
- Per Servings 11.3g Carbs, 29.4g Protein, 24.6g Fat, 528 Calories

Filling Beefy Soup

Servings: 4 | Cooking Time: 15 Minutes

Ingredients:
- 1 small onion, diced
- 3 cloves of garlic, minced
- 1-pound lean ground sirloin
- 3 cups low-sodium beef broth
- 1 bag frozen vegetables of your choice
- 5 tablespoons oil
- Black pepper and salt to taste

Directions:
1. In a large saucepan, heat the oil over medium heat and sauté the onion and garlic until fragrant.
2. Stir in the lean ground sirloin and cook for 3 minutes until lightly golden.
3. Add in the rest of the ingredients and bring the broth to a boil for 10 minutes.
4. Serve warm.

Nutrition Info:
- Per Servings 5.0g Carbs, 29.0g Protein, 34.0g Fat, 334 Calories

Hot Pork With Dill Pickles

Servings: 4 | Cooking Time: 20 Minutes

Ingredients:
- ¼ cup lime juice
- 4 pork chops
- 1 tbsp coconut oil, melted
- 2 garlic cloves, minced
- 1 tbsp chili powder
- 1 tsp ground cinnamon
- 2 tsp cumin
- Salt and black pepper, to taste
- ½ tsp hot pepper sauce
- 4 dill pickles, cut into spears and squeezed

Directions:
1. Using a bowl, combine the lime juice with oil, cumin, salt, hot pepper sauce, pepper, cinnamon, garlic, and chili powder. Place in the pork chops, toss to coat, and refrigerate for 4 hours.
2. Arrange the pork on a preheated grill over medium heat, cook for 7 minutes, turn, add in the dill pickles, and cook for another 7 minutes. Split among serving plates and enjoy.

Nutrition Info:
- Per Servings 2.3g Carbs, 36g Protein, 18g Fat, 315 Calories

Spicy Pork Stew With Spinach

Servings: 4 | Cooking Time: 40 Minutes

Ingredients:
- 1 lb. pork butt, cut into chunks
- 1 onion, chopped
- 4 cloves of garlic, minced
- 1 cup coconut milk, freshly squeezed
- 1 cup spinach leaves, washed and rinsed
- Salt and pepper to taste
- 1 cup water

Directions:
1. In a heavy-bottomed pot, add all ingredients, except for coconut milk and spinach. Mix well.
2. Cover and cook on medium-high fire until boiling. Lower fire to a simmer and cook for 30 minutes undisturbed.
3. Add remaining ingredients and cook on high fire uncovered for 5 minutes. Adjust seasoning if needed.
4. Serve and enjoy.

Nutrition Info:
- Per Servings 7.2g Carbs, 30.5g Protein, 34.4g Fat, 458 Calories

Italian Beef Ragout

Servings: 4 | Cooking Time: 1 Hour 52 Minutes

Ingredients:
- 1 lb chuck steak, trimmed and cubed
- 2 tbsp olive oil
- Salt and black pepper to taste
- 2 tbsp almond flour
- 1 medium onion, diced
- ½ cup dry white wine
- 1 red bell pepper, seeded and diced
- 2 tsp sugar-free Worcestershire sauce
- 4 oz tomato puree
- 3 tsp smoked paprika
- 1 cup beef broth
- Thyme leaves to garnish

Directions:
1. First, lightly dredge the meat in the almond flour and set aside. Place a large skillet over medium heat, add 1 tablespoon of oil to heat and then sauté the onion, and bell pepper for 3 minutes. Stir in the paprika, and add the remaining olive oil.
2. Add the beef and cook for 10 minutes in total while turning them halfway. Stir in white wine, let it reduce by half, about 3 minutes, and add Worcestershire sauce, tomato puree, and beef broth.
3. Let the mixture boil for 2 minutes, then reduce the heat to lowest and let simmer for 1 ½ hours; stirring now and then. Adjust the taste and dish the ragout. Serve garnished with thyme leaves.

Nutrition Info:
- Per Servings 4.2g Carbs, 36.6g Protein, 21.6g Fat, 328 Calories

Pork Medallion With Herbes De Provence

Servings: 2 | Cooking Time: 15 Minutes

Ingredients:
- 8 ounces of pork medallion, trimmed from fat
- ½ teaspoon Herbes de Provence
- ¼ cup dry white wine
- Freshly ground black pepper to taste
- Salt to taste

Directions:
1. Season the meat with black pepper.
2. Place the meat in between sheets of wax paper and pound

on a mallet until about ¼ inch thick.

3. In a nonstick skillet, sear the pork over medium heat for 5 minutes on each side or until the meat is slightly brown.

4. Remove meat from the skillet and sprinkle with herbes de Provence.

5. Using the same skillet, pour the wine and scrape the sides to deglaze. Allow simmering until the wine is reduced.

6. Pour the wine sauce over the pork.

7. Serve immediately.

Nutrition Info:
- Per Servings 1.0g Carbs, 24.0g Protein, 24.0g Fat, 316 Calories

Pork Casserole

Servings: 4 | Cooking Time: 38 Minutes

Ingredients:
- 1 lb ground pork
- 1 large yellow squash, thinly sliced
- Salt and black pepper to taste
- 1 clove garlic, minced
- 4 green onions, chopped
- 1 cup chopped cremini mushrooms
- 1 can diced tomatoes
- ½ cup pork rinds, crushed
- ¼ cup chopped parsley
- 1 cup cottage cheese
- 1 cup Mexican cheese blend
- 3 tbsp olive oil
- ⅓ cup water

Directions:
1. Preheat the oven to 370ºF.
2. Heat the olive oil in a skillet over medium heat, add the pork, season it with salt and pepper, and cook for 3 minutes or until no longer pink. Stir occasionally while breaking any lumps apart.
3. Add the garlic, half of the green onions, mushrooms, and 2 tablespoons of pork rinds. Continue cooking for 3 minutes. Stir in the tomatoes, half of the parsley, and water. Cook further for 3 minutes, and then turn the heat off.
4. Mix the remaining parsley, cottage cheese, and Mexican cheese blend. Set aside. Sprinkle the bottom of a baking dish with 3 tablespoons of pork rinds; top with half of the squash and a season of salt, 2/3 of the pork mixture, and the cheese mixture. Repeat the layering process a second time to exhaust the ingredients.
5. Cover the baking dish with foil and put in the oven to bake for 20 minutes. After, remove the foil and brown the top of the casserole with the broiler side of the oven for 2 minutes. Remove the dish when ready and serve the casserole warm.

Nutrition Info:
- Per Servings 2.7g Carbs, 36.5g Protein, 29g Fat, 495 Calories

Old-style Beef Stew

Servings: 5 | Cooking Time: 40 Minutes

Ingredients:
- 1 ½-pounds beef stew meat, cubed into 1-inch squares
- 16-ounce fresh cremini mushrooms
- 3 medium tomatoes, chopped
- 1 envelope reduced-sodium onion soup mix
- 5 tablespoons butter
- 1 cup water
- Pepper and salt to taste

Directions:
1. Add all ingredients in a pot on high fire and bring to a boil.
2. Once boiling, lower fire to a simmer and cook for 25 minutes.
3. Adjust seasoning to taste.
4. Serve and enjoy.

Nutrition Info:
- Per Servings 11.5g Carbs, 58g Protein, 27.8g Fat, 551 Calories

Sweet Chipotle Grilled Ribs

Servings: 4 | Cooking Time: 32 Minutes

Ingredients:
- 2 tbsp erythritol
- Pink salt and black pepper to taste
- 1 tbsp olive oil
- 3 tsp chipotle powder
- 1 tsp garlic powder
- 1 lb spare ribs
- 4 tbsp sugar-free BBQ sauce + extra for serving

Directions:
1. Mix the erythritol, salt, pepper, oil, chipotle, and garlic powder. Brush on the meaty sides of the ribs and wrap in foil. Sit for 30 minutes to marinate.
2. Preheat oven to 400ºF, place wrapped ribs on a baking sheet, and cook for 40 minutes to be cooked through. Remove ribs and aluminium foil, brush with BBQ sauce, and brown under the broiler for 10 minutes on both sides. Slice and serve with extra BBQ sauce and lettuce tomato salad.

Nutrition Info:
- Per Servings 3g Carbs, 21g Protein, 33g Fat, 395 Calories

Pork Burgers With Caramelized Onion Rings

Servings: 6 | Cooking Time: 20 Minutes

Ingredients:
- 2 lb ground pork
- Pink salt and chili pepper to taste
- 3 tbsp olive oil
- 1 tbsp butter
- 1 white onion, sliced into rings
- 1 tbsp balsamic vinegar
- 3 drops liquid stevia
- 6 low carb burger buns, halved
- 2 firm tomatoes, sliced into rings

Directions:

1. Combine the pork, salt and chili pepper in a bowl and mold out 6 patties.

2. Heat the olive oil in a skillet over medium heat and fry the patties for 4 to 5 minutes on each side until golden brown on the outside. Remove onto a plate and sit for 3 minutes.

3. Meanwhile, melt butter in a skillet over medium heat, sauté the onions for 2 minutes to be soft, and stir in the balsamic vinegar and liquid stevia.

4. Cook for 30 seconds stirring once or twice until caramelized. In each bun, place a patty, top with some onion rings and 2 tomato rings. Serve the burgers with cheddar cheese dip.

Nutrition Info:

- Per Servings 7.6g Carbs, 26g Protein, 32g Fat, 445 Calories

Beef Steak Filipino Style

Servings: 6 | Cooking Time: 25 Minutes

Ingredients:

- 2 tablespoons coconut oil
- 1 onion, sliced
- 4 beef steaks
- 2 tablespoons lemon juice, freshly squeezed
- ¼ cup coconut aminos
- 1 tsp salt
- Pepper to taste

Directions:

1. In a nonstick fry pan, heat oil on medium-high fire.

2. Pan-fry beef steaks and season with coconut aminos.

3. Cook until dark brown, around 7 minutes per side. Transfer to a plate.

4. Sauté onions in the same pan until caramelized, around 8 minutes. Season with lemon juice and return steaks in the pan. Mix well.

5. Serve and enjoy.

Nutrition Info:

- Per Servings 0.7g Carbs, 25.3g Protein, 27.1g Fat, 347 Calories

Lamb Shashlyk

Servings: 4 | Cooking Time: 20 Minutes

Ingredients:

- 1 pound ground lamb
- ¼ tsp cinnamon
- 1 egg
- 1 grated onion
- Salt and ground black pepper, to taste

Directions:

1. Place all ingredients in a bowl. Mix with your hands to combine well. Divide the meat into 4 pieces. Shape all meat portions around previously-soaked skewers. Preheat your grill to medium and grill the kebabs for about 5 minutes per side.

Nutrition Info:

- Per Servings 3.2g Carbs, 27g Protein, 37g Fat, 467 Calories

Bacon Stew With Cauliflower

Servings: 6 | Cooking Time: 40 Minutes

Ingredients:

- 8 ounces mozzarella cheese, grated
- 2 cups chicken broth
- ½ tsp garlic powder
- ½ tsp onion powder
- Salt and black pepper, to taste
- 4 garlic cloves, minced
- ¼ cup heavy cream
- 3 cups bacon, chopped
- 1 head cauliflower, cut into florets

Directions:

1. In a pot, combine the bacon with broth, cauliflower, salt, heavy cream, pepper, garlic powder, cheese, onion powder, and garlic, and cook for 35 minutes, share into serving plates, and enjoy.

Nutrition Info:

- Per Servings 6g Carbs, 33g Protein, 25g Fat, 380 Calories

Veal Stew

Servings: 6 | Cooking Time: 2 Hours

Ingredients:

- 2 tbsp olive oil
- 3 pounds veal shoulder, cubed
- 1 onion, chopped
- 1 garlic clove, minced
- Salt and black pepper, to taste
- 1 cup water
- 1 ½ cups red wine
- 12 ounces canned tomato sauce
- 1 carrot, chopped
- 1 cup mushrooms, chopped
- ½ cup green beans
- 2 tsp dried oregano

Directions:

1. Set a pot over medium-high heat and warm the oil. Brown the veal for 5-6 minutes. Stir in the onion, and garlic, and cook for 3 minutes. Place in the wine, oregano, carrots, pepper, salt, tomato sauce, water, and mushrooms, bring to a boil, reduce the heat to low.

2. Cook for 1 hour and 45 minutes, then in the green beans and cook for 5 minutes. Season with more black pepper and salt, split among serving bowls to serve.

Nutrition Info:

- Per Servings 5.2g Carbs, 44g Protein, 21g Fat, 415 Calories

Beef Italian Sandwiches

Servings: 6 | Cooking Time: 40 Minutes

Ingredients:
- 6 Provolone cheese slices
- 14.5-ounce can beef broth
- 8-ounces giardiniera drained (Chicago-style Italian sandwich mix)
- 3-pounds chuck roast fat trimmed and cut into large pieces
- 6 large lettuce
- Pepper and salt to taste

Directions:
1. Add all ingredients in a pot, except for lettuce and cheese, on high fire, and bring to a boil.
2. Once boiling, lower fire to a simmer and cook for 25 minutes.
3. Adjust seasoning to taste.
4. To make a sandwich, add warm shredded beef in one lettuce leaf and top with cheese.

Nutrition Info:
- Per Servings 3.9g Carbs, 48.6g Protein, 36.4g Fat, 538 Calories

Smoky Baby Back Ribs

Servings: 4 | Cooking Time: 40 Minutes

Ingredients:
- 1 ½ teaspoon barbecue sauce
- 1 ½ teaspoon hoisin sauce
- ½ teaspoon smoked paprika
- 2 ½ pounds baby back ribs
- 1 cup water
- Pepper and salt to taste

Directions:
1. Add all ingredients in a pot on high fire and bring to a boil.
2. Once boiling, lower fire to a simmer and cook for 35 minutes.
3. Adjust seasoning to taste.
4. Serve and enjoy.

Nutrition Info:
- Per Servings 3.7g Carbs, 53.2g Protein, 55.0g Fat, 723 Calories

Garlicky Pork With Bell Peppers

Servings: 4 | Cooking Time: 40 Minutes

Ingredients:
- 3 tbsp butter
- 4 pork steaks, bone-in
- 1 cup chicken stock
- Salt and ground black pepper, to taste
- A pinch of lemon pepper
- 3 tbsp olive oil
- 6 garlic cloves, minced
- 2 tbsp fresh parsley, chopped
- 4 bell peppers, sliced
- 1 lemon, sliced

Directions:

1. Heat a pan with 2 tablespoons oil and 2 tablespoons butter over medium-high heat. Add in the pork steaks, season with pepper and salt, cook until browned; remove to a plate. In the same pan, warm the rest of the oil and butter, add garlic and bell pepper and cook for 4 minutes.
2. Pour the chicken stock, lemon slices, salt, lemon pepper, and black pepper, and cook everything for 5 minutes. Return the pork steaks to the pan and cook for 10 minutes. Split the sauce and steaks among plates and enjoy.

Nutrition Info:
- Per Servings 6g Carbs, 40g Protein, 25g Fat, 456 Calories

Beef Zucchini Boats

Servings: 4 | Cooking Time: 45 Minutes

Ingredients:
- 2 garlic cloves, minced
- 1 tsp cumin
- 1 tbsp olive oil
- 1 pound ground beef
- ½ cup onion, chopped
- 1 tsp smoked paprika
- Salt and ground black pepper, to taste
- 4 zucchinis
- ¼ cup fresh cilantro, chopped
- ½ cup Monterey Jack cheese, shredded
- 1½ cups enchilada sauce
- 1 avocado, chopped, for serving
- Green onions, chopped, for serving
- Tomatoes, chopped, for serving

Directions:

1. Set a pan over high heat and warm the oil. Add the onions, and cook for 2 minutes. Stir in the beef, and brown for 4-5 minutes. Stir in the paprika, pepper, garlic, cumin, and salt; cook for 2 minutes.
2. Slice the zucchini in half lengthwise and scoop out the seeds. Set the zucchini in a greased baking pan, stuff each with the beef, scatter enchilada sauce on top, and spread with the Monterey cheese.
3. Bake in the oven at 350ºF for 20 minutes while covered. Uncover, spread with cilantro, and bake for 5 minutes. Top with tomatoes, green onions and avocado, place on serving plates and enjoy.

Nutrition Info:
- Per Servings 7.8g Carbs, 39g Protein, 33g Fat, 422 Calories

Lettuce Taco Carnitas

Servings: 12 | Cooking Time: 40 Minutes

Ingredients:
- 2 cups shredded Colby-Monterey jack cheese
- 1 can green chilies and diced tomatoes, undrained
- 1 envelope taco seasoning
- 1 boneless pork shoulder butt roast
- Lettuce leaves
- Pepper and salt to taste
- 1 cup water

Directions:

1. Add all ingredients in a pot, except for cheese and lettuce leaves, on high fire, and bring to a boil.
2. Once boiling, lower fire to a simmer and cook for 35 minutes.
3. Adjust seasoning to taste.
4. To serve, add a good amount of shredded pork into the center of one lettuce leaf. Top it with cheese, roll, and enjoy.

Nutrition Info:
- Per Servings 1.7g Carbs, 28.5g Protein, 10.4g Fat, 214 Calories

Paprika Pork Chops

Servings: 4 | Cooking Time: 25 Minutes

Ingredients:
- 4 pork chops
- Salt and black pepper, to taste
- 3 tbsp paprika
- ¾ cup cumin powder
- 1 tsp chili powder

Directions:
1. Using a bowl, combine the paprika with pepper, cumin, salt, and chili. Place in the pork chops and rub them well. Heat a grill over medium temperature, add in the pork chops, cook for 5 minutes, flip, and cook for 5 minutes. Serve with steamed veggies.

Nutrition Info:
- Per Servings 4g Carbs, 41.8g Protein, 18.5g Fat, 349 Calories

Oregano Pork Chops With Spicy Tomato Sauce

Servings: 4 | Cooking Time: 50 Minutes

Ingredients:
- 4 pork chops
- 1 tbsp fresh oregano, chopped
- 2 garlic cloves, minced
- 1 tbsp canola oil
- 15 ounces canned diced tomatoes
- 1 tbsp tomato paste
- Salt and black pepper, to taste
- ¼ cup tomato juice
- 1 red chili, finely chopped

Directions:
1. Set a pan over medium-high heat and warm oil, place in the pork chops, season with pepper and salt, cook for 3 minutes, turn and cook for another 3 minutes; remove to a bowl. Add in the garlic, and cook for 30 seconds.
2. Stir in the tomato paste, tomatoes, tomato juice, and chili; bring to a boil, and reduce heat to medium-low. Place in the pork chops, cover pan and simmer everything for 30 minutes.
3. Remove the pork chops to plates and sprinkle with fresh oregano to serve.

Nutrition Info:
- Per Servings 3.6g Carbs, 39g Protein, 21g Fat, 410 Calories

Onion Swiss Steak

Servings: 6 | Cooking Time: 30 Minutes

Ingredients:
- 1 ½ pounds beef round steak, sliced
- 1 medium onion, sliced
- 2 bay leaves
- ¼ cup coconut oil
- 1/2 cup water
- Salt and pepper to taste

Directions:
1. Place all ingredients in a heavy-bottomed pot on high fire and bring to a boil.
2. Once boiling, lower fire to a simmer.
3. Simmer for 30 minutes.
4. Serve and enjoy.

Nutrition Info:
- Per Servings 0.9g Carbs, 19.3g Protein, 25.3g Fat, 308 Calories

White Wine Lamb Chops

Servings: 6 | Cooking Time: 1 Hour And 25 Minutes

Ingredients:
- 6 lamb chops
- 1 tbsp sage
- 1 tsp thyme
- 1 onion, sliced
- 3 garlic cloves, minced
- 2 tbsp olive oil
- ½ cup white wine
- Salt and black pepper, to taste

Directions:
1. Heat the olive oil in a pan. Add onion and garlic and cook for 3 minutes, until soft. Rub the sage and thyme over the lamb chops. Cook the lamb for about 3 minutes per side. Set aside.
2. Pour the white wine and 1 cup of water into the pan, bring the mixture to a boil. Cook until the liquid is reduced by half. Add the chops in the pan, reduce the heat, and let simmer for 1 hour.

Nutrition Info:
- Per Servings 4.3g Carbs, 16g Protein, 30g Fat, 397 Calories

Chapter 7 Soups, Stew & Salads Recipes

Chapter 7 Soups, Stew & Salads Recipes

Cream Of Thyme Tomato Soup

Servings: 6 | Cooking Time: 20 Minutes

Ingredients:
- 2 tbsp ghee
- 2 large red onions, diced
- ½ cup raw cashew nuts, diced
- 2 cans tomatoes
- 1 tsp fresh thyme leaves + extra to garnish
- 1 ½ cups water
- Salt and black pepper to taste
- 1 cup heavy cream

Directions:
1. Melt ghee in a pot over medium heat and sauté the onions for 4 minutes until softened.
2. Stir in the tomatoes, thyme, water, cashews, and season with salt and black pepper. Cover and bring to simmer for 10 minutes until thoroughly cooked.
3. Open, turn the heat off, and puree the ingredients with an immersion blender. Adjust to taste and stir in the heavy cream. Spoon into soup bowls and serve with low carb parmesan cheese toasts.

Nutrition Info:
- Per Servings 3g Carbs, 11g Protein, 27g Fat, 310 Calories

Celery Salad

Servings: 4 | Cooking Time: 0 Minutes

Ingredients:
- 3 cups celery, thinly sliced
- ½ cup parmigiana cheese, shaved
- 1/3 cup toasted walnuts
- 4 tablespoons extra virgin olive oil
- 1 tablespoon red wine vinegar
- Salt and pepper to taste

Directions:
1. Place the celery, cheese, and walnuts in a bowl.
2. In a smaller bowl, combine the olive oil and vinegar. Season with salt and pepper to taste. Whisk to combine everything.
3. Drizzle over the celery, cheese, and walnuts. Toss to coat.

Nutrition Info:
- Per Servings 3.6g Carbs, 4.3g Protein, 14g Fat, 156 Calories

Coconut Cauliflower Soup

Servings: 10 | Cooking Time: 26 Minutes

Ingredients:
- 1 medium onion, finely chopped
- 3 tablespoons yellow curry paste
- 2 medium heads cauliflower, broken into florets
- 1 carton vegetable broth
- 1 cup coconut milk
- 2 tablespoons olive oil

Directions:
1. In a large saucepan, heat oil over medium heat. Add onion; cook and stir until softened, 2-3 minutes.
2. Add curry paste; cook until fragrant, 1-2 minutes.
3. Add cauliflower and broth. Increase heat to high; bring to a boil. Reduce heat to medium-low; cook, covered, about 20 minutes.
4. Stir in coconut milk; cook an additional minute.
5. Remove from heat; cool slightly.
6. Puree in batches in a blender or food processor.
7. If desired, top with minced fresh cilantro.

Nutrition Info:
- Per Servings 10g Carbs, 3g Protein, 8g Fat, 111 Calories

Caesar Salad With Smoked Salmon And Poached Eggs

Servings: 4 | Cooking Time: 15 Minutes

Ingredients:
- 3 cups water
- 8 eggs
- 2 cups torn romaine lettuce
- ½ cup smoked salmon, chopped
- 6 slices bacon
- 2 tbsp Heinz low carb Caesar dressing

Directions:
1. Boil the water in a pot over medium heat for 5 minutes and bring to simmer. Crack each egg into a small bowl and gently slide into the water. Poach for 2 to 3 minutes, remove with a perforated spoon, transfer to a paper towel to dry, and plate. Poach the remaining 7 eggs.
2. Put the bacon in a skillet and fry over medium heat until browned and crispy, about 6 minutes, turning once. Remove, allow cooling, and chop in small pieces.
3. Toss the lettuce, smoked salmon, bacon, and caesar dressing in a salad bowl. Divide the salad into 4 plates, top with two eggs each, and serve immediately or chilled.

Nutrition Info:
- Per Servings 5g Carbs, 8g Protein, 21g Fat, 260 Calories

Pumpkin & Meat Peanut Stew

Servings: 6 | Cooking Time: 45 Minutes

Ingredients:
- 1 cup pumpkin puree
- 2 pounds chopped pork stew meat
- 1 tbsp peanut butter
- 4 tbsp chopped peanuts
- 1 garlic clove, minced
- ½ cup chopped onion
- ½ cup white wine
- 1 tbsp olive oil

- 1 tsp lemon juice
- ¼ cup granulated sweetener
- ¼ tsp cardamom
- ¼ tsp allspice
- 2 cups water
- 2 cups chicken stock

Directions:

1. Heat the olive oil in a large pot and sauté onion for 3 minutes, until translucent. Add garlic and cook for 30 more seconds. Add the pork and cook until browned, about 5-6 minutes, stirring occasionally. Pour in the wine and cook for one minute.

2. Add in the remaining ingredients, except for the lemon juice and peanuts. Bring the mixture to a boil, and cook for 5 minutes. Reduce the heat to low, cover the pot, and let cook for about 30 minutes. Adjust seasoning and stir in the lemon juice before serving.

3. Ladle into serving bowls and serve topped with peanuts.

Nutrition Info:
- Per Servings 4g Carbs, 27.5g Protein, 33g Fat, 451 Calories

Mushroom Soup

Servings: 8 | Cooking Time: 35 Minutes

Ingredients:
- 1-pound baby portobello mushrooms, chopped
- 2 tablespoons olive oil
- 1 carton reduced-sodium beef broth
- 2 cups heavy whipping cream
- 4 tablespoons butter
- 1/2 cup water

Directions:

1. In a Dutch oven, sauté mushrooms in oil and butter until tender.

2. Add the contents of seasoning packets, broth, and water. Bring to a boil.

3. Reduce heat; cover and simmer for 25 minutes.

4. Add cream and heat through.

Nutrition Info:
- Per Servings 3.6g Carbs, 8g Protein, 26g Fat, 280 Calories

Power Green Soup

Servings: 6 | Cooking Time: 30 Minutes

Ingredients:
- 1 broccoli head, chopped
- 1 cup spinach
- 1 onion, chopped
- 2 garlic cloves, minced
- ½ cup watercress
- 5 cups veggie stock
- 1 cup coconut milk
- 1 tsp salt
- 1 tbsp ghee
- 1 bay leaf
- Salt and black pepper, to taste

Directions:

1. Melt the ghee in a large pot over medium heat. Add onion

and cook for 3 minutes. Add garlic and cook for another minute. Add broccoli and cook for an additional 5 minutes.

2. Pour the stock over and add the bay leaf. Close the lid, bring to a boil, and reduce the heat. Simmer for about 3 minutes.

3. In the end, add spinach and watercress, and cook for 3 more minutes. Stir in the coconut cream, salt and pepper. Discard the bay leaf, and blend the soup with a hand blender.

Nutrition Info:
- Per Servings 5.8g Carbs, 4.9g Protein, 37.6g Fat, 392 Calories

Mediterranean Salad

Servings: 4 | Cooking Time: 10 Minutes

Ingredients:
- 3 tomatoes, sliced
- 1 large avocado, sliced
- 8 kalamata olives
- ¼ lb buffalo mozzarella cheese, sliced
- 2 tbsp pesto sauce
- 2 tbsp olive oil

Directions:

1. Arrange the tomato slices on a serving platter and place the avocado slices in the middle. Arrange the olives around the avocado slices and drop pieces of mozzarella on the platter. Drizzle the pesto sauce all over, and drizzle olive oil as well.

Nutrition Info:
- Per Servings 4.3g Carbs, 9g Protein, 25g Fat, 290 Calories

Bacon And Spinach Salad

Servings: 4 | Cooking Time: 20 Minutes

Ingredients:
- 2 large avocados, 1 chopped and 1 sliced
- 1 spring onion, sliced
- 4 cooked bacon slices, crumbled
- 2 cups spinach
- 2 small lettuce heads, chopped
- 2 hard-boiled eggs, chopped
- Vinaigrette:
- 3 tbsp olive oil
- 1 tsp Dijon mustard
- 1 tbsp apple cider vinegar

Directions:

1. Combine the spinach, lettuce, eggs, chopped avocado, and spring onion, in a large bowl. Whisk together the vinaigrette ingredients in another bowl.

2. Pour the dressing over, toss to combine and top with the sliced avocado and bacon.

Nutrition Info:
- Per Servings 3.4g Carbs, 7g Protein, 33g Fat, 350 Calories

Balsamic Cucumber Salad

Servings: 6 | Cooking Time: 0 Minutes

Ingredients:
- 1 large English cucumber, halved and sliced
- 1 cup grape tomatoes, halved
- 1 medium red onion, sliced thinly
- ¼ cup balsamic vinaigrette
- ¾ cup feta cheese
- Salt and pepper to taste
- ¼ cup olive oil

Directions:
1. Place all ingredients in a bowl.
2. Toss to coat everything with the dressing.
3. Allow chilling before serving.

Nutrition Info:
- Per Servings 9g Carbs, 4.8g Protein, 16.7g Fat, 253 Calories

Green Salad With Bacon And Blue Cheese

Servings: 4 | Cooking Time: 15 Minutes

Ingredients:
- 2 pack mixed salad greens
- 8 strips bacon
- 1 ½ cups crumbled blue cheese
- 1 tbsp white wine vinegar
- 3 tbsp extra virgin olive oil
- Salt and black pepper to taste

Directions:
1. Pour the salad greens in a salad bowl; set aside. Fry bacon strips in a skillet over medium heat for 6 minutes, until browned and crispy. Chop the bacon and scatter over the salad. Add in half of the cheese, toss and set aside.
2. In a small bowl, whisk the white wine vinegar, olive oil, salt, and black pepper until dressing is well combined. Drizzle half of the dressing over the salad, toss, and top with remaining cheese. Divide salad into four plates and serve with crusted chicken fries along with remaining dressing.

Nutrition Info:
- Per Servings 2g Carbs, 4g Protein, 20g Fat, 205 Calories

Salsa Verde Chicken Soup

Servings: 4 | Cooking Time: 15 Minutes

Ingredients:
- ½ cup salsa verde
- 2 cups cooked and shredded chicken
- 2 cups chicken broth
- 1 cup shredded cheddar cheese
- 4 ounces cream cheese
- ½ tsp chili powder
- ½ tsp ground cumin
- ½ tsp fresh cilantro, chopped
- Salt and black pepper, to taste

Directions:
1. Combine the cream cheese, salsa verde, and broth, in a food processor; pulse until smooth. Transfer the mixture to a pot and place over medium heat. Cook until hot, but do not bring to a boil.
2. Add chicken, chili powder, and cumin and cook for about 3-5 minutes, or until it is heated through.
3. Stir in Cheddar cheese and season with salt and pepper to taste. If it is very thick, add a few tablespoons of water and boil for 1-3 more minutes. Serve hot in bowls sprinkled with fresh cilantro.

Nutrition Info:
- Per Servings 3g Carbs, 25g Protein, 23g Fat, 346 Calories

Bacon Tomato Salad

Servings: 6 | Cooking Time: 0 Minutes

Ingredients:
- 6 ounces iceberg lettuce blend
- 2 cups grape tomatoes, halved
- ¾ cup coleslaw salad dressing
- ¾ cup cheddar cheese, shredded
- 12 bacon strips, cooked and crumbled
- Salt and pepper to taste

Directions:
1. Put the lettuce and tomatoes in a salad bowl.
2. Drizzle with the dressing and sprinkle with cheese. Season with salt and pepper to taste then mix.
3. Garnish with bacon bits on top.

Nutrition Info:
- Per Servings 8g Carbs, 10g Protein, 20g Fat, 268 Calories

Grilled Steak Salad With Pickled Peppers

Servings: 4 | Cooking Time: 15 Minutes

Ingredients:
- 1 lb skirt steak, sliced
- Salt and black pepper to season
- 1 tsp olive oil
- 1 ½ cups mixed salad greens
- 3 chopped pickled peppers
- 2 tbsp red wine vinaigrette
- ½ cup crumbled queso fresco

Directions:
1. Brush the steak slices with olive oil and season with salt and pepper on both sides.
2. Heat frying pan over high heat and cook the steaks on each side to the desired doneness, for about 5-6 minutes. Remove to a bowl, cover and leave to rest while you make the salad.
3. Mix the salad greens, pickled peppers, and vinaigrette in a salad bowl. Add the beef and sprinkle with cheese. Serve the salad with roasted parsnips.

Nutrition Info:
- Per Servings 2g Carbs, 18g Protein, 26g Fat, 315 Calories

Mexican Soup

Servings: 4 | Cooking Time: 25 Minutes

Ingredients:
- 1-pound boneless skinless chicken thighs, cut into 3/4-inch pieces
- 1 tablespoon reduced-sodium taco seasoning
- 1 cup salsa
- 1 carton reduced-sodium chicken broth
- 4 tablespoons olive oil

Directions:
1. In a large saucepan, heat oil over medium-high heat. Add chicken; cook and stir 6-8 minutes or until no longer pink. Stir in taco seasoning.
2. Add remaining ingredients; bring to a boil. Reduce heat; simmer, uncovered, 5 minutes to allow flavors to blend. Skim fat before serving.

Nutrition Info:
- Per Servings 5.6g Carbs, 25g Protein, 16.5g Fat, 281 Calories

Lobster Salad With Mayo Dressing

Servings: 4 | Cooking Time: 1 Hour 10 Minutes

Ingredients:
- 1 small head cauliflower, cut into florets
- ⅓ cup diced celery
- ½ cup sliced black olives
- 2 cups cooked large shrimp
- 1 tbsp dill, chopped
- Dressing:
- ½ cup mayonnaise
- 1 tsp apple cider vinegar
- ¼ tsp celery seeds
- A pinch of black pepper
- 2 tbsp lemon juice
- 2 tsp swerve
- Salt to taste

Directions:
1. Combine the cauliflower, celery, shrimp, and dill in a large bowl. Whisk together the mayonnaise, vinegar, celery seeds, black pepper, sweetener, and lemon juice in another bowl. Season with salt to taste.
2. Pour the dressing over and gently toss to combine; refrigerate for 1 hour. Top with olives to serve.

Nutrition Info:
- Per Servings 2g Carbs, 12g Protein, 15g Fat, 182 Calories

Garlic Chicken Salad

Servings: 4 | Cooking Time: 15 Minutes

Ingredients:
- 2 chicken breasts, boneless, skinless, flattened
- Salt and black pepper to taste
- 2 tbsp garlic powder
- 1 tsp olive oil
- 1 ½ cups mixed salad greens
- 1 tbsp red wine vinegar
- 1 cup crumbled blue cheese

Directions:
1. Season the chicken with salt, black pepper, and garlic powder. Heat oil in a pan over high heat and fry the chicken for 4 minutes on both sides until golden brown. Remove chicken to a cutting board and let cool before slicing.
2. Toss salad greens with red wine vinegar and share the salads into 4 plates. Divide chicken slices on top and sprinkle with blue cheese. Serve salad with carrots fries.

Nutrition Info:
- Per Servings 4g Carbs, 14g Protein, 23g Fat, 286 Calories

Strawberry Salad With Spinach, Cheese & Almonds

Servings: 2 | Cooking Time: 20 Minutes

Ingredients:
- 4 cups spinach
- 4 strawberries, sliced
- ½ cup flaked almonds
- 1 ½ cup grated hard goat cheese
- 4 tbsp raspberry vinaigrette
- Salt and black pepper, to taste

Directions:
1. Preheat your oven to 400ºF. Arrange the grated goat cheese in two circles on two pieces of parchment paper. Place in the oven and bake for 10 minutes.
2. Find two same bowls, place them upside down, and carefully put the parchment paper on top to give the cheese a bowl-like shape. Let cool that way for 15 minutes. Divide spinach among the bowls stir in salt, pepper and drizzle with vinaigrette. Top with almonds and strawberries.

Nutrition Info:
- Per Servings 5.3g Carbs, 33g Protein, 34.2g Fat, 445 Calories

Simplified French Onion Soup

Servings: 5 | Cooking Time: 30 Minutes

Ingredients:
- 3 large onions, sliced
- 2 bay leaves
- 5 cups Beef Bone Broth
- 1 teaspoon dried thyme
- 1-oz Gruyere cheese, sliced into 5 equal pieces
- Pepper to taste
- 4 tablespoons oil

Directions:
1. Place a heavy-bottomed pot on medium-high fire and heat pot for 3 minutes.
2. Add oil and heat for 2 minutes. Stir in onions and sauté for 5 minutes.
3. Lower fire to medium-low, continue sautéing onions for 10 minutes until soft and browned, but not burned.
4. Add remaining ingredients and mix well.
5. Bring to a boil, lower fire to a simmer, cover and cook for 5 minutes.
6. Ladle into bowls, top with cheese.
7. Let it sit for 5 minutes.

8. Serve and enjoy.

Nutrition Info:
• Per Servings 9.9g Carbs, 4.3g Protein, 16.8g Fat, 208 Calories

Cobb Egg Salad In Lettuce Cups

Servings: 4 | Cooking Time: 20 Minutes

Ingredients:
• 2 chicken breasts, cut into pieces
• 1 tbsp olive oil
• Salt and black pepper to season
• 6 large eggs
• 1 ½ cups water
• 2 tomatoes, seeded, chopped
• 6 tbsp Greek yogurt
• 1 head green lettuce, firm leaves removed for cups

Directions:
1. Preheat oven to 400ºF. Put the chicken pieces in a bowl, drizzle with olive oil, and sprinkle with salt and black pepper. Mix the ingredients until the chicken is well coated with the seasoning.
2. Put the chicken on a prepared baking sheet and spread out evenly. Slide the baking sheet in the oven and bake the chicken until cooked through and golden brown for 8 minutes, turning once.
3. Bring the eggs to boil in salted water in a pot over medium heat for 6 minutes. Run the eggs in cold water, peel, and chop into small pieces. Transfer to a salad bowl.
4. Remove the chicken from the oven when ready and add to the salad bowl. Include the tomatoes and Greek yogurt; mix evenly with a spoon. Layer two lettuce leaves each as cups and fill with two tablespoons of egg salad each. Serve with chilled blueberry juice.

Nutrition Info:
• Per Servings 4g Carbs, 21g Protein, 24.5g Fat, 325 Calories

Green Mackerel Salad

Servings: 2 | Cooking Time: 25 Minutes

Ingredients:
• 2 mackerel fillets
• 2 hard-boiled eggs, sliced
• 1 tbsp coconut oil
• 2 cups green beans
• 1 avocado, sliced
• 4 cups mixed salad greens
• 2 tbsp olive oil
• 2 tbsp lemon juice
• 1 tsp Dijon mustard
• Salt and black pepper, to taste

Directions:
1. Fill a saucepan with water and add the green beans and salt. Cook over medium heat for about 3 minutes. Drain and set aside.
2. Melt the coconut oil in a pan over medium heat. Add the mackerel fillets and cook for about 4 minutes per side, or until opaque and crispy. Divide the green beans between two salad bowls. Top with mackerel, egg, and avocado slices.

3. In a bowl, whisk together the lemon juice, olive oil, mustard, salt, and pepper, and drizzle over the salad.

Nutrition Info:
• Per Servings 7.6g Carbs, 27.3g Protein, 41.9g Fat, 525 Calories

Citrusy Brussels Sprouts Salad

Servings: 6 | Cooking Time: 3 Minutes

Ingredients:
• 2 tablespoons olive oil
• ¾ pound Brussels sprouts
• 1 cup walnuts
• Juice from 1 lemon
• ½ cup grated parmesan cheese
• Salt and pepper to taste

Directions:
1. Heat oil in a skillet over medium flame and sauté the Brussels sprouts for 3 minutes until slightly wilted. Removed from heat and allow to cool.
2. In a bowl, toss together the cooled Brussels sprouts and the rest of the ingredients.
3. Toss to coat.

Nutrition Info:
• Per Servings 8g Carbs, 6g Protein, 23g Fat, 259 Calories

Chicken Creamy Soup

Servings: 4 | Cooking Time: 15 Minutes

Ingredients:
• 2 cups cooked and shredded chicken
• 3 tbsp butter, melted
• 4 cups chicken broth
• 4 tbsp chopped cilantro
• ⅓ cup buffalo sauce
• ½ cup cream cheese
• Salt and black pepper, to taste

Directions:
1. Blend the butter, buffalo sauce, and cream cheese, in a food processor, until smooth. Transfer to a pot, add the chicken broth and heat until hot but do not bring to a boil. Stir in chicken, salt, black pepper and cook until heated through. When ready, remove to soup bowls and serve garnished with cilantro.

Nutrition Info:
• Per Servings 5g Carbs, 26.5g Protein, 29.5g Fat, 406 Calories

Crispy Bacon Salad With Mozzarella & Tomato

Servings: 2 | Cooking Time: 10 Minutes

Ingredients:
• 1 large tomato, sliced
• 4 basil leaves
• 8 mozzarella cheese slices
• 2 tsp olive oil
• 6 bacon slices, chopped
• 1 tsp balsamic vinegar

- Sea salt, to taste

Directions:

1. Place the bacon in a skillet over medium heat and cook until crispy. Divide the tomato slices between two serving plates. Arrange the mozzarella slices over and top with the basil leaves. Add the crispy bacon on top, drizzle with olive oil and vinegar. Sprinkle with sea salt and serve.

Nutrition Info:
- Per Servings 1.5g Carbs, 21g Protein, 26g Fat, 279 Calories

Chicken Stock And Green Bean Soup

Servings: 6 | Cooking Time:1h 30 Mins

Ingredients:
- 2 tablespoons butter
- 1/2 onion, diced
- 2 ribs celery, diced
- 1 cup green beans
- 6 bacon slices
- What you'll need from the store cupboard:
- 3 cloves garlic, sliced
- 1 quart chicken stock
- 2 1/2 cups water
- 1 bay leaf
- Salt and ground black pepper to taste

Directions:

1. In a large pot over medium-low heat, melt the butter. Add the onions, celery, and sliced garlic, cook for 5-8 minutes, or until onions are soft.
2. Stir in in bacon slices, bay leaf, and green beans. Add chicken stock and water, stirring until well combined, and simmer for 1 hour and 15 minutes, or green beans are soft. Sprinkle with salt and black pepper before serving.

Nutrition Info:
- Per Servings 7g Carbs, 15.1g Protein, 11.3g Fat, 208.6 Calories

Strawberry, Mozzarella Salad

Servings: 3 | Cooking Time: 10 Minutes

Ingredients:
- 5 ounces organic salad greens of your choice
- 2 medium cucumber, spiralized
- 2 cups strawberries, hulled and chopped
- 8 ounces mini mozzarella cheese balls
- ½ cup balsamic vinegar
- 5 tablespoons olive oil
- Salt to taste

Directions:

1. Toss all ingredients in a salad bowl.
2. Allow chilling in the fridge for at least 10 minutes before serving.

Nutrition Info:
- Per Servings 10g Carbs, 7g Protein, 31g Fat, 351 Calories

Creamy Soup With Greens

Servings: 6 | Cooking Time: 20 Minutes

Ingredients:
- ½-pounds collard greens, torn to bite-sized pieces
- 5 cups chicken broth
- 2 cups broccoli florets
- 1 cup diced onion
- 3 tablespoon oil
- 4 tablespoons butter
- Salt and pepper to taste

Directions:

1. Add all ingredients to the pot and bring to a boil.
2. Lower fire to a simmer and simmer for 15 minutes while covered.
3. With an immersion blender, puree soup until creamy.
4. Adjust seasoning to taste.
5. Serve and enjoy.

Nutrition Info:
- Per Servings 6.5g Carbs, 50.6g Protein, 33.5g Fat, 548 Calories

Broccoli Cheese Soup

Servings: 4 | Cooking Time: 20 Minutes

Ingredients:
- ¾ cup heavy cream
- 1 onion, diced
- 1 tsp minced garlic
- 4 cups chopped broccoli
- 4 cups veggie broth
- 2 tbsp butter
- 2 ¾ cups grated cheddar cheese
- ¼ cup cheddar cheese to garnish
- Salt and black pepper, to taste
- ½ bunch fresh mint, chopped

Directions:

1. Melt the butter in a large pot over medium heat. Sauté onion and garlic for 3 minutes or until tender, stirring occasionally. Season with salt and pepper. Add the broth, broccoli and bring to a boil.
2. Reduce the heat and simmer for 10 minutes. Puree the soup with a hand blender until smooth. Add in the cheese and cook about 1 minute. Taste, season with salt and pepper. Stir in the heavy cream.Serve in bowls with the reserved grated Cheddar cheese and sprinkled with fresh mint.

Nutrition Info:
- Per Servings 7g Carbs, 23.8g Protein, 52.3g Fat, 561 Calories

Corn And Bacon Chowder

Servings: 8 | Cooking Time: 23 Minutes

Ingredients:
- ½ cup bacon, fried and crumbled
- 1 package celery, onion, and bell pepper mix
- 2 cups full-fat milk
- ½ cup sharp cheddar cheese, grated
- 5 tablespoons butter
- Pepper and salt to taste
- 1 cup water

Directions:
1. In a heavy-bottomed pot, melt butter.
2. Saute the bacon and celery for 3 minutes.
3. Turn fire on to medium. Add remaining ingredients and cook for 20 minutes until thick.
4. Serve and enjoy with a sprinkle of crumbled bacon.

Nutrition Info:
- Per Servings 4.4g Carbs, 16.6g Protein, 13.6g Fat, 210.5 Calories

Mushroom-broccoli Soup

Servings: 4 | Cooking Time: 20 Minutes

Ingredients:
- 1 onion, diced
- 3 cloves of garlic, diced
- 2 cups mushrooms, chopped
- 2 heads of broccoli, cut into florets
- 1 cup full-fat milk
- 3 cups water
- Pepper and salt to taste

Directions:
1. Place a heavy-bottomed pot on medium-high fire and heat for 3 minutes.
2. Add onion, garlic, water, and broccoli. Season generously with pepper and salt.
3. Cover and bring to a boil. Once boiling, lower fire to a simmer and let it cook for 7 minutes.
4. With a handheld blender, puree mixture until smooth and creamy.
5. Stir in mushrooms and milk, cover, and simmer for another 8 minutes.
6. Serve and enjoy.

Nutrition Info:
- Per Servings 8.5g Carbs, 3.8g Protein, 1.0g Fat, 58.2 Calories

Caesar Salad With Chicken And Parmesan

Servings: 4 | Cooking Time: 1 Hour And 30 Minutes

Ingredients:
- 4 boneless, skinless chicken thighs
- ¼ cup lemon juice
- 2 garlic cloves, minced
- 4 tbsp olive oil
- ½ cup caesar salad dressing, sugar-free
- 12 bok choy leaves
- 3 Parmesan crisps
- Parmesan cheese, grated for garnishing

Directions:
1. Combine the chicken, lemon juice, 2 tbsp of olive oil, and garlic in a Ziploc bag. Seal the bag, shake to combine, and refrigerate for 1 hour. Preheat the grill to medium heat and grill the chicken for about 4 minutes per side.
2. Cut the bok choy leaves lengthwise, and brush it with the remaining olive oil. Grill the bok choy for about 3 minutes. Place on a serving bowl. Top with the chicken and drizzle the caesar salad dressing over. Top with parmesan crisps and sprinkle the grated parmesan cheese over.

Nutrition Info:
- Per Servings 5g Carbs, 33g Protein, 39g Fat, 529 Calories

Traditional Greek Salad

Servings: 4 | Cooking Time: 10 Minutes

Ingredients:
- 5 tomatoes, chopped
- 1 large cucumber, chopped
- 1 green bell pepper, chopped
- 1 small red onion, chopped
- 16 kalamata olives, chopped
- 4 tbsp capers
- 1 cup feta cheese, chopped
- 1 tsp oregano, dried
- 4 tbsp olive oil
- Salt to taste

Directions:
1. Place tomatoes, bell pepper, cucumber, onion, feta cheese and olives in a bowl; mix to combine well. Season with salt. Combine capers, olive oil, and oregano, in a small bowl. Drizzle with the dressing to serve.

Nutrition Info:
- Per Servings 8g Carbs, 9.3g Protein, 28g Fat, 323 Calories

Kale And Brussels Sprouts

Servings: 6 | Cooking Time: 0 Minutes

Ingredients:
- 1 small bunch kale, thinly sliced
- ½ pound fresh Brussels sprouts, thinly sliced
- ½ cup pistachios, chopped coarsely
- ½ cup honey mustard salad dressing
- ¼ cup parmesan cheese, shredded
- Salt and pepper to taste

Directions:
1. Place all ingredients in a salad bowl.
2. Toss to coat everything.
3. Serve.

Nutrition Info:
- Per Servings 9g Carbs, 5g Protein, 15g Fat, 198 Calories

Minty Watermelon Cucumber

Servings: 12 | Cooking Time: 0 Minutes

Ingredients:
- 8 cups cubed seedless watermelon
- 2 English cucumbers, halved and sliced
- ¼ cup minced fresh mint
- ¼ cup balsamic vinegar
- ¼ cup olive oil
- Salt and pepper to taste

Directions:
1. Place everything in a bowl and toss to coat everything.
2. Allow chilling before serving.

Nutrition Info:
- Per Servings 4g Carbs, 0.5g Protein, 8.1g Fat, 95 Calories

Slow Cooker Beer Soup With Cheddar & Sausage

Servings: 8 | Cooking Time: 8 Hr

Ingredients:
- 1 cup heavy cream
- 10 ounces sausages, sliced
- 1 cup celery, chopped
- 1 cup carrots, chopped
- 4 garlic cloves, minced
- 8 ounces cream cheese
- 1 tsp red pepper flakes
- 6 ounces beer
- 16 ounces beef stock
- 1 onion, diced
- 1 cup cheddar cheese, grated
- Salt and black pepper, to taste
- Fresh cilantro, chopped, to garnish

Directions:
1. Turn on the slow cooker. Add beef stock, beer, sausages, carrots, onion, garlic, celery, salt, red pepper flakes, and black pepper, and stir to combine. Pour in enough water to cover all the ingredients by roughly 2 inches. Close the lid and cook for 6 hours on Low.
2. Open the lid and stir in the heavy cream, cheddar, and cream cheese, and cook for 2 more hours. Ladle the soup into bowls and garnish with cilantro before serving. Yummy!

Nutrition Info:
- Per Servings 4g Carbs, 5g Protein, 17g Fat, 244 Calories

Spicy Chicken Bean Soup

Servings: 8 | Cooking Time:1h 20 Mins

Ingredients:
- 8 skinless, boneless chicken breast halves
- 5 cubes chicken bouillon
- 2 cans peeled and diced tomatoes
- 1 container sour cream
- 1 cups frozen cut green beans
- 3 tablespoons. olive oil
- Salt and black pepper to taste
- 1 onion, chopped
- 3 cloves garlic, chopped
- 1 cups frozen cut green beans

Directions:
1. Heat olive oil in a large pot over medium heat, add onion, garlic and cook until tender. Stir in water, chicken, salt, pepper, bouillon cubes and bring to boil, simmer for 1 hour on Low. Remove chicken from the pot, reserve 5 cups broth and slice.
2. Stir in the remaining ingredients in the pot and simmer 30 minutes. Serve and enjoy.

Nutrition Info:
- Per Servings 7.6g Carbs, 26.5g Protein, 15.3g Fat, 275.1 Calories

Creamy Cauliflower Soup With Chorizo Sausage

Servings: 4 | Cooking Time: 40 Minutes

Ingredients:
- 1 cauliflower head, chopped
- 1 turnip, chopped
- 3 tbsp butter
- 1 chorizo sausage, sliced
- 2 cups chicken broth
- 1 small onion, chopped
- 2 cups water
- Salt and black pepper, to taste

Directions:
1. Melt 2 tbsp. of the butter in a large pot over medium heat. Stir in onion and cook until soft and golden, about 3-4 minutes. Add cauliflower and turnip, and cook for another 5 minutes.
2. Pour the broth and water over. Bring to a boil, simmer covered, and cook for about 20 minutes until the vegetables are tender. Remove from heat. Melt the remaining butter in a skillet. Add the chorizo sausage and cook for 5 minutes until crispy. Puree the soup with a hand blender until smooth. Taste and adjust the seasonings. Serve the soup in deep bowls topped with the chorizo sausage.

Nutrition Info:
- Per Servings 5.7g Carbs, 10g Protein, 19.1g Fat, 251 Calories

Tomato Hamburger Soup

Servings: 8 | Cooking Time: 25 Minutes

Ingredients:
- 1-pound ground beef
- 1 can V-8 juice
- 2 packages frozen vegetable mix
- 1 can condensed mushroom soup
- 2 teaspoon dried onion powder
- 5 tablespoons olive oil
- Salt and pepper to taste
- 1 cup water

Directions:
1. Place a pot over medium flame and heat for 2 minutes. Add oil and heat for a minute.
2. Sauté the beef until lightly browned, around 7 minutes.

Season with salt, pepper, and onion powder.

3. Add the mushroom soup and water.

4. Give a good stir to combine everything.

5. Cover and bring to a boil, lower fire to a simmer and cook for 10 minutes.

6. Stir in vegetables. Cook until heated through around 5 minutes. Adjust seasoning if needed.

7. Serve and enjoy.

Nutrition Info:

• Per Servings 10g Carbs, 18.1g Protein, 14.8g Fat, 227 Calories

Coconut, Green Beans, And Shrimp Curry Soup

Servings: 4 | Cooking Time: 20 Minutes

Ingredients:

• 2 tbsp ghee
• 1 lb jumbo shrimp, peeled and deveined
• 2 tsp ginger-garlic puree
• 2 tbsp red curry paste
• 6 oz coconut milk
• Salt and chili pepper to taste
• 1 bunch green beans, halved

Directions:

1. Melt ghee in a medium saucepan over medium heat. Add the shrimp, season with salt and pepper, and cook until they are opaque, 2 to 3 minutes. Remove shrimp to a plate. Add the ginger-garlic puree and red curry paste to the ghee and sauté for 2 minutes until fragrant.

2. Stir in the coconut milk; add the shrimp, salt, chili pepper, and green beans. Cook for 4 minutes. Reduce the heat to a simmer and cook an additional 3 minutes, occasionally stirring. Adjust taste with salt, fetch soup into serving bowls, and serve with cauli rice.

Nutrition Info:

• Per Servings 2g Carbs, 9g Protein, 35.4g Fat, 375 Calories

Homemade Cold Gazpacho Soup

Servings: 6 | Cooking Time: 15 Minutes

Ingredients:

• 2 small green peppers, roasted
• 2 large red peppers, roasted
• 2 medium avocados, flesh scoped out
• 2 garlic cloves
• 2 spring onions, chopped
• 1 cucumber, chopped
• 1 cup olive oil
• 2 tbsp lemon juice
• 4 tomatoes, chopped
• 7 ounces goat cheese
• 1 small red onion, chopped
• 2 tbsp apple cider vinegar
• Salt to taste

Directions:

1. Place the peppers, tomatoes, avocados, red onion, garlic, lemon juice, olive oil, vinegar, and salt, in a food processor.

Pulse until your desired consistency is reached. Taste and adjust the seasoning.

2. Transfer the mixture to a pot. Stir in cucumber and spring onions. Cover and chill in the fridge at least 2 hours. Divide the soup between 6 bowls. Serve very cold, generously topped with goat cheese and an extra drizzle of olive oil.

Nutrition Info:

• Per Servings 6.5g Carbs, 7.5g Protein, 45.8g Fat, 528 Calories

Sour Cream And Cucumbers

Servings: 8 | Cooking Time: 0 Minutes

Ingredients:

• ½ cup sour cream
• 3 tablespoons white vinegar
• 4 medium cucumbers, sliced thinly
• 1 small sweet onion, sliced thinly
• Salt and pepper to taste
• 3 tablespoons olive oil

Directions:

1. In a bowl, whisk the sour cream and vinegar. Season with salt and pepper to taste. Whisk until well-combined.

2. Add in the cucumber and the rest of the ingredients.

3. Toss to coat.

4. Allow chilling before serving.

Nutrition Info:

• Per Servings 4.8g Carbs, 0.9g Protein, 8.3g Fat, 96 Calories

Chicken And Cauliflower Rice Soup

Servings: 8 | Cooking Time: 20 Mins

Ingredients:

• 2 cooked, boneless chicken breast halves, shredded
• 2 packages Steamed Cauliflower Rice
• 1/4 cup celery, chopped
• 1/2 cup onion, chopped
• 4 garlic cloves, minced
• Salt and ground black pepper to taste
• 2 teaspoons poultry seasoning
• 4 cups chicken broth
• ½ cup butter
• 2 cups heavy cream

Directions:

1. Heat butter in a large pot over medium heat, add onion, celery and garlic cloves to cook until tender. Meanwhile, place the riced cauliflower steam bags in the microwave following directions on the package.

2. Add the riced cauliflower, seasoning, salt and black pepper to butter mixture, saute them for 7 minutes on medium heat, stirring constantly to well combined.

3. Bring cooked chicken breast halves, broth and heavy cream to a broil. When it starts boiling, lower the heat, cover and simmer for 15 minutes.

Nutrition Info:

• Per Servings 6g Carbs, 27g Protein, 30g Fat, 415 Calories

Bacon Chowder

Servings: 6 | Cooking Time: 15 Minutes

Ingredients:
- 1-pound bacon strips, chopped
- 1/4 cup chopped onion
- 1 can evaporated milk
- 1 sprig parsley, chopped
- 5 tablespoons butter
- 1/4 teaspoon salt
- 1/4 teaspoon pepper

Directions:
1. In a large skillet, cook bacon over medium heat until crisp, stirring occasionally. Remove with a slotted spoon; drain on paper towels. Discard drippings, reserving 1-1/2 teaspoons in the pan. Add onion to drippings; cook and stir over medium-high heat until tender.
2. Meanwhile, place all ingredients Bring to a boil over high heat. Reduce heat to medium; cook, uncovered, 10-15 minutes or until tender. Reserve 1 cup potato water.
3. Add milk, salt and pepper to the saucepan; heat through. Stir in bacon and onion.

Nutrition Info:
- Per Servings 5.4g Carbs, 10g Protein, 31.9g Fat, 322 Calories

Creamy Cauliflower Soup With Bacon Chips

Servings: 4 | Cooking Time: 25 Minutes

Ingredients:
- 2 tbsp ghee
- 1 onion, chopped
- 2 head cauliflower, cut into florets
- 2 cups water
- Salt and black pepper to taste
- 3 cups almond milk
- 1 cup shredded white cheddar cheese
- 3 bacon strips

Directions:
1. Melt the ghee in a saucepan over medium heat and sauté the onion for 3 minutes until fragrant.
2. Include the cauli florets, sauté for 3 minutes to slightly soften, add the water, and season with salt and black pepper. Bring to a boil, and then reduce the heat to low. Cover and cook for 10 minutes.
3. Puree cauliflower with an immersion blender until the ingredients are evenly combined and stir in the almond milk and cheese until the cheese melts. Adjust taste with salt and black pepper.
4. In a non-stick skillet over high heat, fry the bacon, until crispy. Divide soup between serving bowls, top with crispy bacon, and serve hot.

Nutrition Info:
- Per Servings 6g Carbs, 8g Protein, 37g Fat, 402 Calories

Spinach Fruit Salad With Seeds

Servings: 4 | Cooking Time: 1 Hour 10 Minutes

Ingredients:
- 2 tablespoons sesame seeds
- 1 tablespoon poppy seeds
- 1 tablespoon minced onion
- 10 ounces fresh spinach - rinsed, dried and torn into bite-size pieces
- 1 quart strawberries - cleaned, hulled and sliced
- 1/2 cup stevia
- 1/2 cup olive oil
- 1/4 cup distilled white vinegar
- 1/4 teaspoon Worcestershire sauce
- 1/4 teaspoon paprika

Directions:
1. Mix together the spinach and strawberry in a large bowl, stir in the sesame seeds, poppy seeds, stevia, olive oil, vinegar, paprika, Worcestershire sauce and onion in a medium bowl. Cover and cool for 1 hour.
2. Pour dressing over salad to combine well. Serve immediately or refrigerate for 15 minutes.

Nutrition Info:
- Per Servings 8.6g Carbs, 6g Protein, 18g Fat, 220 Calories

Salmon Salad With Walnuts

Servings: 2 | Cooking Time: 10 Minutes

Ingredients:
- 2 salmon fillets
- 2 tablespoons balsamic vinaigrette, divided
- 1/8 teaspoon pepper
- 2 cups mixed salad greens
- 1/4 cup walnuts
- 2 tablespoons crumbled cheese
- Salt and pepper to taste
- 3 tablespoons olive oil

Directions:
1. Brush the salmon with half of the balsamic vinaigrette and sprinkle with pepper.
2. Grill the salmon over medium heat for 5 minutes on each side.
3. Crumble the salmon and place in a mixing bowl. Add the rest of the ingredients and season with salt and pepper to taste.

Nutrition Info:
- Per Servings 8g Carbs, 5g Protein, 30g Fat, 313 Calories

Quail Eggs And Winter Melon Soup

Servings: 6 | Cooking Time: 40 Minutes

Ingredients:
- 1-pound pork bones
- 4 cloves of garlic, minced
- 1 onion, chopped
- 1 winter melon, peeled and sliced
- 10 quail eggs, pre-boiled and peeled
- Pepper and salt to taste
- 6 cups water, divided
- Chopped cilantro for garnish (optional)

Directions:
1. Place a heavy-bottomed pot on medium-high fire.
2. Add 5 cups water and pork bones. Season generously with pepper.
3. Bring to a boil, lower fire to a simmer, cover and cook for 30 minutes. Discard bones.
4. Add remaining ingredients except for the cilantro. Cover and simmer for another 10 minutes.
5. Adjust seasoning to taste.
6. Serve and enjoy with cilantro for garnish.

Nutrition Info:
• Per Servings 5.6g Carbs, 4.0g Protein, 3.0g Fat, 65 Calories

Brussels Sprouts Salad With Pecorino Romano

Servings: 6 | Cooking Time: 35 Minutes

Ingredients:
• 2 lb Brussels sprouts, halved
• 3 tbsp olive oil
• Salt and black pepper to taste
• 2 ½ tbsp balsamic vinegar
• ¼ red cabbage, shredded
• 1 tbsp Dijon mustard
• 1 cup pecorino romano cheese, grated

Directions:
1. Preheat oven to 400ºF and line a baking sheet with foil. Toss the brussels sprouts with olive oil, a little salt, black pepper, and balsamic vinegar, in a bowl, and spread on the baking sheet in an even layer. Bake until tender on the inside and crispy on the outside, about 20 to 25 minutes.
2. Transfer to a salad bowl and add the red cabbage, Dijon mustard and half of the cheese. Mix until well combined. Sprinkle with the remaining cheese, share the salad onto serving plates, and serve with syrup-grilled salmon.

Nutrition Info:
• Per Servings 6g Carbs, 4g Protein, 18g Fat, 210 Calories

Green Minestrone Soup

Servings: 4 | Cooking Time: 25 Minutes

Ingredients:
• 2 tbsp ghee
• 2 tbsp onion garlic puree
• 2 heads broccoli, cut in florets
• 2 stalks celery, chopped
• 5 cups vegetable broth
• 1 cup baby spinach
• Salt and black pepper to taste

Directions:
1. Melt the ghee in a saucepan over medium heat and sauté the garlic for 3 minutes until softened. Mix in the broccoli and celery, and cook for 4 minutes until slightly tender. Pour in the broth, bring to a boil, then reduce the heat to medium-low and simmer covered for about 5 minutes.
2. Drop in the spinach to wilt, adjust the seasonings, and cook for 4 minutes. Ladle soup into serving bowls. Serve with a sprinkle of grated Gruyere cheese and freshly baked low carb carrot bread.

Nutrition Info:
• Per Servings 2g Carbs, 8g Protein, 20.3g Fat, 227 Calories

Shrimp With Avocado & Cauliflower Salad

Servings: 6 | Cooking Time: 30 Minutes

Ingredients:
• 1 cauliflower head, florets only
• 1 pound medium shrimp
• ¼ cup + 1 tbsp olive oil
• 1 avocado, chopped
• 3 tbsp chopped dill
• ¼ cup lemon juice
• 2 tbsp lemon zest
• Salt and black pepper to taste

Directions:
1. Heat 1 tbsp olive oil in a skillet and cook the shrimp until opaque, about 8-10 minutes. Place the cauliflower florets in a microwave-safe bowl, and microwave for 5 minutes. Place the shrimp, cauliflower, and avocado in a large bowl.
2. Whisk together the remaining olive oil, lemon zest, juice, dill, and some salt and pepper, in another bowl. Pour the dressing over, toss to combine and serve immediately.

Nutrition Info:
• Per Servings 5g Carbs, 15g Protein, 17g Fat, 214 Calories

Chapter 8 Sauces And Dressing Recipes

Chapter 8 Sauces And Dressing Recipes

Keto Ranch Dip

Servings: 8 | Cooking Time: 10 Minutes

Ingredients:
- 1 cup egg white, beaten
- 1 lemon juice, freshly squeezed
- Salt and pepper to taste
- 1 teaspoon mustard paste
- 1 cup olive oil
- Salt and pepper to taste

Directions:
1. Add all ingredients to a pot and bring to a simmer. Stir frequently.
2. Simmer for 10 minutes.
3. Adjust seasoning to taste.

Nutrition Info:
- Per Servings 1.2g Carbs, 3.4g Protein, 27.1g Fat, 258 Calories

Ketogenic-friendly Gravy

Servings: 6 | Cooking Time: 10 Minutes

Ingredients:
- 2 tablespoons butter
- 1 white onion, chopped
- ¼ cup coconut milk
- 2 cups bone broth
- 1 tablespoon balsamic vinegar
- Salt and pepper to taste

Directions:
1. Add all ingredients to a pot and bring to a simmer. Stir frequently.
2. Simmer for 10 minutes.
3. Adjust seasoning to taste.

Nutrition Info:
- Per Servings 1.1g Carbs, 0.2g Protein, 6.3g Fat, 59 Calories

Roasted Garlic Lemon Dip

Servings: 3 | Cooking Time: 30 Minutes

Ingredients:
- 3 medium lemons
- 3 cloves garlic, peeled and smashed
- 5 tablespoons olive oil, divided
- 1/2 teaspoon kosher salt
- Pepper to taste
- Salt
- Pepper

Directions:
1. Arrange a rack in the middle of the oven and heat to 400°F.
2. Cut the lemons in half crosswise and remove the seeds. Place the lemons cut-side up in a small baking dish. Add the garlic and drizzle with 2 tablespoons of the oil.

3. Roast until the lemons are tender and lightly browned, about 30 minutes. Remove the baking dish to a wire rack.
4. When the lemons are cool enough to handle, squeeze the juice into the baking dish. Discard the lemon pieces and any remaining seeds. Pour the contents of the baking dish, including the garlic, into a blender or mini food processor. Add the remaining 3 tablespoons oil and salt. Process until the garlic is completely puréed, and the sauce is emulsified and slightly thickened. Serve warm or at room temperature.

Nutrition Info:
- Per Servings 4.8g Carbs, 0.6g Protein, 17g Fat, 165 Calories

Dijon Vinaigrette

Servings: 4 | Cooking Time: 5 Minutes

Ingredients:
- 2 tablespoons Dijon mustard
- Juice of ½ lemon
- 1 garlic clove, finely minced
- 1½ tablespoons red wine vinegar
- Pink Himalayan salt
- Freshly ground black pepper
- 3 tablespoons olive oil

Directions:
1. In a small bowl, whisk the mustard, lemon juice, garlic, and red wine vinegar until well combined. Season with pink Himalayan salt and pepper, and whisk again.
2. Slowly add the olive oil, a little bit at a time, whisking constantly.
3. Keep in a sealed glass container in the refrigerator for up to 1 week.

Nutrition Info:
- Per Servings 1g Carbs, 1g Protein, 11g Fat, 99 Calories

Keto Thousand Island Dressing

Servings: 10 | Cooking Time: 10 Minutes

Ingredients:
- 1 cup mayonnaise
- 1 tablespoon lemon juice, freshly squeezed
- 4 tablespoons dill pickles, chopped
- 1 teaspoon Tabasco
- 1 shallot chopped finely
- Salt and pepper to taste

Directions:
1. Add all ingredients to a pot and bring to a simmer. Stir frequently.
2. Simmer for 10 minutes.
3. Adjust seasoning to taste.

Nutrition Info:
- Per Servings 2.3g Carbs, 1.7g Protein, 7.8g Fat, 85 Calories

Caesar Dressing

Servings: 4 | Cooking Time: 5 Minutes

Ingredients:
- ½ cup mayonnaise
- 1 tablespoon Dijon mustard
- Juice of ½ lemon
- ½ teaspoon Worcestershire sauce
- Pinch pink Himalayan salt
- Pinch freshly ground black pepper
- ¼ cup grated Parmesan cheese

Directions:
1. In a medium bowl, whisk together the mayonnaise, mustard, lemon juice, Worcestershire sauce, pink Himalayan salt, and pepper until fully combined.
2. Add the Parmesan cheese, and whisk until creamy and well blended.
3. Keep in a sealed glass container in the refrigerator for up to 1 week.

Nutrition Info:
- Per Servings Calories: 2g Carbs, 2g Protein, 23g Fat, 222 Calories

Avocado-lime Crema

Servings: 4 | Cooking Time: 5 Minutes

Ingredients:
- ½ cup sour cream
- ½ avocado
- 1 garlic clove, finely minced
- ¼ cup fresh cilantro leaves
- Juice of ½ lime
- Pinch pink Himalayan salt
- Pinch freshly ground black pepper

Directions:
1. In a food processor (or blender), mix the sour cream, avocado, garlic, cilantro, lime juice, pink Himalayan salt, and pepper until smooth and fully combined.
2. Spoon the sauce into an airtight glass jar and keep in the refrigerator for up to 3 days.

Nutrition Info:
- Per Servings Calories: 2g Carbs, 1g Protein, 8g Fat, 87 Calories

Cheesy Avocado Dip

Cooking Time: 20 Minutes

Ingredients:
- 1/2 medium ripe avocado, peeled and pitted
- 2 crumbled blue cheese
- 1 freshly squeezed lemon juice
- 1/2 kosher salt
- 1/2 cup water

Directions:
1. Scoop the flesh of the avocado into the bowl of a food processor fitted with the blade attachment or blender.
2. Add the blue cheese, lemon juice, and salt. Blend until smooth and creamy, 30 to 40 seconds.

3. With the motor running, add the water and blend until the sauce is thinned and well-combined.

Nutrition Info:
- Per Servings 2.9g Carbs, 3.5g Protein, 7.2g Fat, 86 Calories

Caesar Salad Dressing

Servings: 6 | Cooking Time: 10 Minutes

Ingredients:
- ½ cup olive oil
- 1 tablespoon Dijon mustard
- ½ cup parmesan cheese, grated
- 2/3-ounce anchovies, chopped
- ½ lemon juice, freshly squeezed
- Salt and pepper to taste

Directions:
1. Add all ingredients to a pot and bring to a simmer. Stir frequently.
2. Simmer for 10 minutes.
3. Adjust seasoning to taste.

Nutrition Info:
- Per Servings 1.5g Carbs, 3.4g Protein, 20.7g Fat, 203 Calories

Green Jalapeno Sauce

Servings: 1 | Cooking Time: 0 Minutes

Ingredients:
- ½ avocado
- 1 large jalapeno
- 1 cup fresh cilantro
- 2 tablespoons extra virgin olive oil
- 3 tablespoons water
- Water
- ½ teaspoon salt

Directions:
1. Add all ingredients in a blender.
2. Blend until smooth and creamy.
3. Serve and enjoy.

Nutrition Info:
- Per Servings 10g Carbs, 2.4g Protein, 42g Fat, 407 Calories

Tzatziki

Servings: 4 | Cooking Time: 10 Minutes, Plus At Least 30 Minutes To Chill

Ingredients:
- ½ large English cucumber, unpeeled
- 1½ cups Greek yogurt (I use Fage)
- 2 tablespoons olive oil
- Large pinch pink Himalayan salt
- Large pinch freshly ground black pepper
- Juice of ½ lemon
- 2 garlic cloves, finely minced
- 1 tablespoon fresh dill

Directions:
1. Halve the cucumber lengthwise, and use a spoon to scoop out and discard the seeds.

2. Grate the cucumber with a zester or grater onto a large plate lined with a few layers of paper towels. Close the paper towels around the grated cucumber, and squeeze as much water out of it as you can. (This can take a while and can require multiple paper towels. You can also allow it to drain overnight in a strainer or wrapped in a few layers of cheesecloth in the fridge if you have the time.)

3. In a food processor (or blender), blend the yogurt, olive oil, pink Himalayan salt, pepper, lemon juice, and garlic until fully combined.

4. Transfer the mixture to a medium bowl, and mix in the fresh dill and grated cucumber.

5. I like to chill this sauce for at least 30 minutes before serving. Keep in a sealed glass container in the refrigerator for up to 1 week.

Nutrition Info:
- Per Servings 5g Carbs, 8g Protein, 11g Fat, 149 Calories

Celery-onion Vinaigrette

Servings: 4 | Cooking Time: 0 Minutes

Ingredients:
- 1 tbsp finely chopped celery
- 1 tbsp finely chopped red onion
- 4 garlic cloves, minced
- ½ cup red wine vinegar
- 1 tbsp extra virgin olive oil

Directions:
1. Prepare the dressing by mixing pepper, celery, onion, olive oil, garlic, and vinegar in a small bowl. Whisk well to combine.
2. Let it sit for at least 30 minutes to let flavors blend.
3. Serve and enjoy with your favorite salad greens.

Nutrition Info:
- Per Servings 1.4g Carbs, 0.2g Protein, 3.4g Fat, 41 Calories

Feta Avocado Dip

Servings: 4 | Cooking Time: 0 Minutes

Ingredients:
- 2 avocadoes (mashed)
- ½ cup feta cheese (crumbled)
- 1 plum tomatoes (diced)
- 1 teaspoon garlic (minced)
- ½ lemon (juiced)
- Salt
- Pepper
- 4 tablespoons olive oil

Directions:
1. Fold ingredients together. Do not stir too much to leave chunks of feta and avocado.
2. Serve and enjoy.

Nutrition Info:
- Per Servings 8.1g Carbs, 5g Protein, 19g Fat, 220 Calories

Vegetarian Fish Sauce

Servings: 16 | Cooking Time: 20 Minutes

Ingredients:
- 1/4 cup dried shiitake mushrooms
- 1-2 tbsp tamari (for a depth of flavor)
- 3 tbsp coconut aminos
- 1 ¼ cup water
- 2 tsp sea salt

Directions:
1. To a small saucepan, add water, coconut aminos, dried shiitake mushrooms, and sea salt. Bring to a boil, then cover, reduce heat, and simmer for 15-20 minutes.
2. Remove from heat and let cool slightly. Pour liquid through a fine-mesh strainer into a bowl, pressing on the mushroom mixture with a spoon to squeeze out any remaining liquid.
3. To the bowl, add tamari. Taste and adjust as needed, adding more sea salt for saltiness.
4. Store in a sealed container in the refrigerator for up to 1 month and shake well before use. Or pour into an ice cube tray, freeze, and store in a freezer-safe container for up to 2 months.

Nutrition Info:
- Per Servings 5g Carbs, 0.3g Protein, 2g Fat, 39.1 Calories

Cowboy Sauce

Servings: 6 | Cooking Time: 10 Minutes

Ingredients:
- 1 stick butter
- 2 cloves of garlic, minced
- 1 tablespoon fresh horseradish, grated
- 1 teaspoon dried thyme
- 1 teaspoon paprika powder
- Salt and pepper to taste
- ¼ cup water

Directions:
1. Add all ingredients to a pot and bring to a simmer.
2. Simmer for 10 minutes.
3. Adjust seasoning to taste.

Nutrition Info:
- Per Servings 0.9g Carbs, 1.3g Protein, 20.6g Fat, 194 Calories

Artichoke Pesto Dip

Servings: 1 | Cooking Time: 20 Minutes

Ingredients:
- 1 jar marinated artichoke hearts
- 8 ounces cream cheese (at room temperature)
- 4 ounces parmesan cheese (grated)
- 2 tablespoons basil pesto
- ¼ cup shelled pistachio (chopped, optional)

Directions:
1. Preheat oven to 375oF.
2. Drain and chop artichoke hearts.
3. Mix artichokes, cream cheese, parmesan, and pesto.
4. Pour into 4 ramekins evenly.

5. Bake for 15-20 minutes.

Nutrition Info:
• Per Servings 5g Carbs, 8g Protein, 19g Fat, 214 Calories

Peanut Sauce

Servings: 4 | Cooking Time: 5 Minutes

Ingredients:
• ½ cup creamy peanut butter (I use Justin's)
• 2 tablespoons soy sauce (or coconut aminos)
• 1 teaspoon Sriracha sauce
• 1 teaspoon toasted sesame oil
• 1 teaspoon garlic powder

Directions:
1. In a food processor (or blender), blend the peanut butter, soy sauce, Sriracha sauce, sesame oil, and garlic powder until thoroughly mixed.
2. Pour into an airtight glass container and keep in the refrigerator for up to 1 week.

Nutrition Info:
• Per Servings Calories: 185; Total Fat: 15g; Carbs: 8g; Net Carbs: 6g; Fiber: 2g; Protein: 7g

Simple Tomato Sauce

Servings: 4 | Cooking Time: 20 Minutes

Ingredients:
• 1 can whole peeled tomatoes
• 3 garlic cloves, smashed
• 5 tablespoons olive oil
• Kosher salt
• 2 tablespoons unsalted butter
• Salt

Directions:
1. Purée tomatoes in a food processor until they're as smooth or chunky as you like.
2. Transfer tomatoes to a large Dutch oven or other heavy pot. (Or, use an immersion blender and blend directly in the pot.)
3. Add garlic, oil, and a 5-finger pinch of salt.
4. Bring to a boil and cook, occasionally stirring, until sauce is reduced by about one-third, about 20 minutes. Stir in butter.

Nutrition Info:
• Per Servings 7.6g Carbs, 1.9g Protein, 21.3g Fat, 219 Calories

Alfredo Sauce

Servings: 2 | Cooking Time: 10 Minutes

Ingredients:
• 4 tablespoons butter
• 2 ounces cream cheese
• 1 cup heavy (whipping) cream
• ½ cup grated Parmesan cheese
• 1 garlic clove, finely minced
• 1 teaspoon dried Italian seasoning
• Pink Himalayan salt
• Freshly ground black pepper

Directions:

1. In a heavy medium saucepan over medium heat, combine the butter, cream cheese, and heavy cream. Whisk slowly and constantly until the butter and cream cheese melt.
2. Add the Parmesan, garlic, and Italian seasoning. Continue to whisk until everything is well blended. Turn the heat to medium-low and simmer, stirring occasionally, for 5 to 8 minutes to allow the sauce to blend and thicken.
3. Season with pink Himalayan salt and pepper, and stir to combine.
4. Toss with your favorite hot, precooked, keto-friendly noodles and serve.
5. Keep this sauce in a sealed glass container in the refrigerator for up to 4 days.

Nutrition Info:
• Per Servings 2g Carbs, 5g Protein, 30g Fat, 294 Calories

Fat-burning Dressing

Servings: 6 | Cooking Time: 3 Minutes

Ingredients:
• 2 tablespoons coconut oil
• ¼ cup olive oil
• 2 cloves of garlic, minced
• 2 tablespoons freshly chopped herbs of your choice
• ¼ cup mayonnaise
• Salt and pepper to taste

Directions:
1. Heat the coconut oil and olive oil and sauté the garlic until fragrant in a saucepan.
2. Allow cooling slightly before adding the mayonnaise.
3. Season with salt and pepper to taste.

Nutrition Info:
• Per Servings 0.6g Carbs, 14.1g Protein, 22.5g Fat, 262 Calories

Green Goddess Dressing

Servings: 4 | Cooking Time: 5 Minutes

Ingredients:
• 2 tablespoon buttermilk
• ¼ cup Greek yogurt
• 1 teaspoon apple cider vinegar
• 1 garlic clove, minced
• 1 tablespoon olive oil
• 1 tablespoon fresh parsley leaves

Directions:
1. In a food processor (or blender), combine the buttermilk, yogurt, apple cider vinegar, garlic, olive oil, and parsley. Blend until fully combined.
2. Pour into a sealed glass container and chill in the refrigerator for at least 30 minutes before serving. This dressing will keep in the fridge for up to 1 week.

Nutrition Info:
• Per Servings 1g Carbs, 1g Protein, 6g Fat, 62 Calories

Garlic Aioli

Servings: 4 | Cooking Time: 5 Minutes, Plus 30 Minutes To Chill

Ingredients:
- ½ cup mayonnaise
- 2 garlic cloves, minced
- Juice of 1 lemon
- 1 tablespoon chopped fresh flat-leaf Italian parsley
- 1 teaspoon chopped chives
- Pink Himalayan salt
- Freshly ground black pepper

Directions:
1. In a food processor (or blender), combine the mayonnaise, garlic, lemon juice, parsley, and chives, and season with pink Himalayan salt and pepper. Blend until fully combined.
2. Pour into a sealed glass container and chill in the refrigerator for at least 30 minutes before serving. (This sauce will keep in the fridge for up to 1 week.)

Nutrition Info:
- Per Servings Calories: 3g Carbs, 1g Protein, 22g Fat, 204 Calories

Sriracha Mayo

Servings: 4 | Cooking Time: 5 Minutes

Ingredients:
- ½ cup mayonnaise
- 2 tablespoons Sriracha sauce
- ½ teaspoon garlic powder
- ½ teaspoon onion powder
- ¼ teaspoon paprika

Directions:
1. In a small bowl, whisk together the mayonnaise, Sriracha, garlic powder, onion powder, and paprika until well mixed.
2. Pour into an airtight glass container, and keep in the refrigerator for up to 1 week.

Nutrition Info:
- Per Servings Calories: 2g Carbs, 1g Protein, 22g Fat, 201 Calories

Lemon Tahini Sauce

Servings: 2 | Cooking Time: 5 Minutes

Ingredients:
- 1/2 cup packed fresh herbs, such as parsley, basil, mint, cilantro, dill, or chives
- 1/4 cup tahini
- Juice of 1 lemon
- 1/2 teaspoon kosher salt
- 1 tablespoon water

Directions:
1. Place all the ingredients in the bowl of a food processor fitted with the blade attachment or a blender. Process continuously until the herbs are finely minced, and the sauce is well-blended, 3 to 4 minutes.
2. Serve immediately or store in a covered container in the refrigerator until ready to serve.

Nutrition Info:
- Per Servings 4.3g Carbs, 2.8g Protein, 8.1g Fat, 94 Calories

Chunky Blue Cheese Dressing

Servings: 4 | Cooking Time: 5 Minutes

Ingredients:
- ½ cup sour cream
- ½ cup mayonnaise
- Juice of ½ lemon
- ½ teaspoon Worcestershire sauce
- Pink Himalayan salt
- Freshly ground black pepper
- 2 ounces crumbled blue cheese

Directions:
1. In a medium bowl, whisk the sour cream, mayonnaise, lemon juice, and Worcestershire sauce. Season with pink Himalayan salt and pepper, and whisk again until fully combined.
2. Fold in the crumbled blue cheese until well combined.
3. Keep in a sealed glass container in the refrigerator for up to 1 week.

Nutrition Info:
- Per Servings 3g Carbs, 7g Protein, 32g Fat, 306 Calories

Buttery Dijon Sauce

Servings: 2 | Cooking Time: 0 Minutes

Ingredients:
- 3 parts brown butter
- 1-part vinegar or citrus juice or a combo
- 1-part strong Dijon mustard
- A small handful of flat-leaf parsley (optional)
- 3/4 teaspoon freshly ground pepper
- 1 teaspoon salt

Directions:
1. Add everything to a food processor and blitz until just smooth.
2. You can also mix this up with an immersion blender. Use immediately or store in the refrigerator for up to one day. Blend again before use.

Nutrition Info:
- Per Servings 0.7g Carbs, 0.4g Protein, 34.4g Fat, 306 Calories

Buffalo Sauce

Servings: 8 | Cooking Time: 30 Minutes

Ingredients:
- 8 ounces Cream Cheese (softened)
- ½ cup Buffalo Wing Sauce
- ½ cup Blue Cheese Dressing
- 1 ½ cups Cheddar Cheese (Shredded)
- 1 ¼ cups Chicken Breast (Cooked)

Directions:
1. Preheat oven to 350oF.
2. Blend together buffalo sauce, white salad dressing, cream cheese, chicken, and shredded cheese.
3. Top with any other optional ingredients like blue cheese

chunks.

4. Bake for 25-30 minutes

Nutrition Info:

- Per Servings 2.2g Carbs, 16g Protein, 28g Fat, 325 Calories

Avocado Mayo

Servings: 4 | Cooking Time: 5 Minutes

Ingredients:

- 1 medium avocado, cut into chunks
- ½ teaspoon ground cayenne pepper
- Juice of ½ lime
- 2 tablespoons fresh cilantro leaves (optional)
- Pinch pink Himalayan salt
- ¼ cup olive oil

Directions:

1. In a food processor (or blender), blend the avocado, cayenne pepper, lime juice, cilantro, and pink Himalayan salt until all the ingredients are well combined and smooth.

2. Slowly incorporate the olive oil, adding 1 tablespoon at a time, pulsing the food processor in between.

3. Keep in a sealed glass container in the refrigerator for up to 1 week.

Nutrition Info:

- Per Servings 1g Carbs, 1g Protein, 5g Fat, 58 Calories

Greek Yogurt Dressing

Servings: 2 | Cooking Time: 0 Minutes

Ingredients:

- ¼ tsp ground ginger
- ½ tsp prepared mustard
- 2 tbsp low-fat mayonnaise
- ½ cup plain Greek yogurt
- Salt and pepper to taste

Directions:

1. In a bowl, whisk well all ingredients.
2. Adjust seasoning to taste.
3. Serve and enjoy with your favorite salad greens.

Nutrition Info:

- Per Servings 3.5g Carbs, 3.0g Protein, 2.8g Fat, 51 Calories

Chapter 9 Desserts And Drinks Recipes

Chapter 9 Desserts And Drinks Recipes

Mixed Berry Nuts Mascarpone Bowl

Servings: 4 | Cooking Time: 8 Minutes

Ingredients:
- 4 cups Greek yogurt
- liquid stevia to taste
- 1 ½ cups mascarpone cheese
- 1 ½ cups blueberries and raspberries
- 1 cup toasted pecans

Directions:
1. Mix the yogurt, stevia, and mascarpone in a bowl until evenly combined. Divide the mixture into 4 bowls, share the berries and pecans on top of the cream. Serve the dessert immediately.

Nutrition Info:
- Per Servings 5g Carbs, 20g Protein, 40g Fat, 480 Calories

Choco Coffee Milk Shake

Servings: 1 | Cooking Time: 0 Minutes

Ingredients:
- ½ cup coconut milk
- 1 tbsp cocoa powder
- 1 cup brewed coffee, chilled
- 1 packet Stevia, or more to taste
- ½ tsp cinnamon
- 5 tbsps coconut oil

Directions:
1. Add all ingredients in a blender.
2. Blend until smooth and creamy.
3. Serve and enjoy.

Nutrition Info:
- Per Servings 10g Carbs, 4.1g Protein, 97.4g Fat, 880 Calories

Cream Cheese 'n Coconut Cookies

Servings: 15 | Cooking Time: 17 Minutes

Ingredients:
- 1 Egg
- 1/2 cup Butter softened
- 1/2 cup Coconut Flour
- 1/2 cup Erythritol or other sugar substitutes
- 3 tablespoons Cream cheese, softened
- 1 teaspoon Vanilla extract
- 1/4 teaspoon salt
- 1/2 teaspoon baking powder

Directions:
1. In a mixing bowl, whisk well erythritol, cream cheese, and butter.
2. Add egg and vanilla. Beat until thoroughly combined.
3. Mix in salt, baking powder, and coconut flour.
4. On an 11x13-inch piece of wax paper, place the batter.

Mold into a log shape and then twist the ends to secure. Refrigerate for an hour and then slice into 1-inch circles.
5. When ready, preheat oven to 350oF and line a baking sheet with foil. Place cookies at least 1/2-inch apart.
6. Pop in the oven and bake until golden brown, around 17 minutes.
7. Serve and enjoy.

Nutrition Info:
- Per Servings 3.0g Carbs, 1.0g Protein, 8.0g Fat, 88 Calories

Mint Chocolate Protein Shake

Servings: 4 | Cooking Time: 4 Minutes

Ingredients:
- 3 cups flax milk, chilled
- 3 tsp unsweetened cocoa powder
- 1 avocado, pitted, peeled, sliced
- 1 cup coconut milk, chilled
- 3 mint leaves + extra to garnish
- 3 tbsp erythritol
- 1 tbsp low carb Protein powder
- Whipping cream for topping

Directions:
1. Combine the milk, cocoa powder, avocado, coconut milk, mint leaves, erythritol, and protein powder into a blender, and blend for 1 minute until smooth.
2. Pour into serving glasses, lightly add some whipping cream on top, and garnish with mint leaves.

Nutrition Info:
- Per Servings 4g Carbs, 15g Protein, 14.5g Fat, 191 Calories

Blueberry And Greens Smoothie

Servings: 1 | Cooking Time: 0 Minutes

Ingredients:
- ¼ cup coconut milk
- 2 tbsps blueberries
- ½ cup arugula
- 1 tbsp hemp seeds
- 2 packets Stevia, or as needed
- 1 ½ cups water
- 3 tbsps coconut oil

Directions:
1. Add all ingredients in a blender.
2. Blend until smooth and creamy.
3. Serve and enjoy.

Nutrition Info:
- Per Servings 10.4g Carbs, 3.6g Protein, 59.8g Fat, 572 Calories

Mocha Milk Shake

Servings: 1 | Cooking Time: 0 Minutes

Ingredients:
- 1 cup almond milk
- 2 tbsp cocoa powder
- 2 packet Stevia, or more to taste
- 1 cup brewed coffee, chilled
- 3 tbsps coconut oil

Directions:
1. Add all ingredients in a blender.
2. Blend until smooth and creamy.
3. Serve and enjoy.

Nutrition Info:
- Per Servings 9.9g Carbs, 13.1g Protein, 50.2g Fat, 527 Calories

Mixed Berry Trifle

Servings: 4 | Cooking Time: 3 Minutes + Cooling Time

Ingredients:
- ½ cup walnuts, toasted
- 1 avocado, chopped
- 1 cup mascarpone cheese, softened
- 1 cup fresh blueberries
- 1 cup fresh raspberries
- 1 cup fresh blackberries

Directions:
1. In four dessert glasses, share half of the mascarpone, half of the berries (mixed), half of the walnuts, and half of the avocado, and repeat the layering process for a second time to finish the ingredients. Cover the glasses with plastic wrap and refrigerate for 45 minutes until quite firm.

Nutrition Info:
- Per Servings 8.3g Carbs, 9.8g Protein, 28.5g Fat, 321 Calories

Sea Salt 'n Macadamia Choco Barks

Servings: 10 | Cooking Time: 5 Minutes

Ingredients:
- 1 teaspoon sea salt flakes
- 1/4 cup macadamia nuts, crushed
- 2 Tablespoons erythritol or stevia, to taste
- 3.5 oz 100% dark chocolate, broken into pieces
- 2 Tablespoons coconut oil, melted

Directions:
1. Melt the chocolate and coconut oil over a very low heat.
2. Remove from heat. Stir in sweetener.
3. Pour the mixture into a loaf pan and place in the fridge for 15 minutes.
4. Scatter the crushed macadamia nuts on top along with the sea salt. Lightly press into the chocolate.
5. Place back into the fridge or freezer for 2 hours.

Nutrition Info:
- Per Servings 1.0g Carbs, 2.0g Protein, 8.0g Fat, 84 Calories

No Bake Lemon Cheese-stard

Servings: 8 | Cooking Time: 0 Minutes

Ingredients:
- 1 tsp vanilla flavoring
- 1 tbsp lemon juice
- 2 oz heavy cream
- 8 oz softened cream cheese
- 1 tsp liquid low carb sweetener (Splenda)
- 1 tsp stevia

Directions:
1. Mix all ingredients in a large mixing bowl until the mixture has a pudding consistency.
2. Pour the mixture to small serving cups and refrigerate for a few hours until it sets.
3. Serve chilled.

Nutrition Info:
- Per Servings 1.4g Carbs, 2.2g Protein, 10.7g Fat, 111 Calories

Minty-coco And Greens Shake

Servings: 1 | Cooking Time: 0 Minutes

Ingredients:
- ½ cup coconut milk
- 2 peppermint leaves
- 2 packets Stevia, or as needed
- 1 cup 50/50 salad mix
- 1 tbsp coconut oil
- 1 ½ cups water

Directions:
1. Add all ingredients in a blender.
2. Blend until smooth and creamy.
3. Serve and enjoy.

Nutrition Info:
- Per Servings 5.8g Carbs, 2.7g Protein, 37.8g Fat, 344 Calories

Boysenberry And Greens Shake

Servings: 1 | Cooking Time: 0 Minutes

Ingredients:
- ¼ cup coconut milk
- 2 tbsps Boysenberry
- 2 packets Stevia, or as needed
- ¼ cup Baby Kale salad mix
- 3 tbsps MCT oil
- 1 ½ cups water

Directions:
1. Add all ingredients in a blender.
2. Blend until smooth and creamy.
3. Serve and enjoy.

Nutrition Info:
- Per Servings 3.9g Carbs, 1.7g Protein, 55.1g Fat, 502 Calories

Dark Chocolate Mousse With Stewed Plums

Servings: 6 | Cooking Time: 45 Minutes

Ingredients:
- 12 oz unsweetened chocolate
- 8 eggs, separated into yolks and whites
- 2 tbsp salt
- ¾ cup swerve sugar
- ½ cup olive oil
- 3 tbsp brewed coffee
- Stewed Plums
- 4 plums, pitted and halved
- ½ stick cinnamon
- ½ cup swerve
- ½ cup water
- ½ lemon, juiced

Directions:
1. Put the chocolate in a bowl and melt in the microwave for 1 ½ minutes. In a separate bowl, whisk the yolks with half of the swerve until a pale yellow has formed, then, beat in the salt, olive oil, and coffee. Mix in the melted chocolate until smooth.
2. In a third bowl, whisk the whites with the hand mixer until a soft peak has formed. Sprinkle the remaining swerve sugar over and gently fold in with a spatula. Fetch a tablespoon full of the chocolate mixture and fold in to combine. Pour in the remaining chocolate mixture and whisk to mix.
3. Pour the mousse into 6 ramekins, cover with plastic wrap, and refrigerate overnight. The next morning, pour water, swerve, cinnamon, and lemon juice in a saucepan and bring to a simmer for 3 minutes, occasionally stirring to ensure the swerve has dissolved and a syrup has formed.
4. Add the plums and poach in the sweetened water for 18 minutes until soft. Turn the heat off and discard the cinnamon stick. Spoon a plum each with syrup on the chocolate mousse and serve.

Nutrition Info:
- Per Servings 6.9g Carbs, 9.5g Protein, 23g Fat, 288 Calories

Strawberry Yogurt Shake

Servings: 1 | Cooking Time: 0 Minutes

Ingredients:
- ½ cup whole milk yogurt
- 4 strawberries, chopped
- 1 tbsp cocoa powder
- 3 tbsp coconut oil
- 1 tbsp pepitas
- 1 ½ cups water
- 1 packet Stevia, or more to taste

Directions:
1. Add all ingredients in a blender.
2. Blend until smooth and creamy.
3. Serve and enjoy.

Nutrition Info:
- Per Servings 10.5g Carbs, 7.7g Protein, 49.3g Fat, 496 Calories

Berry Tart

Servings: 4 | Cooking Time: 45 Minutes

Ingredients:
- 4 eggs
- 2 tsp coconut oil
- 2 cups berries
- 1 cup coconut milk
- 1 cup almond flour
- ¼ cup sweetener
- ½ tsp vanilla powder
- 1 tbsp powdered sweetener
- A pinch of salt

Directions:
1. Preheat the oven to 350ºF. Place all ingredients except coconut oil, berries, and powdered sweetener, in a blender; blend until smooth. Gently fold in the berries. Grease a baking dish with the oil. Pour the mixture into the prepared pan and bake for 35 minutes. Sprinkle with powdered sugar to serve.

Nutrition Info:
- Per Servings 4.9g Carbs, 15g Protein, 26.5g Fat, 305 Calories

Lettuce Green Shake

Servings: 1 | Cooking Time: 0 Minutes

Ingredients:
- ¾ cup whole milk yogurt
- 2 cups 5-lettuce mix salad greens
- 3 tbsp MCT oil
- 1 tbsp chia seeds
- 1 ½ cups water
- 1 packet Stevia, or more to taste

Directions:
1. Add all ingredients in a blender.
2. Blend until smooth and creamy.
3. Serve and enjoy.

Nutrition Info:
- Per Servings 6.1g Carbs, 8.1g Protein, 47g Fat, 483 Calories

Ice Cream Bars Covered With Chocolate

Servings: 15 | Cooking Time: 4 Hours And 20 Minutes

Ingredients:
- Ice Cream:
- 1 cup heavy whipping cream
- 1 tsp vanilla extract
- ¾ tsp xanthan gum
- ½ cup peanut butter
- 1 cup half and half
- 1 ½ cups almond milk
- ⅓ tsp stevia powder
- 1 tbsp vegetable glycerin
- 3 tbsp xylitol
- Chocolate:
- ¾ cup coconut oil
- ¼ cup cocoa butter pieces, chopped
- 2 ounces unsweetened chocolate
- 3 ½ tsp THM super sweet blend

Directions:

1. Blend all ice cream ingredients until smooth. Place in an ice cream maker and follow the instructions. Spread the ice cream into a lined pan, and freezer for about 4 hours.

2. Combine all chocolate ingredients in a microwave-safe bowl and heat until melted. Allow cooling. Remove the ice cream from the freezer and slice into bars. Dip them into the cooled chocolate mixture and return to the freezer for about 10 minutes before serving.

Nutrition Info:

• Per Servings 5g Carbs, 4g Protein, 32g Fat, 345 Calories

Hazelnut-lettuce Yogurt Shake

Servings: 1 | Cooking Time: 0 Minutes

Ingredients:

• 1 cup whole milk yogurt
• 1 cup lettuce chopped
• 1 tbsp Hazelnut chopped
• 1 packet Stevia, or more to taste
• 1 tbsp olive oil
• 1 cup water

Directions:

1. Add all ingredients in a blender.
2. Blend until smooth and creamy.
3. Serve and enjoy.

Nutrition Info:

• Per Servings 8.8g Carbs, 9.4g Protein, 22.2g Fat, 282 Calories

Berry Merry

Servings: 4 | Cooking Time: 6 Minutes

Ingredients:

• 1 ½ cups blackberries
• 1 cup strawberries + extra for garnishing
• 1 cup blueberries
• 2 small beets, peeled and chopped
• 2/3 cup ice cubes
• 1 lime, juiced

Directions:

1. For the extra strawberries for garnishing, make a single deep cut on their sides; set aside.
2. Add the blackberries, strawberries, blueberries, beet, and ice into the smoothie maker and blend the ingredients at high speed until smooth and frothy, for about 60 seconds.
3. Add the lime juice, and puree further for 30 seconds. Pour the drink into tall smoothie glasses, fix the reserved strawberries on each glass rim, stick a straw in, and serve the drink immediately.

Nutrition Info:

• Per Servings 8g Carbs, 2.7g Protein, 3g Fat, 83 Calories

Raspberry-choco Shake

Servings: 1 | Cooking Time: 0 Minutes

Ingredients:

• ¼ cup heavy cream, liquid
• 1 tbsp cocoa powder
• 1 packet Stevia, or more to taste
• ¼ cup raspberries
• 1 ½ cups water

Directions:

1. Add all ingredients in a blender.
2. Blend until smooth and creamy.
3. Serve and enjoy.

Nutrition Info:

• Per Servings 11.1g Carbs, 3.8g Protein, 45.0g Fat, 438 Calories

Green Tea Brownies With Macadamia Nuts

Servings: 4 | Cooking Time: 28 Minutes

Ingredients:

• 1 tbsp green tea powder
• ¼ cup unsalted butter, melted
• 4 tbsp swerve confectioner's sugar
• A pinch of salt
• ¼ cup coconut flour
• ½ tsp low carb baking powder
• 1 egg
• ¼ cup chopped macadamia nuts

Directions:

1. Preheat the oven to 350°F and line a square baking dish with parchment paper. Pour the melted butter into a bowl, add sugar and salt, and whisk to combine. Crack the egg into the bowl.

2. Beat the mixture until the egg has incorporated. Pour the coconut flour, green tea, and baking powder into a fine-mesh sieve and sift them into the egg bowl; stir. Add the nuts, stir again, and pour the mixture into the lined baking dish. Bake for 18 minutes, remove and slice into brownie cubes. Serve warm.

Nutrition Info:

• Per Servings 2.2g Carbs, 5.2g Protein, 23.1g Fat, 248 Calories

Almond Butter Fat Bombs

Servings: 4 | Cooking Time: 3 Minutes + Cooling Time

Ingredients:

• ½ cup almond butter
• ½ cup coconut oil
• 4 tbsp unsweetened cocoa powder
• ½ cup erythritol

Directions:

1. Melt butter and coconut oil in the microwave for 45 seconds, stirring twice until properly melted and mixed. Mix in cocoa powder and erythritol until completely combined.
2. Pour into muffin moulds and refrigerate for 3 hours to harden.

Nutrition Info:

• Per Servings 2g Carbs, 4g Protein, 18.3g Fat, 193 Calories

Green And Fruity Smoothie

Servings: 2 | Cooking Time: 0 Minutes

Ingredients:
- 1 cup spinach, packed
- ½ cup strawberries, chopped
- ½ avocado, peeled, pitted, and frozen
- 1 tbsp almond butter
- ¼ cup packed kale, stem discarded, and leaves chopped
- 1 cup ice-cold water
- 5 tablespoons MCT oil or coconut oil

Directions:
1. Blend all ingredients in a blender until smooth and creamy.
2. Serve and enjoy.

Nutrition Info:
- Per Servings 10g Carbs, 1.6g Protein, 47.3g Fat, 459 Calories

Raspberry Sorbet

Servings: 1 | Cooking Time: 3 Minutes

Ingredients:
- ¼ tsp vanilla extract
- 1 packet gelatine, without sugar
- 1 tbsp heavy whipping cream
- ⅓ cup boiling water
- 2 tbsp mashed raspberries
- 1 ½ cups crushed Ice
- ⅓ cup cold water

Directions:
1. Combine the gelatin and boiling water, until completely dissolved; then transfer to a blender. Add the remaining ingredients. Blend until smooth and freeze for at least 2 hours.

Nutrition Info:
- Per Servings 3.7g Carbs, 4g Protein, 10g Fat, 173 Calories

Coconut Raspberry Bars

Servings: 12 | Cooking Time: 20 Minutes

Ingredients:
- 1 cup coconut milk
- 3 cups desiccated coconut
- 1/3 cup erythritol powder
- 1 cup raspberries, pulsed
- ½ cup coconut oil or other oils

Directions:
1. Preheat oven to 380oF.
2. Combine all ingredients in a mixing bowl.
3. Pour into a greased baking dish.
4. Bake in the oven for 20 minutes.
5. Let it rest for 10 minutes.
6. Serve and enjoy.

Nutrition Info:
- Per Servings 8.2g Carbs, 1.5g Protein, 14.7g Fat, 170 Calories

Cinnamon Cookies

Servings: 4 | Cooking Time: 25 Minutes

Ingredients:
- 2 cups almond flour
- ½ tsp baking soda
- ¾ cup sweetener
- ½ cup butter, softened
- A pinch of salt
- Coating:
- 2 tbsp erythritol sweetener
- 1 tsp cinnamon

Directions:
1. Preheat your oven to 350ºF. Combine all cookie ingredients in a bowl. Make 16 balls out of the mixture and flatten them with hands. Combine the cinnamon and erythritol. Dip the cookies in the cinnamon mixture and arrange them on a lined cookie sheet. Cook for 15 minutes, until crispy.

Nutrition Info:
- Per Servings 1.5g Carbs, 3g Protein, 13g Fat, 131 Calories

No Nuts Fudge

Servings: 15 | Cooking Time: 4 Hours

Ingredients:
- ¼ cup cocoa powder
- ½ teaspoon baking powder
- 1 stick of butter, melted
- 4 tablespoons erythritol
- 6 eggs, beaten
- Salt to taste.

Directions:
1. Mix all ingredients in a slow cooker.
2. Add a pinch of salt.
3. Mix until well combined.
4. Cover pot.
5. Press the low settings and adjust the time to 4 hours.

Nutrition Info:
- Per Servings 1.3g Carbs, 4.3g Protein, 12.2g Fat, 132 Calories

Avocado And Greens Smoothie

Servings: 1 | Cooking Time: 0 Minutes

Ingredients:
- ½ cup coconut milk
- ¼ avocado fruit
- ½ cup spring mix greens
- 3 tbsps avocado oil
- 1 ½ cups water
- 2 packets Stevia, or as needed

Directions:
1. Add all ingredients in a blender.
2. Blend until smooth and creamy.
3. Serve and enjoy.

Nutrition Info:
- Per Servings 10.3g Carbs, 3.8g Protein, 77.4g Fat, 764 Calories

Keto Lemon Custard

Servings: 8 | Cooking Time: 50 Minutes

Ingredients:
- 1 Lemon
- 6 large eggs
- 2 tbsp lemon zest
- 1 cup Lakanto
- 2 cups heavy cream

Directions:
1. Preheat oven to 300oF.
2. Mix all ingredients.
3. Pour mixture into ramekins.
4. Put ramekins into a dish with boiling water.
5. Bake in the oven for 45-50 minutes.
6. Let cool then refrigerate for 2 hours.
7. Use lemon slices as garnish.

Nutrition Info:
- Per Servings 4.0g Carbs, 7.0g Protein, 21.0g Fat, 233 Calories

Strawberry-choco Shake

Servings: 1 | Cooking Time: 0 Minutes

Ingredients:
- ½ cup heavy cream, liquid
- 1 tbsp cocoa powder
- 1 packet Stevia, or more to taste
- 4 strawberries, sliced
- 1 tbsp coconut flakes, unsweetened
- 1 ½ cups water
- 3 tbsps coconut oil

Directions:
1. Add all ingredients in a blender.
2. Blend until smooth and creamy.
3. Serve and enjoy.

Nutrition Info:
- Per Servings 10.1g Carbs, 2.6g Protein, 65.3g Fat, 610 Calories

Brownies With Coco Milk

Servings: 10 | Cooking Time: 6 Hours

Ingredients:
- ¾ cup coconut milk
- 1 teaspoon erythritol
- 2 tablespoons butter, melted
- 4 egg yolks, beaten
- 5 tablespoons cacao powder

Directions:
1. In a bowl, mix well all ingredients.
2. Lightly grease your slow cooker with cooking spray and pour in batter.
3. Cover and cook on low for six hours.
4. Serve and enjoy.

Nutrition Info:
- Per Servings 1.2g Carbs, 1.5g Protein, 8.4g Fat, 86 Calories

Five Greens Smoothie

Servings: 4 | Cooking Time: 5 Minutes

Ingredients:
- 6 kale leaves, chopped
- 3 stalks celery, chopped
- 1 ripe avocado, skinned, pitted, sliced
- 1 cup ice cubes
- 2 cups spinach, chopped
- 1 large cucumber, peeled and chopped
- Chia seeds to garnish

Directions:
1. In a blender, add the kale, celery, avocado, and ice cubes, and blend for 45 seconds. Add the spinach and cucumber, and process for another 45 seconds until smooth.
2. Pour the smoothie into glasses, garnish with chia seeds and serve the drink immediately.

Nutrition Info:
- Per Servings 2.9g Carbs, 3.2g Protein, 7.8g Fat, 124 Calories

Crispy Zucchini Chips

Servings: 5 | Cooking Time: 20 Mins

Ingredients:
- 1 large egg, beaten
- 1 cup. almond flour
- 1 medium zucchini, thinly sliced
- 3/4 cup Parmesan cheese, grated
- Cooking spray

Directions:
1. Preheat oven to 400 degrees F. Line a baking pan with parchment paper.
2. In a bowl, mix together Parmesan cheese and almond flour.
3. In another bowl whisk the egg. Dip each zucchini slice in the egg, then the cheese mixture until finely coated.
4. Spray zucchini slices with cooking spray and place in the prepared oven.
5. Bake for 20 minutes until crispy. Serve.

Nutrition Info:
- Per Servings 16.8g Carbs, 10.8g Protein, 6g Fat, 215.2 Calories

Blackberry Cheese Vanilla Blocks

Servings: 5 | Cooking Time: 20mins

Ingredients:
- ½ cup blackberries
- 6 eggs
- 4 oz mascarpone cheese
- 1 tsp vanilla extract
- 4 tbsp stevia
- 8 oz melted coconut oil
- ½ tsp baking powder

Directions:
1. Except for blackberries, blend all ingredients in a blender until smooth.
2. Combine blackberries with blended mixture and transfer to

a baking dish.

3. Bake blackberries mixture in the oven at 320°F for 20 minutes. Serve.

Nutrition Info:
- Per Servings 15g Carbs, 13g Protein, 4g Fat, 199 Calories

Spicy Cheese Crackers

Servings: 4 | Cooking Time: 10 Mins

Ingredients:
- 3/4 cup almond flour
- 1 egg
- 2 tablespoons cream cheese
- 2 cups shredded Parmesan cheese
- 1/2 teaspoon red pepper flakes
- 1 tablespoon dry ranch salad dressing mix

Directions:
1. Preheat oven to 425 degrees F.
2. Combine Parmesan and cream cheese in a microwave safe bowl and microwave in 30 second intervals. Add the cheese to mix well, and whisk along the almond flour, egg, ranch seasoning, and red pepper flakes, stirring occasionally.
3. Transfer the dough in between two parchment-lined baking sheets. Form the dough into rolls by cutting off plum-sized pieces of dough with dough cutter into 1-inch square pieces, yielding about 60 pieces.
4. Place crackers to a baking sheet lined parchment. Bake for 5 minutes, flipping halfway, then continue to bake for 5 minutes more. Chill before serving.

Nutrition Info:
- Per Servings 18g Carbs, 17g Protein, 4g Fat, 235 Calories

Eggnog Keto Custard

Servings: 8 | Cooking Time: 10 Minutes

Ingredients:
- ¼ tsp nutmeg
- ¼ Truvia
- ½ cup heavy whipping cream
- 1 cup half and half
- 4 eggs

Directions:
1. Blend all ingredients together.
2. Pour evenly into 6 ramekins (microwave safe).
3. Microwave at 50% power for 4 minutes then stir thoroughly.
4. Microwave for another 3-4 minutes at 50% power then stir well again.
5. Serve either cool or hot.

Nutrition Info:
- Per Servings 1.0g Carbs, 3.0g Protein, 6.0g Fat, 70 Calories

Coconut-mocha Shake

Servings: 1 | Cooking Time: 0 Minutes

Ingredients:
- 2 tbsp cocoa powder
- 1 tbsp coconut flakes, unsweetened
- 2 packet Stevia, or more to taste
- 1 cup brewed coffee, chilled
- 3 tbsps coconut oil

Directions:
1. Add all ingredients in a blender.
2. Blend until smooth and creamy.
3. Serve and enjoy.

Nutrition Info:
- Per Servings 9g Carbs, 2.4g Protein, 43.7g Fat, 402 Calories

Chia And Blackberry Pudding

Servings: 2 | Cooking Time: 10 Minutes

Ingredients:
- 1 cup full-fat natural yogurt
- 2 tsp swerve
- 2 tbsp chia seeds
- 1 cup fresh blackberries
- 1 tbsp lemon zest
- Mint leaves, to serve

Directions:
1. Mix together the yogurt and the swerve. Stir in the chia seeds. Reserve 4 blackberries for garnish and mash the remaining ones with a fork until pureed. Stir in the yogurt mixture
2. Chill in the fridge for 30 minutes. When cooled, divide the mixture between 2 glasses. Top each with a couple of raspberries, mint leaves, lemon zest and serve.

Nutrition Info:
- Per Servings 4.7g Carbs, 7.5g Protein, 10g Fat, 169 Calories

Garden Greens & Yogurt Shake

Servings: 1 | Cooking Time: 0 Minutes

Ingredients:
- 1 cup whole milk yogurt
- 1 cup Garden greens
- 3 tbsp MCT oil
- 1 tbsp flaxseed, ground
- 1 cup water
- 1 packet Stevia, or more to taste

Directions:
1. Add all ingredients in a blender.
2. Blend until smooth and creamy.
3. Serve and enjoy.

Nutrition Info:
- Per Servings 7.2g Carbs, 11.7g Protein, 53g Fat, 581 Calories

Granny Smith Apple Tart

Servings: 8 | Cooking Time: 65 Minutes

Ingredients:
- 6 tbsp butter
- 2 cups almond flour
- 1 tsp cinnamon
- ⅓ cup sweetener
- Filling:
- 2 cups sliced Granny Smith
- ¼ cup butter
- ¼ cup sweetener
- ½ tsp cinnamon
- ½ tsp lemon juice
- Topping:
- ¼ tsp cinnamon
- 2 tbsp sweetener

Directions:
1. Preheat your oven to 370ºF and combine all crust ingredients in a bowl. Press this mixture into the bottom of a greased pan. Bake for 5 minutes.
2. Meanwhile, combine the apples and lemon juice in a bowl and let them sit until the crust is ready. Arrange them on top of the crust. Combine the rest of the filling ingredients, and brush this mixture over the apples. Bake for about 30 minutes.
3. Press the apples down with a spatula, return to oven, and bake for 20 more minutes. Combine the cinnamon and sweetener, in a bowl, and sprinkle over the tart.
4. Note: Granny Smith apples have just 9.5g of net carbs per 100g. Still high for you? Substitute with Chayote squash, which has the same texture and rich nutrients, and just around 4g of net carbs .

Nutrition Info:
- Per Servings 6.7g Carbs, 7g Protein, 26g Fat, 302 Calories

Coconut Fat Bombs

Servings: 4 | Cooking Time: 22 Minutes +cooling Time

Ingredients:
- 2/3 cup coconut oil, melted
- 1 can coconut milk
- 18 drops stevia liquid
- 1 cup unsweetened coconut flakes

Directions:
1. Mix the coconut oil with the milk and stevia to combine. Stir in the coconut flakes until well distributed. Pour into silicone muffin molds and freeze for 1 hour to harden.

Nutrition Info:
- Per Servings 2g Carbs, 4g Protein, 19g Fat, 214 Calories

Strawberry Vanilla Shake

Servings: 4 | Cooking Time: 2 Minutes

Ingredients:
- 2 cups strawberries, stemmed and halved
- 12 strawberries to garnish
- ½ cup cold unsweetened almond milk
- 2/3 tsp vanilla extract
- ½ cup heavy whipping cream
- 2 tbsp swerve

Directions:
1. Process the strawberries, milk, vanilla extract, whipping cream, and swerve in a large blender for 2 minutes; work in two batches if needed . The shake should be frosty.
2. Pour into glasses, stick in straws, garnish with strawberry halves, and serve.

Nutrition Info:
- Per Servings 3.1g Carbs, 16g Protein, 22.6g Fat, 285 Calories

Nutritiously Green Milk Shake

Servings: 1 | Cooking Time: 5 Minutes

Ingredients:
- 1 cup coconut cream
- 1 packet Stevia, or more to taste
- 1 tbsp coconut flakes, unsweetened
- 2 cups spring mix salad
- 3 tbsps coconut oil
- 1 cup water

Directions:
1. Add all ingredients in a blender.
2. Blend until smooth and creamy.
3. Serve and enjoy.

Nutrition Info:
- Per Servings 10g Carbs, 10.5g Protein, 95.3g Fat, 887 Calories

Raspberry Nut Truffles

Servings: 4 | Cooking Time: 6 Minutes + Cooling Time

Ingredients:
- 2 cups raw cashews
- 2 tbsp flax seed
- 1 ½ cups sugar-free raspberry preserves
- 3 tbsp swerve
- 10 oz unsweetened chocolate chips
- 3 tbsp olive oil

Directions:
1. Line a baking sheet with parchment paper and set aside. Grind the cashews and flax seeds in a blender for 45 seconds until smoothly crushed; add the raspberry and 2 tbsp of swerve.
2. Process further for 1 minute until well combined. Form 1-inch balls of the mixture, place on the baking sheet, and freeze for 1 hour or until firmed up.
3. Melt the chocolate chips, oil, and 1tbsp of swerve in a microwave for 1 ½ minutes. Toss the truffles to coat in the chocolate mixture, put on the baking sheet, and freeze further for at least 2 hours.

Nutrition Info:
- Per Servings 3.5g Carbs, 12g Protein, 18.3g Fat, 251 Calories

Vanilla Bean Frappuccino

Servings: 4 | Cooking Time: 6 Minutes

Ingredients:
- 3 cups unsweetened vanilla almond milk, chilled
- 2 tsp swerve
- 1 ½ cups heavy cream, cold
- 1 vanilla bean
- ¼ tsp xanthan gum
- Unsweetened chocolate shavings to garnish

Directions:
1. Combine the almond milk, swerve, heavy cream, vanilla bean, and xanthan gum in the blender, and process on high speed for 1 minute until smooth. Pour into tall shake glasses, sprinkle with chocolate shavings, and serve immediately.

Nutrition Info:
- Per Servings 6g Carbs, 15g Protein, 14g Fat, 193 Calories

Blackberry-chocolate Shake

Servings: 1 | Cooking Time: 0 Minutes

Ingredients:
- ½ cup half and half
- 1 tbsp blackberries
- 3 tbsps MCT oil
- 1 tbsp Dutch-processed cocoa powder
- 2 tbsp Macadamia nuts, chopped
- 1 ½ cups water
- 1 packet Stevia, or more to taste

Directions:
1. Add all ingredients in a blender.
2. Blend until smooth and creamy.
3. Serve and enjoy.

Nutrition Info:
- Per Servings 10.1g Carbs, 2.7g Protein, 43.9g Fat, 463 Calories

Walnut Cookies

Servings: 12 | Cooking Time: 25 Minutes

Ingredients:
- 1 egg
- 2 cups ground pecans
- ¼ cup sweetener
- ½ tsp baking soda
- 1 tbsp butter
- 20 walnuts halves

Directions:
1. Preheat the oven to 350ºF. Mix the ingredients, except the walnuts, until combined. Make 20 balls out of the mixture and press them with your thumb onto a lined cookie sheet. Top each cookie with a walnut half. Bake for about 12 minutes.

Nutrition Info:
- Per Servings 0.6g Carbs, 1.6g Protein, 11g Fat, 101 Calories

Blackcurrant Iced Tea

Servings: 4 | Cooking Time: 8 Minutes

Ingredients:
- 6 unflavored tea bags
- 2 cups water
- ½ cup sugar-free blackcurrant extract
- Swerve to taste
- Ice cubes for serving
- Lemon slices to garnish, cut on the side

Directions:
1. Pour the ice cubes in a pitcher and place it in the fridge.
2. Bring the water to boil in a saucepan over medium heat for 3 minutes and turn the heat off. Stir in the sugar to dissolve and steep the tea bags in the water for 2 minutes.
3. Remove the bags after and let the tea cool down. Stir in the blackcurrant extract until well incorporated, remove the pitcher from the fridge, and pour the mixture over the ice cubes.
4. Let sit for 3 minutes to cool and after, pour the mixture into tall glasses. Add some more ice cubes, place the lemon slices on the rim of the glasses, and serve the tea cold.

Nutrition Info:
- Per Servings 5g Carbs, 0g Protein, 0g Fat, 22 Calories

Choco-coco Bars

Servings: 12 | Cooking Time: 10 Minutes

Ingredients:
- 1/3 cup Virgin Coconut Oil, melted
- 2 cups shredded unsweetened coconut
- 2 droppers Liquid Stevia
- 2 droppers of Liquid Stevia
- 3 squares Baker's Unsweetened Chocolate
- 1 tablespoon oil

Directions:
1. Lightly grease an 8x8-inch silicone pan.
2. In a food processor, process shredded unsweetened coconut, coconut oil, and Stevia until it forms a dough. Transfer to prepared pan and press on the bottom to form a dough. Place in the freezer to set.
3. Meanwhile, in a microwave-safe Pyrex cup, place chocolate, coconut oil, and Stevia. Heat for 10-second intervals and mix well. Do not overheat, just until you have mixed the mixture thoroughly. Pour over dough.
4. Return to the freezer until set.
5. Serve and enjoy.

Nutrition Info:
- Per Servings 4.0g Carbs, 2.0g Protein, 22.0g Fat, 222 Calories

Eggless Strawberry Mousse

Servings: 6 | Cooking Time: 6 Minutes + Cooling Time

Ingredients:
- 2 cups chilled heavy cream
- 2 cups fresh strawberries, hulled
- 5 tbsp erythritol
- 2 tbsp lemon juice
- ¼ tsp strawberry extract
- 2 tbsp sugar-free strawberry preserves

Directions:
1. Beat the heavy cream, in a bowl, with a hand mixer at high speed until a stiff peak forms, for about 1 minute; refrigerate immediately. Puree the strawberries in a blender and pour into a saucepan.
2. Add erythritol and lemon juice, and cook on low heat for 3 minutes while stirring continuously. Stir in the strawberry extract evenly, turn off heat and allow cooling. Fold in the whipped cream until evenly incorporated, and spoon into six ramekins. Refrigerate for 4 hours to solidify.
3. Garnish with strawberry preserves and serve immediately.

Nutrition Info:
- Per Servings 5g Carbs, 5g Protein, 24g Fat, 290 Calories

Almond Milk Hot Chocolate

Servings: 4 | Cooking Time: 7 Minutes

Ingredients:
- 3 cups almond milk
- 4 tbsp unsweetened cocoa powder
- 2 tbsp swerve
- 3 tbsp almond butter
- Finely chopped almonds to garnish

Directions:
1. In a saucepan, add the almond milk, cocoa powder, and swerve. Stir the mixture until the sugar dissolves. Set the pan over low to heat through for 5 minutes, without boiling.
2. Swirl the mix occasionally. Turn the heat off and stir in the almond butter to be incorporated. Pour the hot chocolate into mugs and sprinkle with chopped almonds. Serve warm.

Nutrition Info:
- Per Servings 0.6g Carbs, 4.5g Protein, 21.5g Fat, 225 Calories

Cranberry White Chocolate Barks

Servings: 6 | Cooking Time: 5 Minutes

Ingredients:
- 10 oz unsweetened white chocolate, chopped
- ½ cup erythritol
- ⅓ cup dried cranberries, chopped
- ⅓ cup toasted walnuts, chopped
- ¼ tsp pink salt

Directions:
1. Line a baking sheet with parchment paper. Pour chocolate and erythritol in a bowl, and melt in the microwave for 25 seconds, stirring three times until fully melted. Stir in the cranberries, walnuts, and salt, reserving a few cranberries and walnuts

for garnishing.
2. Pour the mixture on the baking sheet and spread out. Sprinkle with remaining cranberries and walnuts. Refrigerate for 2 hours to set. Break into bite-size pieces to serve.

Nutrition Info:
- Per Servings 3g Carbs, 6g Protein, 21g Fat, 225 Calories

Strawberry And Yogurt Smoothie

Servings: 3 | Cooking Time: 5 Minutes

Ingredients:
- 1/2 cup yogurt
- 1 cup strawberries
- 1 teaspoon almond milk
- 1 teaspoon lime juice
- 1 1/2 teaspoons stevia

Directions:
1. Place all ingredients in a blender, blender until finely smooth. Serve and enjoy.

Nutrition Info:
- Per Servings 6.3g Carbs, 4.6g Protein, 12.4g Fat, 155.2 Calories

Blueberry Ice Pops

Servings: 6 | Cooking Time: 5 Minutes + Cooling Time

Ingredients:
- 3 cups blueberries
- ½ tbsp lemon juice
- ¼ cup swerve
- ¼ cup water

Directions:
1. Pour the blueberries, lemon juice, swerve, and water in a blender, and puree on high speed for 2 minutes until smooth. Strain through a sieve into a bowl, discard the solids.
2. Mix in more water if too thick. Divide the mixture into ice pop molds, insert stick cover, and freeze for 4 hours to 1 week. When ready to serve, dip in warm water and remove the pops.

Nutrition Info:
- Per Servings 7.9g Carbs, 2.3g Protein, 1.2g Fat, 48 Calories

Brownie Fudge Keto Style

Servings: 10 | Cooking Time: 6 Hours

Ingredients:
- ¾ cup coconut milk
- 1 teaspoon erythritol
- 2 tablespoons butter, melted
- 4 egg yolks, beaten
- 5 tablespoons cacao powder

Directions:
1. Mix all ingredients in a slow cooker and cook on low settings for 6 hours.
2. Serve and enjoy.

Nutrition Info:
- Per Servings 1.2g Carbs, 1.5g Protein, 8.4g Fat, 86 Calories

Coconut Macadamia Nut Bombs

Servings: 4 | Cooking Time: 0 Mins

Ingredients:
- 2 packets stevia
- 5 tbsps unsweetened coconut powder
- 10 tbsps coconut oil
- 3 tbsps chopped macadamia nuts
- Salt to taste

Directions:
1. Heat the coconut oil in a pan over medium heat. Add coconut powder, stevia and salt, stirring to combined well; then remove from heat.
2. Spoon mixture into a lined mini muffin pan. Place in the freezer for a few hours.
3. Sprinkle nuts over the mixture before serving.

Nutrition Info:
- Per Servings 0.2g Carbs, 1.1g Protein, 15.2g Fat, 143 Calories

Coco-ginger Fat Bombs

Servings: 10 | Cooking Time: 10 Minutes

Ingredients:
- 1 cup coconut oil
- 1 cup shredded coconut
- 1 teaspoon erythritol
- 1 teaspoon ginger powder
- ¼ cup water

Directions:
1. Add all ingredients and pour ¼ cup water in a saucepan on the medium-low fire.
2. Stir constantly for 10 minutes.
3. Turn off and scoop small balls from the mixture.
4. Allow to set in the fridge for 1 hour.

Nutrition Info:
- Per Servings 2.2g Carbs, 0.5g Protein, 12.8g Fat, 126 Calories

Berry-choco Goodness Shake

Servings: 1 | Cooking Time: 0 Minutes

Ingredients:
- ½ cup half and half
- ¼ cup raspberries
- ¼ cup blackberry
- ¼ cup strawberries, chopped
- 3 tbsps avocado oil
- 1 packet Stevia, or more to taste
- 1 tbsp cocoa powder
- 1 ½ cups water

Directions:
1. Add all ingredients in a blender.
2. Blend until smooth and creamy.
3. Serve and enjoy.

Nutrition Info:
- Per Servings 7g Carbs, 4.4g Protein, 43.3g Fat, 450 Calories

Italian Greens And Yogurt Shake

Servings: 1 | Cooking Time: 0 Minutes

Ingredients:
- ½ cup half and half
- ½ cup Italian greens
- 1 packet Stevia, or more to taste
- 1 tbsp hemp seeds
- 3 tbsp coconut oil
- 1 cup water

Directions:
1. Add all ingredients in a blender.
2. Blend until smooth and creamy.
3. Serve and enjoy.

Nutrition Info:
- Per Servings 10.3g Carbs, 5.2g Protein, 46.9g Fat, 476 Calories

Nutty Choco Milk Shake

Servings: 1 | Cooking Time: 0 Minutes

Ingredients:
- ¼ cup half and half
- 1 tbsp cocoa powder
- 1 packet Stevia, or more to taste
- 4 pecans
- 1 tbsp macadamia oil
- 1 ½ cups water
- 3 tbsp coconut oil

Directions:
1. Add all ingredients in a blender.
2. Blend until smooth and creamy.
3. Serve and enjoy.

Nutrition Info:
- Per Servings 9.4g Carbs, 4.8g Protein, 73g Fat, 689 Calories

Nutty Greens Shake

Servings: 1 | Cooking Time: 0 Minutes

Ingredients:
- ½ cup half and half, liquid
- 1 packet Stevia, or more to taste
- 3 pecan nuts
- 3 macadamia nuts
- 1 cup spring mix salad greens
- 1 ½ cups water
- 3 tablespoons coconut oil

Directions:
1. Add all ingredients in a blender.
2. Blend until smooth and creamy.
3. Serve and enjoy.

Nutrition Info:
- Per Servings 10.5g Carbs, 7.0g Protein, 65.6g Fat, 628 Calories

Ice Blueberry Milk Smoothie

Servings: 3 | Cooking Time: 5 Mins

Ingredients:
- 2 blueberries
- 2 cups almond milk
- 1/2 cup butter
- 2 tablespoons stevia, or to taste
- 2 cups ice cubes

Directions:
1. Combine all ingredients in a blender; process until well blended, about 30 seconds.

Nutrition Info:
- Per Servings 6g Carbs, 12.8g Protein, 17g Fat, 228 Calories

Vanilla Flan With Mint

Servings: 4 | Cooking Time: 10 Minutes

Ingredients:
- ⅓ cup erythritol, for caramel
- 2 cups almond milk
- 4 eggs
- 1 tbsp vanilla
- 1 tbsp lemon zest
- ½ cup erythritol, for custard
- 2 cup heavy whipping cream
- Mint leaves, to serve

Directions:
1. Heat the erythritol for the caramel in a deep pan. Add 2-3 tablespoons of water, and bring to a boil. Reduce the heat and cook until the caramel turns golden brown. Divide between 4-6 metal tins. Set aside and let them cool.
2. In a bowl, mix the eggs, remaining erythritol, lemon zest, and vanilla. Add the almond milk and beat again until well combined.
3. Pour the custard into each caramel-lined ramekin and place them into a deep baking tin. Fill over the way with the remaining hot water. Bake at 345 ºF for 45-50 minutes. Using tongs, take out the ramekins and let them cool for at least 4 hours in the fridge. Run a knife slowly around the edges to invert onto a dish. Serve with dollops of whipped cream, scattered with mint leaves.

Nutrition Info:
- Per Servings 1.7g Carbs, 7.6g Protein, 26g Fat, 269 Calories

Raspberry Creamy Smoothie

Servings: 1 | Cooking Time: 0 Minutes

Ingredients:
- ¼ cup coconut milk
- 1 ½ cups brewed coffee, chilled
- 2 tbsps raspberries
- 2 tbsps avocado meat
- 1 tsp chia seeds
- 2 packets Stevia or more to taste
- 3 tbsps coconut oil

Directions:
1. Add all ingredients in a blender.

2. Blend until smooth and creamy.
3. Serve and enjoy.

Nutrition Info:
- Per Servings 8.2g Carbs, 4.9g Protein, 33.2g Fat, 350 Calories

Coco-loco Creamy Shake

Servings: 1 | Cooking Time: 0 Minutes

Ingredients:
- ½ cup coconut milk
- 2 tbsp Dutch-processed cocoa powder, unsweetened
- 1 cup brewed coffee, chilled
- 1 tbsp hemp seeds
- 1-2 packets Stevia
- 3 tbsps MCT oil or coconut oil

Directions:
1. Add all ingredients in a blender.
2. Blend until smooth and creamy.
3. Serve and enjoy.

Nutrition Info:
- Per Servings 10.2g Carbs, 5.4g Protein, 61.1g Fat, 567 Calories

Lemon 'n Cashew Bars

Servings: 12 | Cooking Time: 25 Minutes

Ingredients:
- ¼ cup cashew
- ¼ cup fresh lemon juice, freshly squeezed
- ¾ cup coconut milk
- ¾ cup erythritol
- 1 cup desiccated coconut
- 1 teaspoon baking powder
- 2 eggs, beaten
- 2 tablespoons coconut oil
- A dash of salt

Directions:
1. Preheat oven to 350oF and lightly grease an 8x8-inch square pan.
2. Combine all ingredients thoroughly in a mixing bowl.
3. Pour batter in prepared pan and bake for 20-25 minutes.
4. Serve and enjoy.

Nutrition Info:
- Per Servings 3.9g Carbs, 2.6g Protein, 10.2g Fat, 118 Calories

Dark Chocolate Mochaccino Ice Bombs

Servings: 4 | Cooking Time: 2 Hours And 10 Minutes

Ingredients:
- ½ pound cream cheese
- 4 tbsp powdered sweetener
- 2 ounces strong coffee
- 2 tbsp cocoa powder, unsweetened
- 1 ounce cocoa butter, melted
- 2 ½ ounces dark chocolate, melted

Directions:

1. Combine cream cheese, sweetener, coffee, and cocoa powder, in a food processor. Roll 2 tbsp. of the mixture and place on a lined tray.
2. Mix the melted cocoa butter and chocolate, and coat the bombs with it. Freeze for 2 hours.

Nutrition Info:
- Per Servings 1.4g Carbs, 1.9g Protein, 13g Fat, 127 Calories

Creamy Coconut Kiwi Drink

Servings: 4 | Cooking Time: 3 Minutes

Ingredients:
- 6 kiwis, pulp scooped
- 3 tbsp erythritol or to taste
- 3 cups unsweetened coconut milk
- 2 cups coconut cream
- 7 ice cubes
- Mint leaves to garnish

Directions:
1. In a blender, process the kiwis, erythritol, milk, cream, and ice cubes until smooth, about 3 minutes. Pour into four serving glasses, garnish with mint leaves, and serve.

Nutrition Info:
- Per Servings 1g Carbs, 16g Protein, 38g Fat, 425 Calories

Strawberry Vanilla Extract Smoothie

Servings: 3 | Cooking Time: 5 Mins

Ingredients:
- 1 cup almond milk
- 14 frozen strawberries
- 1 1/2 teaspoons stevia
- What you'll need from the store cupboard:
- 1/2 teaspoon vanilla extract

Directions:
1. Place almond milk and strawberries in a blender, blend until creamy. Add vanilla and stevia if desired, blend again and serve.

Nutrition Info:
- Per Servings 5g Carbs, 12.8g Protein, 18.8g Fat, 240.4 Calories

Lime Strawberry Smoothie

Servings: 3 | Cooking Time: 3 Mins

Ingredients:
- 4 ice cubes
- 1/4 fresh strawberry
- 1 large avocado, diced
- 1 cup lime juice

Directions:
1. In a food processor, combine all ingredients and puree on High until a smooth smoothie is formed. Serve and enjoy.

Nutrition Info:
- Per Servings 4g Carbs, 3g Protein, 11g Fat, 127 Calories

Vanilla Jello Keto Way

Servings: 6 | Cooking Time: 6 Minutes

Ingredients:
- 1 cup heavy cream
- 1 teaspoon vanilla extract
- 2 tablespoons gelatin powder, unsweetened
- 3 tablespoons erythritol
- 1 cup boiling water

Directions:
1. Place the boiling water in a small pot and bring to a simmer.
2. Add the gelatin powder and allow to dissolve.
3. Stir in the rest of the ingredients.
4. Pour the mixture into jello molds.
5. Place in the fridge to set for 2 hours.

Nutrition Info:
- Per Servings 5.2g Carbs, 3.3g Protein, 7.9g Fat, 105 Calories

Lemon Gummies

Servings: 4 | Cooking Time: 15 Minutes

Ingredients:
- 1/4 cup fresh lemon juice
- 2 Tablespoons gelatin powder
- 2 Tablespoons stevia, to taste
- ½ cup half and half
- 1 Tablespoon water

Directions:
1. In a small saucepan, heat up water and lemon juice.
2. Slowly stir in the gelatin powder and the rest of the ingredients. Heating and mixing well until dissolved.
3. Pour into silicone molds.
4. Freeze or refrigerate for 2+ hours until firm.

Nutrition Info:
- Per Servings 1.0g Carbs, 3.0g Protein, 7g Fat, 88 Calories

Coffee Fat Bombs

Servings: 6 | Cooking Time: 3 Minutes + Cooling Time

Ingredients:
- 1 ½ cups mascarpone cheese
- ½ cup melted butter
- 3 tbsp unsweetened cocoa powder
- ¼ cup erythritol
- 6 tbsp brewed coffee, room temperature

Directions:
1. Whisk the mascarpone cheese, butter, cocoa powder, erythritol, and coffee with a hand mixer until creamy and fluffy, for 1 minute. Fill into muffin tins and freeze for 3 hours until firm.

Nutrition Info:
- Per Servings 2g Carbs, 4g Protein, 14g Fat, 145 Calories

Coconut-melon Yogurt Shake

Servings: 1 | Cooking Time: 0 Minutes

Ingredients:
- ¼ cup half and half
- 3 tbsp coconut oil
- ½ cup melon, slices
- 1 tbsp coconut flakes, unsweetened
- 1 tbsp chia seeds
- 1 ½ cups water
- 1 packet Stevia, or more to taste

Directions:
1. Add all ingredients in a blender.
2. Blend until smooth and creamy.
3. Serve and enjoy.

Nutrition Info:
- Per Servings 8g Carbs, 2.4g Protein, 43g Fat, 440 Calories

Lychee And Coconut Lassi

Servings: 4 | Cooking Time: 2 Hours 28 Minutes

Ingredients:
- 2 cups lychee pulp, seeded
- 2 ½ cups coconut milk
- 4 tsp swerve
- 2 limes, zested and juiced
- 1 ½ cups plain yogurt
- 1 lemongrass, white part only, crushed
- Toasted coconut shavings for garnish

Directions:
1. In a saucepan, add the lychee pulp, coconut milk, swerve, lemongrass, and lime zest. Stir and bring to boil on medium heat for 2 minutes, = stirring continually. Then reduce the heat, and simmer for 1 minute. Turn the heat off and let the mixture sit for 15 minutes.
2. Remove the lemongrass and pour the mixture into a smoothie maker or a blender, add the yogurt and lime juice, and process the ingredients until smooth, for about 60 seconds.
3. Pour into a jug and refrigerate for 2 hours until cold; stir. Serve garnished with coconut shavings.

Nutrition Info:
- Per Servings 1.5g Carbs, 5.3g Protein, 26.1g Fat, 285 Calories

Strawberry And Basil Lemonade

Servings: 4 | Cooking Time: 3 Minutes

Ingredients:
- 4 cups water
- 12 strawberries, leaves removed
- 1 cup fresh lemon juice
- ⅓ cup fresh basil
- ¾ cup swerve
- Crushed Ice
- Halved strawberries to garnish
- Basil leaves to garnish

Directions:
1. Spoon some ice into 4 serving glasses and set aside. In a pitcher, add the water, strawberries, lemon juice, basil, and swerve. Insert the blender and process the ingredients for 30 seconds.
2. The mixture should be pink and the basil finely chopped. Adjust the taste and add the ice in the glasses. Drop 2 strawberry halves and some basil in each glass and serve immediately.

Nutrition Info:
- Per Servings 5.8g Carbs, 0.7g Protein, 0.1g Fat, 66 Calories

White Choco Fatty Fudge

Servings: 6 | Cooking Time: 10 Minutes

Ingredients:
- 1/4 cup coconut butter
- 1/4 cup cashew butter
- 2 tbsp cacao butter
- 1/4 teaspoon vanilla powder
- 10–12 drops liquid stevia, or to taste
- 2 tbsp coconut oil

Directions:
1. Over low heat, place a small saucepan and melt coconut oil, cacao butter, cashew butter, and coconut butter.
2. Remove from the heat and stir in the vanilla and stevia.
3. Pour into a silicone mold and place it in the freezer for 30 minutes.
4. Store in the fridge for a softer consistency.

Nutrition Info:
- Per Servings 1.7g Carbs, 0.2g Protein, 23.7g Fat, 221 Calories

Fast 'n Easy Cookie In A Mug

Servings: 1 | Cooking Time: 5 Minutes

Ingredients:
- 1 tablespoon butter
- 3 tablespoons almond flour
- 1 tablespoon erythritol
- 1 egg yolk
- 1/8 teaspoon vanilla extract
- A dash of cinnamon
- A pinch of salt

Directions:
1. Mix all ingredients in a microwave-safe mug.
2. Nuke in the microwave for 3 minutes.
3. Let it rest for a minute.
4. Serve and enjoy.

Nutrition Info:
- Per Servings 1.4g Carbs, 3.5g Protein, 17.8g Fat, 180 Calories

Brownie Mug Cake

Servings: 1 | Cooking Time: 5 Minutes

Ingredients:
- 1 egg, beaten
- ¼ cup almond flour
- ¼ teaspoon baking powder
- 1 ½ tablespoons cacao powder
- 2 tablespoons stevia powder
- A pinch of salt
- 1 teaspoon cinnamon powder
- ¼ teaspoon vanilla extract (optional)

Directions:
1. Combine all ingredients in a bowl until well-combined.
2. Transfer in a heat-proof mug.
3. Place the mug in a microwave.
4. Cook for 2 minutes. Let it sit for another 2 minutes to continue cooking.
5. Serve and enjoy.

Nutrition Info:
- Per Servings 4.1g Carbs, 9.1g Protein, 11.8g Fat, 159 Calories

Chocolate Cakes

Servings: 6 | Cooking Time: 25 Minutes

Ingredients:
- ½ cup almond flour
- ¼ cup xylitol
- 1 tsp baking powder
- ½ tsp baking soda
- 1 tsp cinnamon, ground
- A pinch of salt
- A pinch of ground cloves
- ½ cup butter, melted
- ½ cup buttermilk
- 1 egg
- 1 tsp pure almond extract
- For the Frosting:
- 1 cup double cream
- 1 cup dark chocolate, flaked

Directions:
1. Preheat the oven to 360°F. Use a cooking spray to grease a donut pan.
2. In a bowl, mix the cloves, almond flour, baking powder, salt, baking soda, xylitol, and cinnamon. In a separate bowl, combine the almond extract, butter, egg, buttermilk, and cream. Mix the wet mixture into the dry mixture. Evenly ladle the batter into the donut pan. Bake for 17 minutes.
3. Set a pan over medium heat and warm double cream; simmer for 2 minutes. Fold in the chocolate flakes; combine until all the chocolate melts; let cool. Spread the top of the cakes with the frosting.

Nutrition Info:
- Per Servings 10g Carbs, 4.8g Protein, 20g Fat, 218 Calories

Strawberry-coconut Shake

Servings: 1 | Cooking Time: 0 Minutes

Ingredients:
- ½ cup whole milk yogurt
- 3 tbsp MCT oil
- ¼ cup strawberries, chopped
- 1 tbsp coconut flakes, unsweetened
- 1 tbsp hemp seeds
- 1 ½ cups water
- 1 packet Stevia, or more to taste

Directions:
1. Add all ingredients in a blender.
2. Blend until smooth and creamy.
3. Serve and enjoy.

Nutrition Info:
- Per Servings 10.2g Carbs, 6.4g Protein, 50.9g Fat, 511 Calories

30 Day Meal Plan

	Breakfast	Lunch	Dinner
Day 1	Easy Chicken Meatloaf	Chicken And Zucchini Bake	Garlic Chicken Salad
Day 2	Chicken Paella With Chorizo	Chicken Garam Masala	Cobb Egg Salad In Lettuce Cups
Day 3	Parsley Beef Burgers	Fried Chicken Breasts	Green Mackerel Salad
Day 4	Keto Enchilada Bake	Sticky Cranberry Chicken Wings	Citrusy Brussels Sprouts Salad
Day 5	Tofu Sandwich With Cabbage Slaw	Easy Chicken Vindaloo	Strawberry, Mozzarella Salad
Day 6	Crispy Chorizo With Cheesy Topping	Basil Turkey Meatballs	Creamy Soup With Greens
Day 7	Parmesan Crackers	Spicy Chicken Kabobs	Broccoli Cheese Soup
Day 8	Zucchini Lasagna With Ricotta And Spinach	Chicken And Spinach Stir Fry	Corn And Bacon Chowder
Day 9	Walnuts With Tofu	Buttered Duck Breast	Traditional Greek Salad
Day 10	Morning Granola	Paprika Chicken With Cream Sauce	Kale And Brussels Sprouts
Day 11	Vegetable Burritos	Greek Chicken With Capers	Minty Watermelon Cucumber
Day 12	Strawberry Mug Cake	Pesto Chicken	Sour Cream And Cucumbers
Day 13	Spicy Devilled Eggs With Herbs	Chicken And Green Cabbage Casserole	Chicken And Cauliflower Rice Soup
Day 14	Greek-style Zucchini Pasta	Stewed Chicken Salsa	Salmon Salad With Walnuts
Day 15	Curried Tofu	Chicken Curry	Mixed Berry Nuts Mascarpone Bowl

Day 16	Yummy Chicken Queso	Pork Osso Bucco	Coconut Cauliflower Soup
Day 17	Bbq Pork Pizza With Goat Cheese	Pork Nachos	Celery Salad
Day 18	Garlic Beef & Egg Frittata	Moroccan Style Beef Stew	Mushroom Soup
Day 19	Keto Beefy Burritos	Italian Shredded Beef	Mediterranean Salad
Day 20	Beef Stovies	Slow Cooker Pork	Bacon And Spinach Salad
Day 21	Easy Garlic Keto Bread	Garlic Pork Chops	Balsamic Cucumber Salad
Day 22	Herb Cheese Sticks	Grilled Fennel Cumin Lamb Chops	Green Salad With Bacon And Blue Cheese
Day 23	Fat Burger Bombs	Roast Rack Of Lamb	Salsa Verde Chicken Soup
Day 24	Onion Cheese Muffins	Pork Chops And Peppers	Bacon Tomato Salad
Day 25	Bacon Jalapeno Poppers	Ribeye Steak With Shitake Mushrooms	Grilled Steak Salad With Pickled Peppers
Day 26	Tasty Cream Cheese Stuffed Mushrooms	Mushroom Beef Stew	Mint Chocolate Protein Shake
Day 27	Zucchini Noodles	Simple Pulled Pork	Berry Tart
Day 28	Sausage Roll	Beef Enchilada Stew	Strawberry Yogurt Shake
Day 29	Kale Cheese Waffles	Caribbean Beef	Lettuce Green Shake
Day 30	Easy Vanilla Granola	Pork Lettuce Cups	Hazelnut-lettuce Yogurt Shake

S

Salad Green
Green Salad With Bacon And Blue Cheese 98
Lettuce Green Shake 117

Salmon
Chipotle Salmon Asparagus 45
Bacon And Salmon Bites 46
Avocado And Salmon 48
Dilled Salmon In Creamy Sauce 48
Simple Steamed Salmon Fillets 48
Cedar Salmon With Green Onion 49
Mustard-crusted Salmon 49
Asian-style Fish Salad 49
Salmon And Cauliflower Rice Pilaf 51
Lemon Marinated Salmon With Spices 51
Salmon Panzanella 52
Steamed Mustard Salmon 54
Chili-garlic Salmon 54
Parmesan Fish Bake 54
Pistachio-crusted Salmon 54
Salmon Salad With Walnuts 105

Sausage
Cocktail Kielbasa With Mustard Sauce 23
Sausage Roll 28
Slow Cooker Beer Soup With Cheddar & Sausage 103

Scallop
Asian Seafood Stir-fry 55

Shrimp
Cilantro Shrimp 45
Shrimp Stuffed Zucchini 46
Yummy Shrimp Fried Rice 47
Angel Hair Shirataki With Creamy Shrimp 49
Rosemary-lemon Shrimps 50
Shrimp Spread 52
Grilled Shrimp With Chimichurri Sauce 53
Steamed Asparagus And Shrimps 55
Lobster Salad With Mayo Dressing 99
Shrimp With Avocado & Cauliflower Salad 106

Skirt Steak
Adobo Beef Fajitas 84
Beef And Egg Rice Bowls 87
Grilled Steak Salad With Pickled Peppers 98

Spaghetti Squash
Spaghetti Squash With Eggplant & Parmesan 34

Spinach
Creamy Artichoke And Spinach 29
Bacon And Spinach Salad 97
Strawberry Salad With Spinach, Cheese & Almonds 99
Spinach Fruit Salad With Seeds 105
Green And Fruity Smoothie 119
Five Greens Smoothie 120

Squash
Baked Chicken With Acorn Squash And Goat's Cheese 72

Strawberry
Strawberry Mug Cake 36
Strawberry, Mozzarella Salad 101
Strawberry Yogurt Shake 117
Berry Merry 118
Strawberry-choco Shake 120
Strawberry Vanilla Shake 122
Eggless Strawberry Mousse 124
Strawberry And Yogurt Smoothie 124
Berry-choco Goodness Shake 125
Strawberry Vanilla Extract Smoothie 127
Strawberry And Basil Lemonade 128
Strawberry-coconut Shake 129

Swiss
Zesty Balsamic Chard 20
Chard Swiss Dip 29

Swiss Cheese
Herb Cheese Sticks 21

T

Tilapia Fillet
Steamed Chili-rubbed Tilapia 46
Five-spice Steamed Tilapia 47
Tilapia With Olives & Tomato Sauce 50
Red Cabbage Tilapia Taco Bowl 52

Tofu
Sriracha Tofu With Yogurt Sauce 38

Tomato
Vegan Cheesy Chips With Tomatoes 27
Briam With Tomato Sauce 32
Egg And Tomato Salad 33
Greek Salad With Poppy Seed Dressing 35
Sautéed Celeriac With Tomato Sauce 43
Greek Chicken With Capers 62

W

Y

Z

Made in the USA
Monee, IL
16 February 2023

28028720R00079